Glorious Adventure

For Franklin

Glorious Adventure

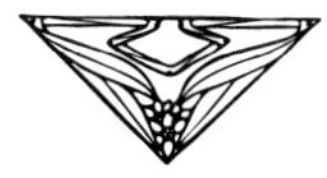

Carter Catlett Williams

Pioneer Network in Culture Change

Published by Pioneer Network in Culture Change
P.O. Box 18648
Rochester, NY 14618
www.PioneerNetwork.net

Portions of Chapter 1 originally appeared in *Aging and the Meaning of Time*, Chapter 6: Voyage in Time p. 113–119, reproduced with the permission of Springer Publishing, LLC, New York, NY 10036.

Designed by Geri McCormick

ISBN: 978-0-615-22298-1

CONTENTS

PREFACE

"Letters act upon you," my daughter said in an early morning phone call. "I was reading your book late into the night—finished it, and then was so much in my grandfather's world I couldn't sleep." Her voice had a faraway sound not because she was calling from Virginia, but because she was just emerging from my father's world and time.

How well I know this feeling: for thirteen years my father's letters have acted upon me. No amount of hearing about my father could bring him to me, into my life, as reading his own words has. His thoughts, hopes, miseries, passions, uncertainties and delights poured out on paper three quarters of a century ago have brought encounters between the two of us. I, too, have often felt as though I had gone back in time, to another world, and been with him.

I am compelled to share this story of finding my father through his letters. I suspect that I need to establish him for all the world to see, and make up for his long absence. And I want others to know that an adventure such as this is possible in later life. Indeed, this stage of life may be the best time for something that goes so deeply into the heart and bears such fruit. My father's letters have given me new life to be reckoned with and reconsideration of the old. I hope readers will be similarly prompted toward interior adventures of their own.

Pen and ink and paper are inanimate things that give no hint of power until words are fashioned by means of them, then they become a vehicle that goes where it will. After the encounter, the reader is not the same. Penetrating the heart, the writer becomes an active force in the reader's life, as my father has become in mine.

Acknowledgements

I never knew it took so many people to write a book. This one would not have come into being without a legion of friends, colleagues and relatives who gave help in many forms, from coaching me in the art of writing, to reading and re-reading different versions of the manuscript, to steadfast encouragement. I want to call them by name, asking forgiveness of any one who is neglected because of my imperfect memory, and taking full responsibility myself for the final manuscript.

First and foremost is my husband, Thomas Franklin Williams, who after almost a half-century of marriage, adjusted to a writing wife, whose preoccupation with her new calling at times caused mysterious silences and intense emotions. Franklin not only weathered it all, but gave me and my project whole-hearted emotional and practical support. Our daughter, Mary Williams Montague, a fine writer herself, has given me much helpful feedback and particularly wrestled with title ideas, as have our grandson, John Williams Damron and granddaughter, Catharine Carter Damron. Our son, Thomas Nelson Williams, brought his keen eye to the choosing of appropriate photographs, and his understanding of my need to have unbroken morning writing time. Our younger grandchildren, Edward Thomas Williams and Mary Berkeley Breckinridge Montague, have borne up under prolonged family discussions of the book. My first cousin, Letitia Montague Grant, has been constant in her support, reading a complete draft, supplying pictures, filling in gaps in family information and unfailingly offering encouragement.

The earliest appreciation of my project from any group came in the form of an invitation about eight years ago from the people who lived on Friendship 4 West at Monroe Community Hospital in Rochester. All listened intently as I read selections from my father's letters and encouraged me in my project. One gentleman, who had been a member of a flight crew in World War II, later helped me understand the love and lure of flight.

Nicky Harmon and Carol Podgorski read all the letters straight through and encouraged me in my writing. Two friends at St. Luke and St. Simon Cyrene Episcopal Church, Sylvia Kannapel and Toni Burr, read the first year of letters, and affirmed the interest they hold for the general reader. My friend Gladys Reeves read and encouraged my early recollections, which stirred memories of her own Southern childhood, and led to our laughter about an artifact we held in common—brutal, yellow Octagon soap.

Colleagues in the movement to transform nursing homes graciously accepted my pulling back from work in the movement. Cathy Unsino and Rose Marie Fagan have given me their support and strong encouragement throughout the many years of transcribing and writing, and Bill and Jude Thomas, Barry Barkan, Joanne Rader, Charlene Boyd and Bonnie Kantor have never flagged in their belief in my work. Barbara Frank and Beth Baker have read the manuscript at critical junctures and offered valuable suggestions.

Pam Klainer carried me through many rough spots with her expressions of confidence and her sensitive comments on the manuscript, and gave me a treasure-trove of pictures. Phyllis Ladrigan, always interested and encouraging, led me to Monica Weis who gave me vital encouragement at a crucial time. Dr. Jeffry Lyness read the manuscript and spoke of the value it holds for others. Friends Tom Rogers and Elaine McCorry never failed to express their interest and good wishes, as has been true of Connie Bowen, Janet Gelein, Bernadette Mallaret and Pat Kraus.

Elsa Verbyla, editor of the *Gloucester-Mathews Gazette-Journal*, generously responded to my inquiries about Gloucester in earlier years, and Mimi Ulsaker informed me about commercial shipping and passenger docks used by the Chesapeake Bay steamships in the early 1900s. The Rev. Dennis Wienk made my grandfather's Latin phrases accessible to me.

Therapist Connie Donaldson, LCSW, was a steadying guide and wonderful perceiver of elements in my life I did not recognize, building wholeness and healing.

To Thomas Cole I am hugely indebted for urging me to read my father's letters. He understood their importance for me, when I had no inkling, and has stood by me on this journey. To Karen van Meenen and Gail Hosking Gilberg I give my warm appreciation for editorial assistance, Karen meeting with me through thick and thin over the course of two years, and Gail stepping in at a crucial time to increase my writing skills and cheer me on.

Wendy Lustbader has been sister and companion to me throughout this journey. No detail has been too small to escape her interest, or bewilderment on my part too great for her to turn it around with expressions of confidence.

To all I am deeply grateful.

Author's note: the two voices in this story, my father's and mine, are signified by specific fonts. Original spelling has been maintained in the letters, while punctuation has been modified to aid the reader's understanding. The reader is invited to peruse the endnotes for each chapter for references and additional relevant information.

INTRODUCTION

Thomas R. Cole

If you haven't suffered the loss of a parent at an early age, it is almost impossible to appreciate the bewilderment or the terrible, endless ache of unknown origin that casts such a long shadow over your life, or the emptiness you can't identify. There is the grief of the unremembered love which brought you into the world and the yearning for connection, and for a truth that will make sense of it all.

I first met Carter Catlett Williams at a Gerontological Society meeting in the late 1980's. I knew immediately that we were kindred spirits. At the time, I thought that our spiritual kinship was grounded solely in a common concern for meaning and human values in aging, and in advocating respect for the personal experience of each individual elder. But as we got to know each other, it became clear that we had something else in common: the tragic deaths of our fathers when we were very young. Carter was not yet two years old in 1925, when her father, Landon Carter Catlett, Jr., died in a plane crash. The first clues on a path toward recovering her father's love and consciously mourning his death did not appear for almost seventy years. My father, Burton David Michel, had committed suicide when I was four years old in 1953. Thirty-five years later, I was still searching for him.

When Carter's mother, Catharine Mott Catlett, died in 1986, she passed on to her daughter a box of letters written by Carter's father. I was terribly envious of this treasure trove. My grandmother had kept a collection of letters from my father's army days. But when I asked to see them, it turned out that they'd accidentally been thrown away. For years, I kept prodding Carter to read her father's letters.

In 1995, Carter began the journey of recovery, healing, reconstruction and historical transmission which culminates in this marvelous book, *Glorious Adventure*. First came the shocking joy and grief of encountering her father as a real person. On one afternoon, she decided to read all the letters written after her birth on September 2,

1923. "There," she later wrote in a letter to him. "I found both the wonder of your love and the loss of it. I cried in happiness—and in anguish."

Next came the slow work of organizing and mastering the letters for herself. Over a period of five years, Carter arranged and transcribed every letter and postcard. During this period from 1995 to 2001, she was also a primary force in the national movement to transform the culture of nursing homes. This struggle to transform bureaucratic regimes of routinized care into the personalized work of individual caring and relationship demanded a great deal of time and energy. Increasingly, Carter found that her public commitment to nursing home reform competed with her private need to open the "gifts" of her father's life, love and death.

Carter Williams is a passionate and determined human being. Sensitive to injustice, she has always advocated for the vulnerable and for the victims of prejudice. As she put it to me, "I have always empathized with the underdog and the powerless. I have identified with people whom society perceived as somehow inferior." (Personal communication, 5/1/2008) Carter's ire is not limited to prejudice against classes of people, but is especially aimed at any attempt to erase the uniqueness or to deny the right to personhood of each individual human being.

When Carter turned more deeply to her father's letters, she began the painstaking work of reclaiming his unique life and of coming to terms with the cosmic injustice of losing him. She spent years excerpting the letters and constructing material that filled in historical and biographical lacunae in his story. Meanwhile she wrote letters to him, filling him in on her own life, reacting to his letters, going through a long, painful and joyous process of coming to know him and letting him go.

This book takes a unique form which perfectly suits its intention to tell several stories at once—the story of her father's life; the story of her family and of Gloucester County in the first quarter of the twentieth century; and the story of Carter's search to know her father, to have a personal relationship with him, and to mourn his death. In a magical background chapter, Carter transports readers to Gloucester County in the Virginia Tidewater, where her parents were born less than forty years after the Civil War. The writing is so vivid that a reader can smell the honeysuckle and the farm animals, feel the morning mists rising over the tidewater, and see the steamboats pulling up to the wharves.

Glorious Adventure opens with a prologue and message to her father. It is the beginning of a fascinating and paradoxical dialogue between a living daughter and a dead father, carried out in alternating sections. In the process, Carter's father becomes a living presence in her life. We follow him from the Fall of 1914, when he leaves home to attend an Episcopal boarding school, through a year and a half at the University of Virginia, a stint in the Army Air Service, three years at the United States Military Academy at West Point, courtship, marriage, the birth of his daughter Catharine (Carter), and back to his first love flying in the Army Air Service. Each chapter about his life is followed by a letter from Carter to her father, responding directly to his letters and commenting on her own emotional journey. Hence, the book alternates primarily between two stories: the story of her father's life and the story of Carter's spiritual journey reacting, responding to, and commenting on her father's life and letters.

Having undertaken this long and strenuous journey, Carter now finds herself enjoying "a peace I've not known before." Readers of *Glorious Adventure* will themselves be amply rewarded as they undertake a journey on which they meet an intrepid, passionate, and sensitive individual with the rare courage to explore, to face, to know, and to shape the existential depths of her soul.

Thomas R. Cole, Ph.D.

Director, McGovern Center for Health, Humanities and the Human Spirit

University of Texas, Health Science Center, Houston

BACKGROUND: GLOUCESTER
In the Virginia Tidewater

Gloucester County, where my parents were born and raised over a century ago, and I grew up, is water-bound by inlets of the southern Chesapeake Bay. Viewed from the air, the tidal waters not only form the eastern boundary of the County, but reach far into the land making a lace-work tracery of multiple creeks and coves.

It's a land of horizontals—water, marsh grass, gentle riverbanks, and piney woods, with no heights to yield breath-taking views. All is low and soft and embracing, though sometimes foreboding in its sultry weather and forests thick with impenetrable vines. Morning mists rise over water and field in the warm months, and in certain weathers, there is the fresh and briney scent of salt water. At other times, the fragrances of pine and bay, or magnolia and honeysuckle prevail. Summers can be hot almost beyond human toleration, but spring is a glorious and prolonged unfolding of bloom. In the fall, there is a welcome clarity in the air, and black gum and maple display their scarlet and gold.

The culture of the County is shaped both by its geographic location and events of time past. In 1898 and 1900, the birth years of my father and mother, the Civil War had ended less than forty years earlier. The poverty which pervaded the South after the war was very much in evidence, but the ante-bellum sense of family and aristocracy remained, and segregation of people according to race was enforced by Jim Crow state laws. In 1910 there were almost as many black people in this completely rural county as white, the total number of all souls being twelve and a half thousand. Most were in general farming except for those who lived in Guinea, a neck of land between the York and Severn Rivers, who were known as watermen. They worked the rivers and bay for their abundant fish, crabs, and oysters, which they sold commercially. Because few black families owned farms—the promised "forty acres and a mule" never having materialized—most were farm laborers and domestic workers.

By the close of the nineteenth century, the homes of several hundred people clustered around the county seat, so the sole village in the

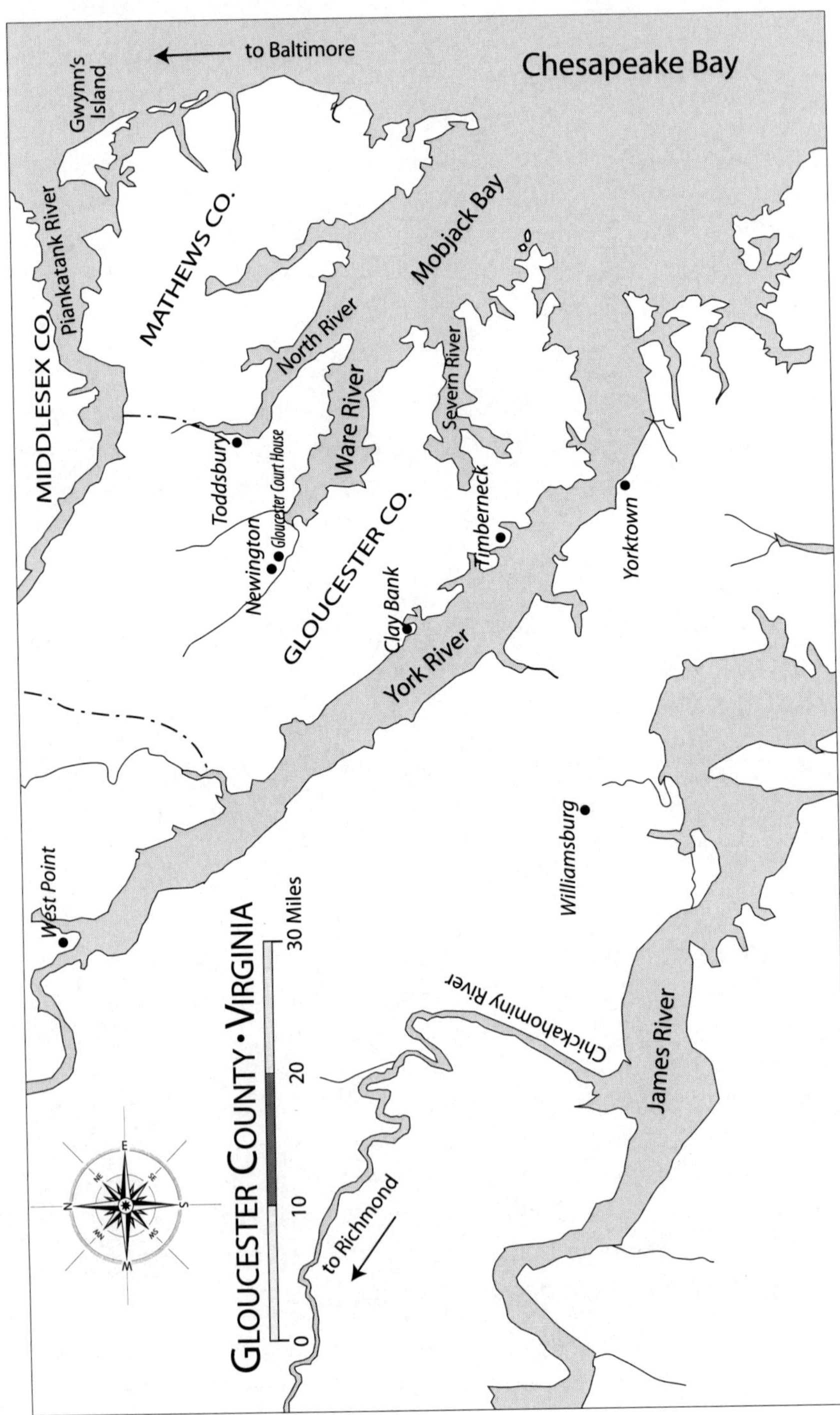

to Baltimore
Chesapeake Bay
Gwynn's Island
Piankatank River
MIDDLESEX CO.
MATHEWS CO.
Mobjack Bay
North River
Ware River
Severn River
Toddsbury
Gloucester Court House
Newington
GLOUCESTER CO.
Timberneck
Clay Bank
York River
Yorktown
Williamsburg
West Point
GLOUCESTER COUNTY • VIRGINIA
0
10
20
30 Miles
Chickahominy River
James River
to Richmond

county was—and is—called Gloucester Court House. The county had no railroad, and roads were sorry things, particularly in rainy spells, but in the early nineteen hundreds it had as many as thirteen commercial wharves open for shipping and passenger service at varying times of the year. Usually at least one wharf on each of the rivers—York, Severn, Ware and North—was open year round. Commerce depended on shipping goods by boat the length of the Chesapeake Bay to Baltimore and points north, or up the York River to the small town of West Point, from where passengers and freight could go by rail to Richmond and points beyond.

The Chesapeake Bay steamers offered more than a means of shipping freight. In my mother's childhood, the captain of the Mobjack, which came to Dixondale wharf on the North River three times a week bringing mail, telegrams, coal and other necessities, obliged the ladies by purchasing threads in Baltimore that matched the colors of their latest sewing projects.

General farming and fruit orchards characterized local agriculture, rather than the cotton, tobacco and peanuts of the counties farther south. Farm and orchard products were shipped to market by the Bay steamers, the loading facilitated by trolley tracks that ran the lengths of the long wharves. In the early nineteen hundreds a few people began to grow jonquils (the local name for the narcissus or daffodil), and ship them to Baltimore, but not until after World War I were they grown in such quantity that they became a significant cash crop.

Some families who had been in Gloucester for generations, held on, and were often identified by their old homes dating from pre-revolutionary days, now in varying states of disrepair. These homes were usually situated on the rivers—like Timberneck, an eighteenth century house on the York River, which was the Catlett home for many generations. Toddsbury, where my mother was born and grew up, was even older, dating from the mid-seventeenth century. My father was born and raised at Newington, in Gloucester Court House, five miles from Toddsbury. His father's brother, the eldest son in the family, lived at Timberneck.

To some extent, there was a river society and an inland social group more centered around Gloucester Court House. On the rivers, communication with neighbors was easier by boat than by traveling the long lanes leading down to each house from the main road. Both lanes and main roads were unpaved and so filled with mud holes during wet spells that they could become almost impassable for buggy or wagon.

Schooling was affected by the difficulties in getting around. On North River, three or four families hired a teacher who lived with each family several months at a time and taught all the children in a one-room log cabin in the yard of Elmington, another large house about a mile down-river from Toddsbury. The children, including my mother, aunts and uncle, walked and rowed to school. They splashed each other with quick smacks of their oars on the water—even in winter—causing them to arrive at school with hands streaked with red dye from their wet, hand-knit mittens. By contrast, my father's home at the Court House was almost next door to the county public school, so there were no impediments to his schooling.

River dwelling and inland folk met and mingled at church, occasional social events, and the bimonthly court days when the circuit court judge heard cases and people gathered from all over the county to do business. It was a fine opportunity to catch up on news and sell seasonal produce.

My father and mother grew up in the same church, Ware Episcopal Parish. It, too, had a long and significant history, having been founded in the late sixteen hundreds when Anglicanism was the established church in Virginia. Before the Revolution, all citizens, including those who dissented from the established church, were required by law to attend services at regular intervals as well as pay taxes to support the church. Generally people of the plantation society were not among the dissenters, thus, even as late as the early nineteen hundreds, church denomination was often indicative of class.

Hospitality in the home was generous and abundant, from the frequent presence of friends and additional family at table, to overnight visitors, the latter often spending one or more weeks. Both of my parents' families often had visitors requiring board and lodging, some paying for these accommodations on a regular basis. Everyone gathered for each meal, the mid-day meal being the big one of the day, and Sunday dinner the culinary high point of the week. Food was seasonal, the best that garden and farm produced. To this richness was added the bounty of the surrounding waters—fresh fish, oysters, clams and crab, the last to be had in abundance by simply going down to the nearest dock with a crab net and dropping into the water a chicken neck at the end of a line.

* * *

For one who grew up there, Gloucester is a place in the heart. It's sun and heat, flowers and scented air. It's sun-sparked water in the morning, and often by late afternoon, it's green, white-capped, churlish water as the wind howls, thunder claps, lightning streaks, and on occasion a massive tree crashes to the ground. It's winter-time maples etched black against the evening sky, and the early greening of the willows. It's marsh grass and the thick smell of oozy black mud. It's the snuffling of the horses as they graze beneath our windows at night, the slow trek of the sheep at midday across the yard to the shade of the great willow oak, and the profiles of their lambs as they gambol on the river bank. It's the cows standing belly-deep in the water switching their tails and cooling themselves, and the ill-tempered geese clamping their bills around the tails of the calves and flapping behind the frightened animals. It's swimming from the row boat on stifling afternoons, standing watch for each other so as to make stinging-nettle sightings. It's the pine and shining holly and magnolia, ivy and cedar making a festival of evergreens at Christmas, and the wind on a stormy winter night playing the loose window panes like timpani.

And Gloucester is community, where everybody knows who you are, and you know who they are, and there's family everywhere.

When a real man sees an

opportunity of great service,

of high honor,

of glorious adventure,

he seizes it.

Only the sluggard lives painfully

in accord with the great law of

self-preservation.

—Landon Carter Catlett, Jr.
January 30, 1921

Elders [are] explorers without
maps.

We . . . draw our maps as we go—
not knowing where the road will
lead us,

or just what lies ahead, but
daring the

explorer's adventure to which I
believe [we] are called.

—Carter Catlett Williams
March 24, 1998

1

PROLOGUE

My father, Landon Carter Catlett, Jr., a second lieutenant in the U.S. Army Air Service, was killed in a plane crash in Hawaii in 1925 at age 27 when I, his only child, was barely 23 months old. My mother, Catharine Mott Catlett, then age 25, returned with me to Gloucester County, Virginia, where both her parents and my father's parents lived. There I grew up, and from there I departed for college and a larger world. Marriage, child-raising and, later, social work occupied me full time.

I have no memory of my father. For me he was only the man in the pictures on my mother's bureau, a distant icon, not a flesh and blood person, but I knew from occasional comments that he was much admired by those who remembered him. I was aware that my mother had a box of his letters, and once, in my early forties, I looked at a few of them. They made me sad, so I put them back in the box and gave no thought of returning to them again. Busy with child-raising, being a supportive wife to an even busier husband and enthralled in one good cause or another, the notion of taking time out to read more letters never entered my head.

But then came old age, and with it unguarded moments of reflection on earlier parts of my life and, at intervals, surprising moments of awareness.

I was 63 when my mother died. At her funeral, the minister offered a prayer for both my parents—"Remember thy servants Catharine and Landon Carter, O Lord, according to the favour which thou bearest unto thy people, and grant that, increasing in knowledge and love of thee, they may go from strength to strength . . . " Hearing their names together both startled and reassured me that indeed I had once had two living parents. As unlikely as it may seem to those who grew up in "regular" families, it was a moment of revelation and comfort to me—the prayer accomplished what the pictures on the bureau had failed to do.

With Mother's death came the awareness there was no longer anyone standing as a buffer between me and the end of my own life. But I did not dwell on that thought. I had other things to think about and much advocacy work to do, and I hardly paused.

In fact, looking back, I see now that I resolutely avoided exploring strong emotions that welled up on occasion after my mother's death, and threatened to undo me. The first I recall occurred one night when I was going through a box of papers from my mother's family. I noticed a letter in very different handwriting that I thought might be my father's. It was indeed a letter written by him to his mother on Mother's Day in 1925, and it was filled with news of me, his twenty-one-month-old daughter. "I don't try to sneak away when I leave the house," he wrote. "I kiss my hand to her and say 'bye-bye' and she runs to the window and climbs into the rocker to wave and kiss her hand as long as she can see me" (5-10-25). This glimpse of my father and me brought tears, but the possibility of learning more about my life with him did not cross my mind.

The next morning, when I returned to sorting in Mother's attic, another and much larger box caught my attention. I made my way through piles of books, bed trays, chamber pots, Christmas ornaments and other relics of four generations to get to it, but the light was too dim for me to see what was inside, so I maneuvered the box down the narrow stairs to a spot by the dining room window.

Inside the box lay carefully folded army uniforms, a three-quarter-length gray coat conspicuous for its many rows of brass buttons, and, wrapped in a yellowing towel, an American flag folded in a triangle. Though I had never seen them before, I knew from pictures that these were my father's uniforms and his West Point brass-buttoned coat. I spread them out on the dining room table, but, mindful of the sorting task that still awaited me in the attic, I did not linger over them. As I began to pack them away again, I smoothed the rough wool uniforms, and suddenly knew I was stroking and comforting my father's broken body. Choking back tears, I quickly sealed the box, and sealed off that moment, speaking to no one about it.

Six or seven years later, another summons came, and this one finally made me stop and explore. It happened one day when I passed the collection of photos I had put together for my mother's nursing home room, to aid her memory and sense of place. There were pictures of Toddsbury, the old house on the river where Mother had been born and where I had grown up, and of the steamship Mobjack that came up the river three times a week, as well as pictures of family—her parents and sisters and brother, with the ever-present animals that roamed the yard. There was one of her and my father in their courting days, and then one of them with me as a newborn. All of these I had selected from the big black photo albums Mother stored under her bed, the same albums I used to pore over as a child. The scenes and the people were familiar, except for those of my own original family.

The photo collection now hangs in our upstairs hall, and that particular day as I passed it, I thought bleakly, "This was my life—now it's all over and done with, dead and gone, and nobody knows about it." My sadness and emptiness were so great that I wrote about my feelings in an effort to understand. I shared my writing with my friend, historian Tom Cole, and was brought up short by his response: "These pictures are not your life—they are your mother's life!" He added that I needed to explore that emptiness within, but I had no idea how to do that.

Tom had been asking me at intervals if I was reading the letters from my father that I had once mentioned to him, but the letters remained untouched in the battered little box that had been moved from attic to attic for close to three quarters of a century.

Continuing to disappoint Tom's repeated inquiries made me ashamed that I was not carving out time from professional work to pay attention to my father. After all, at the age of 72, the number of years I could hope for was shrinking. In January 1995 I finally decided to open the box.

But before that I wrote a letter to my father.

* * *

My dear Father,

This seems a formal way to address you, but the truth of the matter is I don't know what to call you. Mother called her parents Mother and Father, and I suppose you did the same with yours. But I don't know what you taught me because all I remember was simply "your father" when others spoke to me of you.

I have waiting for me a box of letters written by you and saved by Granny, who handed them on to Mother. They've been in our attic since Mother's death seven years ago. Now, in response to the urging of a wise friend, I'm going to set aside time to read them.

As I'm poised to learn something of your life directly from you, it occurs to me that I should tell you a little about mine, but, at age 72, there's a prodigious amount of living to reflect upon, and far too much to write about in one sitting, so I'll settle for opening just a few windows in time.

At the first window, you see me focused on getting the best education Mother and I can manage, and eager to get beyond Gloucester's confines into a wider world. Following in the footsteps of your sisters, I attend Wellesley College in Massachusetts (for the four years of World War II), graduating in 1945. Two years later, after returning to Virginia and working in Gloucester's welfare department, I go to Simmons College School of Social Work in Boston and earn my Master of Social Work degree in 1949.

During these Boston years, I meet another student from the South, Thomas Franklin Williams of North Carolina, who is studying medicine at Harvard, and in 1951 we marry. Our children, all North Carolinians, are Mary Wright, born in 1956, Thomas Nelson, born in 1959 and Landon Carter. Landon's birth brings tragedy and grieving—born prematurely April 19, 1960, he survives only 12 hours.

Franklin is a very busy junior faculty member at the University of North Carolina Medical School, and I am occupied with the children and not attempting to do social work, but both of us are deeply involved in the civil rights movement to eliminate racial segregation.

In 1968, during our middle years, we move to Rochester, New York, for Franklin to become Medical Director of Monroe Community Hospital and a professor of medicine at the University of Rochester Medical School. Having had a sabbatical year in Nashville, Tennesee, a year earlier, and having been influenced by the lives and thinking of our clergy friend John Harmon and his wife Nicky, we decide to live in the city and escape the sameness of suburbia. We choose a house in an older part of Rochester, with neighbors that assure diversity—on one side, a group home for women well enough to leave the county psychiatric hospital, and on the other, a small, old-world synagogue referred to as a schul. Branches of the YMCA and the public library are at the foot of our block.

Franklin's attention and professional interests become increasingly focused on care of elders. I return to part-time social work to help out with our children's education expenses. By chance, I too start working with elders, both in their own homes and nursing homes. And we, especially Franklin, devote considerable time to working for the establishment of a high-school-without-walls in the city public school system. Mary's dissatisfaction with the highly routine character of the city high schools lends urgency to our work.

In 1983, Franklin accepts an appointment as Director of the National Institute on Aging of the National Institutes of Health, and we have eight interesting years in Washington. I am surprised that they become years of professional development for me as I pursue answers to urgent questions growing out of my work with elders, the most troubling of which is the practice of tying them down in physical restraints. Having seen restraint-free care in a Swedish nursing home, I help spread the message, speaking about it across the country at every opportunity.

Now to 1995, the present, and a glimpse through the last window. We are back in Rochester, and Franklin has shifted gears. He is working part time as Distinguished Physician with the Veteran's Administration, and is again at Monroe Community Hospital in a pro bono teaching role. I am very much absorbed in the national movement to end the use of physical restraints, as well as promoting change in the culture of nursing homes.

Photograph by Wendy Lustbader

Thomas Franklin and Carter Catlett Williams, 1995.

We've had joys and distresses along the way—joys in our children and our work, as well as concerns about both, and we've lived in turbulent times of war and social change. In all, the life we share is a rich one.

I wish so much that you could have known your son-in-law and grandchildren.

Your daughter,
Catharine Carter

About my name: After your death, Mother changed my middle name from Mott to Carter, and always called me Catharine Carter, as did everyone else. But when I went off to school, there were three Catharines in my class. Mine was soon dropped, and I've been Carter ever since.

* * *

I was aware of mixed feelings as I opened the battered little box and began to sort the letters that lay in complete disarray.

But soon curiosity overcame fear, and I began to open envelopes and read randomly, knowing that later I would have to discipline myself to read in chronological order. But at first this was not possible. Suddenly I was a starving person with a feast set before me. Taking letter after letter from its envelope, I devoured each one. There was no reaching satiety. I ricocheted back and forth, with no context in terms of the life stage and situation in which each letter was written. There were my father's letters from the Military Aeronautics School at Cornell and from rough flying fields in Georgia and Florida, from Granny at home in Gloucester or on a visit to her sisters and brothers, condolence letters from the time of his death, long letters while away at school for the first time, and letters from Daddy Catlett expressing great confidence his son's bright future. I read in haste, gobbling them up.

* * *

It took days just to get these letters into chronological order. I counted 400 letters and postcards written between 1914 and 1925. Of these, 264 were from my father, the remaining 136 from his parents, sisters and other relatives and friends. Also among them were several from Mother, as well as those devastating condolence letters.

There were eleven years of hopeful, vital letters—encouraging, instructing, reporting on big and little daily events, anticipating—so much dreaming and anticipating, and then my father went up in his pursuit plane one morning and for some unknown reason, crashed in the blue-green waters of Hawaii.

Photograph by Maribeth Romslo

The letters are now in order.

2

CARTER, THE SCHOOLBOY, AND LETTERS FROM HOME

Fall, 1914–Spring, 1916

I enter my father's life September 12, 1914 when he is sixteen years old. He takes leave of his Gloucester home and family—his parents, Letitia Nelson and Landon Carter Catlett, Sr., and his two younger sisters, Mary Mann and Fanny—in order to attend the Episcopal High School, a boarding school near Alexandria, Virginia.

I picture him that September morning, a boy of slight build with bright brown eyes, whose father has just delivered him by buggy to Clay Bank wharf on the York River. He is to travel by boat to connect at West Point with the train to Richmond, where he will stop off for two nights at The Cedars with his aunts and uncles who run a dairy farm near the city. The next day, he writes his family about the first leg of his journey:

Sep. 12, 1914

Dear Parents and Sistren (as opposed to brethren),

Fine as silk and hope you are the same! I have slept thirteen hours since leaving home. I slept from before 5 PM straight through and for that reason I didn't write . . . Likewise I hadn't read any from the Bible during the day and so missed for the first time since last Christmas.

Getting used to traveling now. I no longer have so much anxiety about my baggage. Porter brought my suitcase on the boat after I had forgotten it as clean as a whistle . . .

I remain in life, about to surrender my liberty for the pursuit of learning.

Your loving son [and] brother

The Mobjack, one of the steamers that plied the Chesapeake Bay, the York, and other Gloucester Rivers.

Letters from each of his parents soon follow, full of longing for their son and news of his life at school. They report the latest family happenings and exhort him to follow the Christian life, albeit in the context of a racist culture:

[Gloucester, Va.]
Sept. 13, 1914

My precious boy,

It will be good to hear from you again & to know how you are getting on. I have missed you all the time, but especially when the children have all come home from school in the evening. I shed eloquent tears, every now and then as an accompaniment to my *eloquent thoughts*, on the subject of my first born & only son leaving home, so sad *I be*, & then I hear your father say "my boy is gone and I have lost him *forever*," & I just have to laugh . . . I am so thankful to know you are to have the advantages you are to have, though, that I am not grieving that you are gone all the time. I want to know that you are *well* & *happy* & not working too hard & something of how the days pass . . .

I gave your brushes to Seth as your parting gift & he said he needed a shirt very much so I turned it over to him. Of course he got into it as that race can wear anything you know. Your Cousin Mary Lee seemed to think your clothes you left were worth a great deal for Fitzhugh, so I carted them over to them—& thought of "My Little boy blue," you know, but we have Xmas to look forward to haven't we & the everlasting Future? . . .

Write soon to your devoted Mother Letitia Nelson Catlett

His father writes the same day:

Gloucester, Va.

My dear Boy,

. . . I do want to see you take a high stand [at the High School] but I do not want you to study too hard. Above every thing I want you to grow up to be a clean and pure man and a faithful follower of the Christ. He came that we might have life and that we might have it more abundantly. Never get the false idea that you give up anything that is worth while in order to be a Christian. The fullest and most complete life is the Christian life.

Of course we miss you. I went out this morning and picked about 2 qts. of raspberries and then I got peaches and then I gathered a lot of James grapes. I ate a few raspberries and grapes that, [including peaches], I might say I had all three for breakfast . . .

[T]his afternoon . . . [nephew] Chas. and Debra came . . . I was afraid Debra [who is expecting] would make herself sick.

We had peaches for dinner . . . and she raved over the apples and kept eating them. We went to the grape tree and she pitched [in] with good heart. Then we went to the peach tree and I peeled peaches for her. She said she also ate a pear. We gave her all the apples we could get in the buggy. I think we put in six buckets full. She seemed to want all she could get. Tish gave her carrots and beets. I called a halt on the beets as I want them for my garden exhibit [at the Fair] . . .

With every good wish for your health and happiness,

Your father

Several weeks pass before Carter writes more than postcards:

Class Room/Study Hall
Oct. 1, 1914
Thursday night 9:15

Dear, dear Mother,

. . . I am doing my best to make the best of my opportunities, especially physical. I eat all I can and foot-ball, which pulls weight off some people . . . has not robbed me a bit. I weigh more than on the day I came . . . Dressed I will weigh probably 142 . . .

Friday Night 9:15.—I must explain that we are allowed to write letters after 9:15 but the reason I haven't done it before is because I have needed the time for study. The little boys, or rather those under fifteen, because I'm not a giant myself—are allowed to leave the hall at 9:15.

We had scrimmage with the second team [today]. I played the whole time—thank goodness, it wasn't very long. I am right guard if you should happen to meet anybody who wants to know where I play. I didn't do any wonders against the second—very few of us did—but I came in for some praise . . .

[In reply to your question] . . . I have no before-breakfast accomplishments [bowel movements] but speedy dressing and waking all the old boys in dorm who are not awake at

> 7:20. I got only one demerit for being late for breakfast last week . . .
>
> Yes, the hazing is about over or at least in a lull. We have "rat relay" to wake up the old boys. Crump is "head rat" . . . and Wetmore goes around at 7:00 and puts down all the windows, if it is cold, Conner goes at 7:15 and wakes up the crowd. I wake up those who have gone back to sleep at 7:20 and Randolph goes at 7:25 . . .
>
> I must close now to go to church. I miss you and love you all very much.
>
> Your loving son,
> Carter

As the school year progresses, Carter studies hard, and plays hard—at football, basketball and baseball, each in its season, but team membership eludes him. His intensely competitive approach to his studies comes through one day when he bests another boy who had given him unsolicited instruction at an exam break time about how to work more quickly. When the grades are posted, Carter takes "fiendish joy" in earning one point more than the boy who had given him the gratuitous advice (3-20-15). His grades at the end of his first term are excellent—stars are awarded him in Latin, Greek, Trigonometry, Geometry and English. He is relieved and proud, ending his letter with the hope that he is "not impressing people as the conceitedest skunk in town" (1–10–15).

His parents send warm and enthusiastic congratulations, both son and parents now being reassured that he can meet the standards of the Episcopal High School. Through his fine scholarship, his mother hopes he may retrieve a "cultured atmosphere" this branch of the family has had to forego for several generations in order to make a living at farming:

> The atmosphere makes for something you know. You inherit some of the "Atmosphere" too if one goes back a little but a lot of dairy, pigs, cows, chickens, plow, hoe, rake spraying

> machines, & market wagons have taken the place of books very often (1-20-15).

Carter, however, is not impressed:

> I don't think much of a classic atmosphere and now while I am lonely . . . I feel as though I would give my knowledge of books for an equivalent knowledge of practical mechanics . . . Staige Blackford is the only one of the atmosphere I like very much. I utterly despise Wickham. There's no use denying I am jealous of him. I just plain despise and would like to beat him better than I would like to win anything (1-24-15).

Whereupon his mother, ever-mindful of the importance of character-building, warns him of the dangers inherent in jealousy:

> . . . [D]on't allow jealousy at any time, pray against the green eyed monster, & a lover of flattery as you would against the bubonic plaque. Of all things never . . . be jealous of W[ickham] . . . Never be envious or jealous of any man! . . . Now if you are going to be jealous of any body let it be of those who do good & give pleasure, comfort, to others. As Henry Van Dyke says, "envy no body anything but kindness of heart & gentleness of manner" (1-26-15)!

A few days later, Carter tones down his feelings toward Wickham:

> Let us hope my jealousy of W. is not very serious. Don't feel at all ill-disposed toward him, though I have no admiration for him. I am perfectly willing to admit that he has more brains than I have, but I do not envy him . . . (1-31-15).

Later he confides his worries about faith and self-discipline, writing his mother at length about his deficiencies:

> The lack of concentration bothers me more in religion than in knowledge. I study very well in study hall but I can not keep my mind on a sermon . . . Then the various services I go through mechanically and without proper spirit . . .
>
> I rarely get time to say my prayers properly. In the morning it is too cold to say them undressed (and I seldom remember

> it anyway) and I generally stay in bed to the last minute and dress in a hurry. At night there is always talking outside and you know how that always affected me . . .
>
> Sometimes I've forgotten my Bible reading entirely and at others there has been a lot of talking outside. I am sincerely glad that I have read the Bible through three times because the reading I am doing now isn't adding much to my knowledge.
>
> So my life at present leaves much to be improved. Sometimes I feel ashamed that so much money is being spent on me and feel afraid of my task to be worth it.
>
> But don't think from this that I dislike school or am unhappy. It's very much the other way. These things don't worry me as much as they ought to. I fear that I need some misfortune to make me more thoughtful and sincere. The main trouble I see in my self is that I am so self-centered. I congratulate the boys on their new honors but in nine cases out of ten I don't care a snap what they do just so I get my slice. And yet I like people to congratulate me and enjoy nothing more than flattery if it isn't put on so thick that I recognize it (2-28-15)!

His mother responds:

> All you write about yourself is quite natural, & you are all right as long as you know your duty & pray to do it & you don't have to stop anything to pray thank God! Many of us have learned that our most fervent prayers can be put up . . . [while we are] worked to death with duties, & not a moment to stop . . .
>
> The very fact that you think about these matters is evidence that you are on the right side[.] [T]he majority don't think. So pray instead of worrying . . . (3-3-15).

In his second term, feelings of loneliness and recurring homesickness plague Carter. Classes are held Tuesday through Saturday, Sunday is crammed with church services and Bible study, and Monday, his free day, is when homesickness attacks:

> . . . [O]f all the mean days a Monday here is the most miserable! About one half of the boys it seems are gone to

> Washington or somewhere else . . . There's nothing to do that you want to do and a whole lot to do that you don't want to do. So I always get so starving homesick I'm no good for anything. It might be different if I took long walks with some chum but there were no chums at home to-day. I read my English parallel in the morning . . . I played basketball in the gym and caught baseball till after five and loafed till six and then dressed for supper. I bought a pie from the bakery wagon that came to bring bread. It was not extra good pie but it tasted good to me (1-25-15).

Several weeks later he crowds a postcard with details of an expensive attempt to chase away another attack of Monday blues:

> Tuesday night
> [Feb. 9, 1915]
>
> Dear Mother,
>
> I haven't time to write but I am homesick again. It seems a Monday makes me homesick whether I go or stay. Ramsay and I . . . took dinner at the Washington Lunch. We spent a great deal more money than usual. [W]e felt like eating all day. We went to the medical museum but soon got enough of that. It didn't make me sick but I just didn't like it. Then we strolled down to the capital and into the gallery of the [H]ouse but they weren't doing anything but arguing about the cost of a post office to be built in a short time . . . In the Senate chamber the Republicans we[re] filibustering the shipping bill and that was better . . . I recognized the Vice-President by his face, LaFollette by his pompadou, & Ollie James by his height (6 ft 5 in). We went up in the dome of the Capitol. For the rest of the day we walked & walked & went to a "movie." I had to buy a doz. new collars . . . I spent all my check.for $2.50 dated 10 days ahead. I spent too much but it is less than most boys spend. With a heart full of love, Carter

His mother consoles him—she is glad he had the trip to Washington, wants him to take advantage of such opportunities, and "as you don't get there often, of course you have to spend some money, & a growing boy needs to eat (2-11-15)." She also recommends that when he feels lonesome and homesick he should "look around for someone else to give some pleasure to (1-26-15)."

In the same letter, she muses on aloneness and reflects on how she may have felt differently when she was young:

> It was perfectly natural that you should be homesick some, there is no loneliness like that felt in a crowd of strangers. I am peculiarly constituted. I like to be alone a good deal . . . [F]or myself I don't seem to care a cent for popularity. I couldn't have the trouble of nurturing it for anything. I can't bear to be put forward, I don't like conspicuous places, & nothing but duty will make me allow myself to be put forward. Maybe I was different when I was young. I think I was, very ambitious for worldly things, & it mortified me awfully not to have a chance to go to schools, & shine generally. With much fervent prayer on the subject I got over that pretty effectually, I think (1-26-15).

Miss Lila Jones, a former grammar school teacher of Carter's who now boards with the Catlett family, weighs in with advice about homesickness also: "There are 800 texts in the Bible commanding us to rejoice so it [is] your duty to be glad always (2-11-15)." Carter disagrees:

> I enjoy Miss Lila's letters and will try to profit by them but I refuse to accept "rejoicing" as a duty . . . If she looked in Jeremiah and Lamentations she will find a great many commanding us to weep and some of the weeping was to be done by the Jews "who sat by the waters of Babylon." Was it not? I don't think her argument goes. There is a time to laugh, and a time to weep and the Jews got homesick as well as other people (2-4-15).

Episcopal High awards many prizes and medals, and Carter, even in his first year, is eager to win some of them, so he enters most competitions and tracks others' grades as well as his own. By the end of his first year, he has placed second in six contests:

[5-25-15]

Dear Father,

. . . Strubing has won the math medal and I feel that pretty keenly . . . I am sure I am second because my Math is so much easier. Don't I ride my old second place? I have a lot to be thankful for, I know, but I did want a medal so bad! Of course, I know without being told that everything happens for the best but that doesn't comfort me . . . Oh, well, I'll try next year for nine medals and every prize I'm eligible for . . . Well, I'm not unhappy for I'm coming home!

Lovingly, Carter

In addition to intense competition for medals, rivalry is keen in the debates between the Blackford and Fairfax literary societies, and Carter becomes a member of the Blackford Society debating team. The subject for the final debate is Women's Suffrage, with Carter and his debating partner, the previously disliked Wickham, speaking in the affirmative. They lose the debate, despite diligent preparation and what classmates deem good argument and delivery. The substitute moderator misunderstands instructions and incorrectly shortens Carter's rebuttal time by four minutes—a vital four minutes in Carter's opinion:

> If the contest was so close what might I have done with four more minutes for rebuttal? I shall always believe that that four minutes would have made us come nearer winning . . . Even a lot of Fairfax fellows say we won the debate and should have gotten the decision. I gave up a lot of good sleep and outdoor exercise for this debate and lost six or seven pounds preparing for it . . . I can't forgive that wretched mistake about the time for my rebuttal (5-2-15).

There are also competitions in Reading and Declaiming at the High School, for which Carter chooses both classical and dialect pieces, such as a "Negro sermon" beginning with these lines:

Rev. Gave Tucker's Remarks

You may notch it on de palin' as a mighty risky plan
To make yo' judgement by de clothes dat kivers up a man
For I hardly needs to tell you how you often come across
A Fifty-dollar saddle on a twenty-dollar horse.
An', workin' in de low-groun's, you diskiver as you go
Dat de fines' shuck may hide de meanes' nubbin in de row . . .
(1-24-15).

Carter's mother admires the writing of two white practitioners of dialect, Joel Chandler Harris, author of the Uncle Remus stories, and Thomas Nelson Page, a distant cousin, and she suggests that Carter use more dialect pieces. He gets something of a reputation for his renderings of Uncle Remus stories, at times being asked to tell them at the weekend evening gatherings in faculty homes. His mother also comments appreciatively on minstrel shows:

> We had a jolly minstrel show last night[.] Mr. Turner had it in charge and made it quite brilliant[.] [H]e was leader as you were but in full dress as the "white man[.]" In some respects you were ahead of them & more natural, & Negro fied. They had a troup of fifteen, & good deal of dancing . . . You know how they can dance—they went off the stage with the "Bunny Hug" I suppose . . . (5-29-15).

Not all correspondence concerns Carter's life at school. Many of his parents' letters report on home and community events, except when his mother finds the Gloucester social scene "emensly dull (1-17-15)." The work days of both parents are long and full—his father's with his duties as Gloucester County's first Agricultural Demonstration Agent and the running of his own small farm, on which the family depends for virtually all its food and some of its income. His mother's days are relentlessly busy too, caring for nine and eleven year old daughters, raising chickens and running a household which often includes boarders.

The monetary returns for their constant work are small. In addition to a regular, but often-late and always-small salary for his father's

Demonstration work, the family supplements its income by small sales of fruit, breeding fowls, eggs and cream, as well as daffodils that they ship by boat to Baltimore. Sale of timber is a last resort, used only to raise some funds for Carter's schooling and to purchase a car. Intermittent boarders also bring in a little money, but Carter's father has times of despair:

> I thought I had money enough to settle all my bills at the C[ourt] H[ouse]. Your mother got Corr's [Store] bill and it was $92.00 (about) that lays me out again. I am going to make one more effort to pay up and get on a cash basis. You had better make up your mind to start life on a cash basis . . .
>
> Maud Wiatt sold us three pigs yesterday for three dollars a piece. They are small. I did not have the money to pay for them. I have not received any part of my Oct. salary yet (11-8-14).

Despite their precarious finances, Carter's father, described in his obituary as being "identified with nearly every progressive movement in Gloucester County from boyhood on," pursues and supports numerous projects for the betterment of the community—raising money to pave roads, bringing telephone service to Gloucester and trying (unsuccessfully) to bring in a railroad, establishing a potato growers' cooperative, and at intervals, taking part in amateur plays.

At times his mother is concerned that Carter may be embarrassed by his lack of money, saying, "We . . . [are] short but let me know how you are. You mustn't be intirely out or have to borrow" (9-28-14). But when Carter has to wear a dress suit for the big debate, he makes good sport of assembling a borrowed outfit:

> When I went to Mr. Hoxton [the Headmaster] about the suit he lent me his! Wasn't that handsome? But his had a black vest and then there are other things about evening attire not included in a dress suit, so I wore Mr. Hoxton's coat and trousers, Frost's shirt, Hinkle's vest, Hamburger's collar, Crump's white bow tie, Speer's pumps, Gambrill's brass shirt studs and Scott's suspenders. My sox and underwear belonged to Carter Catlett (4-18-15).

Carter periodically worries that he is not contributing to family support. He writes as his graduation approaches, "My heart may be somewhat uplifted by all the good time I've been having but I'll be right down glad to get home and do something besides spend your money" (5-31-16).

When Carter's father attends a two-week training session for Agricultural Agents at Virginia Polytechnic Institute in western Virginia, Carter is particularly concerned about the extra burden of work that falls on his mother. Despite careful instructions to Seth, the hired "colored man," necessary things do not get done. Upon learning that Seth has failed to attend to some of the heaviest chores, Carter writes his mother:

> Good heavens! If Seth doesn't empty the slops who does? It certainly is shameful for you to be there with water to pump and other still worse work to do while [F]ather and I are away. Of course it's a pity for father to have those things to do too because he has worked enough in his life to deserve some ease (1-17-15).

In reply, his mother reflects on the possible reason for Seth's behavior:

> Seth is a comfort, but I have to tell him every day to fill up the buckets with water or it isn't done you know, & the reason I remarked upon the slops was that it seemed so remarkable that knowing there was no one to do it but he should pass them day after day in that way. He is doing a little better though. No doubt he thinks the white folk do very little of the worlds work, & he is doing a good deed to get some out of them occasionally (1-20-15).

After long consideration, Carter's parents conclude they must let Seth go as part of their plan to buy a car, which his father needs for traveling about the County in his Demonstration work. Their ancient work horse, Punch, on whom Carter's father has been relying for buggy travel, is so worn out that one Sunday his father decides to walk the two and a half miles to church "so as to let Punch have a real Sunday" (10-18-14).

With the sale of some timber and the money saved by not paying Seth, they see their way clear to buying a Ford. They promptly dub it Betsy, and enjoy the first family outing by motor:

> Gloucester, Va
> April 26, 1915
>
> My precious boy,
>
> . . . We have come over 75 miles in "Betsy" today, from the Cedars, & we got here about 3 this aft. Most of the time was taken up . . . putting [in] cold water, & letting out the hot [,] crossing rivers, & getting through the deep sand of Hanover, & King & Queen [Counties]. We went up to the Cedars Sat. & have had the time of my life! It was a beautiful trip & I injoyed in the full . . . All were so glad to see us, & it gave your Grand Pa the greatest pleasure I have seen anything give him for years . . . Often wished for you. If you had been there to help your father run the machine he would have injoyed it more, but he certainly made her fly on some of the road, which was beautiful, & we could see the course clear for a mile . . .
>
> We left the Cedars directly after breakfast . . . & stopped six times to cool, water the engine & cross the ferry . . .
>
> I must close & God bless my boy. Lovingly Mother with love from everybody.

Carter's mother is a great believer in "healthy pleasures," of which motoring is only one:

> Now I want you to be ready for any healthy pleasure that comes along, & feel that it is just as much a part of your building as the most serious work. If you learn to enjoy everything in life you can [be] sympathetic with young people & old, & be much more capable of cheering the down trodden, & afflicted (3-1-15).

Dancing is among those healthy pleasures. Earlier she had written Carter about the benefits of it, but he, anticipating a friend's desire to attend dances, is loathe to invite the friend to Gloucester. She buttresses her approval of dancing by noting that Generals Washington and Lee danced:

> It is a pleasant side of your . . . [county] life you have yet to get a glimpse of as a part of your education. Of course I haven't ever wanted my children to be taken up with such things to interfere with their physical or mental development, but it is a side of life to know something about, even if one hasn't much time for it . . . Gen Wash[ington] danced—Gen Lee too I suppose . . . It has always occupied a place in the world & in every nation's history, so the bible even says there is a time to dance, & a time to sing songs, etc, etc (1-20-15).

By the fall of 1915 when Carter begins his second year at the High School, he is a more confident student and determines not only to win medals but also to end hazing of new students—"the rats." He has endured the experience himself, writing his parents of one such occasion that occurred at the end of his first month at the school:

> [After telling ghost stories] . . . someone called for my piece about the cat-fight, and of course two boys who came in in the middle of the recitation had to hear it over again . . . Buck Wimberly . . . came in shortly after and gave me a paddling. Just then the dorm bell rang (9:45) and he started to conduct me to my room. The missionary store is just at the foot of the stairs as I go up to my room and when we got there he dragged me in . . . and he and Spruill began to hugging me and laughing. They often try that on new boys to see how much they can embarrass them and of course it works pretty well with bashful boys. I put an arm around the neck of each and kissed *at* them, remarking to the audience, "Gentlemen, I am between the devil and the deep sea." . . . I broke away and ran upstairs because I didn't want to get stuck. They came up . . . and made some more fun of me . . .
>
> After the gail of laughter blew over, though, and I was in bed I thought more of home than ever. These fellows think of me only as something to laugh at and everyone who loves me is at home (10-19-14).

Carter writes his father soon after his return to school, "I'm treating the rats the best I know how and I hope to make warm friends among them" (9-23-15). In October, after being "unanimously voted . . . Editor-in-Chief of *The Monthly Chronicle,*" the school magazine, he writes an editorial against hazing (10-4-15). His stand sets him up in the eyes of some as a spoil-sport:

> I have fitted into the school life and have some close friends, many pleasant acquaintances and a few enemies. I am proud to say that my stand on hazing and also . . . my conceit seem to have brought . . . [my enemies] into the open. Scott heard one of them say he thought that the old boys ought to agree not to speak to the rats but he knew that d-n Catlett would go ahead and speak to a lot of them first thing. I can give you oceans of hazing information when I get home. In the meantime, the right is conquering . . . (11-28-15).

Carter meets the challenge of editing and producing a monthly magazine with gusto, encouraging submissions and striving to make rejections as constructive as possible. Word of his respectful treatment of would-be authors gets around:

> I had a great compliment tonight from a boy who is not generally thought to be over half-hard. Fact is, I don't know that I disagree with the general opinion but the boy came to me and said he had a joke for the Chronicle and he was showing it to me of all the editors because he knew I would give him a fair deal and not make fun of him (12-5-15).

Carter's courses require serious study. In his first spring term he is reading Horace's *Satires,* studying trigonometry, Tennyson's *Idylls of the King,* which "fascinates" him, and doing parallel reading "in the Southern poets, [of whom] Poe and Lanier are the chief but there are about twenty in all" (3-16-15). In his final term he reports being "almost through four books of Xenophon's *Anabasis*" and expecting to start *The Iliad* soon (4-15-16). On his approach to the classic languages he comments:

> There's one thing that always has pulled for me in Latin and Greek especially. My vivid imagination can supply the gaps in my translation so that I have never since I can remember blanked anything considerable on an examination (2-10-16).

Reading gives Carter's imagination full play. On a Sunday in April, 1916, fully aware of Sunday rules excluding frivolous reading, he writes his mother:

> Do you know your son well enough to understand him when he says he is just sobering up from one of his sprees? I've been intensely wicked and I'm not very repentant yet. I've been reading Kipling most of the time since church this morning . . . My taste is satisfied now and I have no desire to read any more . . . You know how I read? Eyes, ears, sense of smell, all intent, though the fire burn low and the night wane far (4-2-16).

Scholarship is important to Carter, but he also has other interests and goals:

> I am trying—and have been trying since last September and for two years before that—to cultivate popularity. That's a rather bold confession isn't it? I do not sacrifice my own self-respect and independence of course but try to be courteous to all, friendly to those I respect and servile to none . . .
>
> A great college professor writing in the Youth's Companion said there were three different aims for which boys strive at college. One is scholarship, the second popularity, and the third athletics . . .
>
> Of course with me scholarship comes first, athletics second, and popularity third (1-17-15).

Scholarship ranks first, but does not exclude raucous and rule-breaking schoolboy times too—particularly with Hippo Minor:

> "Hippo" and I broke a door the other day. We were romping and I chased him into the laboratory. As he went in he tried to jerk the door shut after him. I struck it edge-on and broke the rotten wood off the lower hinge. I'm sorry of it because they will use the $5.00 deposited to pay for it but it is a public

> benefit as that door had no catch to shut on and one panel gone (1-24-15).
>
> Whew! The mails brought me a lot of good fortune last week! Two letters from each of you, one from Miss Lila, the cake and raisins, and a jar of sweet pickle from Sally. I ate about half a pint of sweet pickle one night after inspection. It was the first real nourishment I had since Christmas. Then I sprinkled talcum powder about the room so Flick wouldn't smell pickle. I shared my pickle with Hippo Minor . . . "Hip" says it saved his life (1-31-15).

Athletics indeed rank a strong second with Carter. Despite his small frame and light weight, he doggedly, but unsuccessfully, pursues a place on the football team. He fares no better in basketball, but again he persists even though it means playing only on a dorm team. Membership in the baseball team, his greatest love, also eludes him, but not for want of trying:

> Never a word did Old Nick . . . [the coach] give me of encouragement, praise, advice or blame and he kept me catching all during the whole batting practice. You know catching isn't easy work and batting is. Picture me with some inherited surplus energy concentrated on the desire to bat, with every muscle tingling for it, standing there and jumping in every direction to catch the miserable ball that none of the pitchers could put over the plate . . . and it does seem hard to get so much of the wrong end of the mule. Of course, I know it is good for me. "It is good for the man that he bear the yoke in his youth" but Jeremiah doesn't comfort you much better than Job's friends. So I fret and chafe. I've been doing it all spring, first with exaltation and then with despair (4-6-16).

He maintains this high level of physical activity, all the while combating what he calls a cold, which he says has hung on for three years. His mother calls it catarrh, and she is deeply worried about it:

> Do pray try to learn how not to have those colds . . . You ought to avoid bathing too soon after being heated or staying wet for too long. You are not quick enough bathing & drying

> yourself. Long lecture—but must give you line upon line you know—for some people conquer these diseases & I would like to see you do it (10-15-14).

Carter is not deterred by his symptoms. He is determined and resourceful, particularly at the crucial time of the debate on Women's Suffrage:

> I had a vile cough last week and had to get the doctor Thursday . . . I was taking Scott's Emulsion too, but getting no better. The doctor gave me capsules of liquid creosote and a throat spray . . . I also got two lemons and sucked one then and there . . .
>
> When I came back I read my speech over at the hall and then went up to dorm to go to bed. I pulled off shoes and coat and got between the blankets but I found I was wheezing so long and loud that there was no chance of a nap. I felt desperate then and got up and sprayed my throat until I choked and spit up some vile stuff which relieved me. I got to sleep at a quarter past five and slept an hour. Then I got up and took a shower and put on all that part of my dress attire which belonged to me—my underclothes. Of course I put on other clothes too. I drank a glass of milk at supper and got excused to dress. I took a dose of Scott's Emulsion, a dose of creosote, sprayed my nose, sprayed my throat several times, and took a potash tablet. Right up until then I had been coughing in spells but after supper I didn't have a bit of trouble until after the debate was over (5-2-15)!

He yearns to hold elected office, and is confident he could serve the literary society better than the sports heroes who are invariably chosen. He has many ideas about improving the society meetings but claims he doesn't "despair of human nature because the voters elect such poor officials. I am a democrat and an optimist and I shall not try to squirm into office (1-9-16)."

Carter's father also thinks of himself as a democrat, and is deeply perturbed at his elitist feelings when Carter wants to take a certain girl to a Botetourt High School graduation occasion. His wife writes their son:

> I was *pleased* at your selection of . . . [this girl], looking on I liked your taste, & thought this the *pick of the school as a girl* not knowing of her at all. Your father who has been among her people a good deal, & has been thrown with *the men,* was rather shocked in a quiet way, & I was surprised when he gave me the benefit of his feelings that night to find that he had been so much upset, & the fear that was aroused. He thought he was democratic, but had struck a snag . . . (4-18-15).

In another context, Carter's mother presses him to consider the worth of each individual, regardless of status, quoting Tennyson:

> Tis only noble to be good.
> Kind hearts are more than coronets,
> and simple faith than Norman blood.

Writing to his family is important to Carter, and on at least one occasion, the cause of a fight between him and his roommate:

> My writing is due to an injured thumb . . . [Scotti] bent it back till it was unbearable and I surrendered. He then eased on the thumb but tried to squeeze my hand up. However, he is ticklish and I got one hand in his ribs with ominous results. I ended up by sitting on top of him . . . What started the row was Scott's singing "My Old Kentucky Home" in a cracked quaver while I was sitting down to write [you] (10-31-15).

Carter also makes a discovery: "I like to write letters! (2-6-16)"

At his graduation June 7, 1916, he is not only valedictorian of his class but is able finally to bring home "a piece of gold"—two gold medals, in fact, one for Excellence in Latin and Greek, and one in Reading. But despite his great longing for the whole family to be with him, only his father is on hand for the big day. A quarantine in Alexandria, because of an epidemic of scarlet fever, prevents his mother and sisters from coming.

Landon Carter Catlett, Jr., when he graduated from Episcopal High School, June 1916.

Dear Schoolboy,

Surely I know you better now than most daughters know their fathers.

I love this boy who is so ambitious that he tries for every medal awarded by the school, who is doggedly determined to be an athlete though he has no particular athletic talent, who is sought out by another boy for being the one who won't laugh at him when he offers something to be published in the school magazine, who campaigns against hazing, who gets drunk on reading a good book, who admits his "fiendish joy" when he bests a certain other student, and fights his roommate when that boy teases him about his letter-writing to his parents. Here you are in all your stars and warts.

But I have to tell you, I do not share your pleasure in one aspect of your world. Instead of confronting you with it now, however, I want to take it up directly with your parents—my dear grandparents, who remain always in my heart.

With love from your grateful daughter,

Catharine Carter

Dear Granny and Daddy Catlett,

Your words lay in a box for close to a century, mute. Now they have a reader—your eldest granddaughter—and defenseless, you open yourselves to me. You in turn enter my heart and spirit, to such a degree that some days this communion consumes me. At any moment—as I bathe and dress, go about household tasks, take a walk—I am thinking of you, ruminating on your lives, savoring your relationships, giving thanks for the good and wonderful things you handed on to me, and wrestling, at painful intervals, with the dark part of that inheritance.

You come back to me: the slow cadence of your speech and its archaic Tidewater Virginia "broad A" in which you place a "y" after a consonant and eliminate "r" sounds, as in "She drove the cyah to the gyahden." And I recall particularly your gentle, bemused way of speaking, Granny. I see your somber expression, Daddy Catlett, and hear your sighs, and I savor your asparagus, rhubarb and raspberries.

Granny, you were lavish with hugs and kisses, and I enjoyed special attention from Aunt Mary Mann and Aunt Fanny who wrote verses for me, and introduced me to Winnie the Pooh and the Walrus and the Carpenter, which they recited with wonderfully exaggerated expression. I also remember squirming down from your lap, Granny, wanting to be on the run rather than to sit still and be hugged.

I feel parts of myself in you—or is it the other way round? I am at one with you, Daddy Catlett, and your garden, though I'm not nearly as knowledgeable and skilled as you. Also, I think I know just what you mean when you say toward the end of a letter, "I think I shall eat one more pear and then if nothing comes to me I shall go to bed"—food may bring inspiration! And you warm my heart with your efforts to give Punch a restful Sunday.

While my interests don't run to better roads, railroads, telephones, potato cooperatives and prohibition, I harbor strong progressive and reformist yearnings. You have a sense of mission about a better life for your beloved Gloucester County and Virginia. I have a sense of mission about civil rights, about freeing elders from physical restraints and from nursing home environments that trap them in meaningless lives. It strengthens me to know I am in the company of my grandfather.

One more thing, Daddy Catlett. We meet across the years and generations when I read your reaction upon learning that your son liked a certain girl. You thought you were a democrat, but in Granny's apt phrase, you "struck a snag." You were steeped in the strong sense of family and pride in ancestry as Virginians can be, yet equally convinced, on the basis of faith and commitment to democratic principles, in the worth of all people. Your son's interest in a girl whose men-folk you did not admire put you between a rock and a hard place. It distressed you to find how un-democratic your reactions could be. I'm familiar with this struggle.

With you, Granny, I recognize commonalities over a range of things, but first and foremost, it's your passion for education I respond to. Having been denied such education yourself—perhaps after the seventh grade—because of those hard, impoverished post-Civil War years, you dealt with your bitter disappointment as best you could, through prayer and an unyielding resolve to see that your daughters went to college. And not just any college. I've learned that your beloved and greatly admired Cousin Jennie Nelson was a classics teacher in the first faculty at Wellesley College when it opened in 1875, and you must have determined then that it would be the place of choice for any daughters you might have. I owe my privilege of a Wellesley education directly to you, because I wanted to follow in the footsteps of my young aunts.

You and Daddy Catlett accomplished what any reasonable person would have told you was impossible: each of your three children had two years in preparatory school and four years in college, though family income was always meager and uncertain. At home you had neither telephone nor radio, and I remember no electric refrigerator, only the large wooden ice-box on the side porch. You are quoted by one of your daughters as saying, when chastised by a friend for not having a radio, "We . . . [are] just buying meat and potatoes, and education."

Knowing you both at a deeper level leads me toward a new comprehension of my own life, lived in times so different from yours, but grounded in yours nonetheless. This knowing does not eliminate the dark side of the legacy handed on to me, however, or free me from the periodic wrestling with it that has plagued me most of my adult life. For the darkness in the legacy of all my Southern forbears—all my family on both sides, as well as the legacy of my church and the whole community, local and regional—was the oppression of black people as part and parcel of everyday living.

It shocks me how insidious this was in its normalcy. We addressed all "colored people" by their first names, repeated and laughed at their words and rich expressions, and, without hesitating, dressed at Halloween in "blackface." We didn't go to school with "them," eat with "them" or share bathrooms or drinking fountains. Routinely, the one black member of Ware Parish received the bread and wine of the Holy Communion alone after all the white people had knelt together and received first. I seem to remember being told he was a doctor from the West Indies. In any case, the sight of him kneeling alone at the communion rail is etched in my mind. For all I know, you and Daddy Catlett didn't like that either.

Granny, it hurts to read some of your words, and absorb the implications of your saying "that race"—I know right off something derisive will follow.

And yet, unlike many white people of your day, you could place yourself in Seth's shoes for a moment, and speculate that he "thinks the white folk do very little of the world's work, & he is doing a good deed to get some out of them occasionally."

But your—and my schoolboy father's—enjoyment of minstrel shows reveals no consciousness of the searing shame they caused black people. You don't see that the very attributes derided in the minstrel show are the result of the white population's laws and social customs that deprived them of education, all but menial employment and any hope for a different future.

I cannot mesh the profession of our Christian faith and the racial oppression that permeated every part of our culture. Still in my mind is the often-used prayer that began: "Almighty God, who hast made of one blood all nations of men for to dwell on the face of the whole earth . . . " Sunday after Sunday, we heard such words as those from the Book of Common Prayer, and always Jesus' injunction, "Love thy neighbor as thyself." In the midst of so much love and eloquent language was this loathsome thing, this degradation and fear and oppression of the other that governed our lives.

The scents and scenes of Toddsbury, a setting so full of grace and beauty, remain deep in my mind and spirit. And this is what comes to me now: the stench of the pig-sty behind the barn pierced the fragrance of the honeysuckle and magnolia all around us, as our degrading of the other fouled our society. It was the stinking thing in our midst. For me, the struggle to make peace with our "sweet world and the horror that kept it going" is more than a snag—it harrows my heart and mind, and drags on my spirit.

In gratitude, and distress,

Your eldest granddaughter,

Catharine Carter

3

UNIVERSITY, AND WAR

Fall, 1916–Fall, 1917

I rejoin my father in the fall of 1916, as he begins his freshman year at the University of Virginia, Charlottesville. He is a far more confident young man than when he set off alone two years earlier to enter a school where he knew no one. He sees many old friends from Episcopal High School who are also at the University, and he settles in happily at Mrs. McIlhaney's boarding house, pleased to have the Ryan Scholarship for support, and liking his new roommate, Charlie Wilson from Baltimore. He notes that he is the only student of the classics among the boarders, the others being rather equally divided between engineering, medicine and law, except for one each in science and the ministry (10-22-16).

Though Carter is serious about his studies, discussions of them occupy far less space in his letters than at the High School. He takes Latin, Greek, German, Math and Government, the last being a considerable disappointment. He finds the professor "an interesting talker but the work is too elemental (10-12-16)." In his second year he studies economics and chemistry, but says he "can't claim much as a scientist. I love the work but am naturally slow and a poor observer of phenomena" (11-17-17).

Carter is into sports as much as ever, coping with the same handicaps in weight and size, but says he must always have exercise. He makes his sole disparaging remark about his height:

> As usual I am outweighed in football . . . Most of our line men are 175 pounders . . . By hard work and prodigious eating I have attained unto 149 pounds, a gain of perhaps 15 since I left Gloucester and 5 above my Christmas dinner weight last year. On account of my lightness I have often been left over from the scrimmage but I got in for the last half this evening and the way I handled a 170-lb. man was a caution (10-12-16).
>
> Exercise I must have and plenty of it. I don't believe an afternoon's study does me any good. I feel strenuous and I want to grow. If I stay the size I am now [5 ft. 8 in.] I shall despise myself (12-3-16).

One afternoon late in the season, when he has just come in from football practice, he is exuberant:

> My ears are tingling and my nose is running and every part of me feels good—especially my appetite. I haven't had a sore throat or increase of cold and cough this fall and go with a bare neck and head in football and get in a perspiration in the open air. I believe I ha[ve] learned some things about taking care of myself. I have never felt so well in my life. The hard work of the season ends to morrow . . . I will be glad. Everybody is happy when a football season begins or ends. Such a lot of good fun and hard work lies between (11-21-16).

On the social front, Carter's shyness with girls continues:

> A family of Joneses live next door, very nice. The youngest boy is a First Year man and we go to football practice together every day. The daughters are all trained nurses I believe. One of them is . . . at home now and I met her yesterday evening

> when I went in to play checkers with the son. She was sitting out on the porch a half an hour ago and the boys wanted me to take them over and introduce them. I was loath but Mrs. McIlhany sent down a message saying that she wished that some of us would call so we prepared to go. I was to introduce Lewis and Martin, who were to do the talking. Charlie and Berkeley were not to go, being New Men and not necessary for an introduction. But just before we set out a beau came to see the lady and we gave it up. As usual having once braced myself for the ordeal I held on till the last though not very aggressively (10-15-16).

His extra-curricular activities center around the Episcopal Church and its mountain mission, and the Jefferson Literary Society, of which, he proudly notes, Edgar Allen Poe and Woodrow Wilson were members in their student days. He is leery of fraternities and when he goes with Charlie "to some kind of soiree . . . [of] a fraternity that wants to look us over," he reassures his prohibitionist parents: "Don't worry, they won't get me in a hurry and I'm going to smell any liquid they offer me" (9-20-16). Several days later, he reports to his father that he and Charlie were invited to join:

> I wouldn't have joined any crowd who served beer anyhow but the fellow was so polite that I didn't tell him that. I told him the perfect truth when I said I couldn't afford it . . . I don't covet any Greek letters after my name but O B K (Phi Beta Kappa) (9-23-16).

During the Fall, he is intensely interested in the presidential election:

> Mr. Hughes is a fine man but he has made a very cold, unmagnetic candidate and if he is beaten, the Republican politicians will drop him like a hot biscuit. Whoever wins we will have a good man for President but I believe Wilson will be stronger as a leader than "the bearded lady" as Hughes is called in Democratic circles. Everything is so solidly democratic here that we can form no fair estimate over the country but feel very hopeful. I'm going over to Madison Hall

> early Tuesday night and stay as long as there is any news to be gotten (11-5-16).

Carter likes his roommate from the start, and a warm friendship develops. He not only feels sympathy for Charlie who lost both parents at an early age—noting that "he has never known very much home life and has had very little mothering or fathering"—but also is concerned about his health and habits:

> Wilson left me and went to a soiree tonight. He is a teetotaler, thank Goodness, and I had him pledged not to smoke tonight. He has no idea but I intend to break him from smoking before the year is over if prayer can help. He and I are more completely in each other's confidence than I have ever been with anyone in my whole life, even Giles. He is gay and carefree but as straight a fellow as anyone can be and he worships fine women like Mrs. Mac as if they were angels (10-26-16).

He admires Charlie's ease in social situations:

> Charlie is more delightful socially than I am and we have the largest, most public room in the house so we have a great deal of merry company. It sometimes cuts us out of an hour of much needed study but it is on the whole well worth the cost. We are making a fine circle of acquaintances and some warm friends (11-21-16).

In summing up his experience of the first term at the University, Carter says, "Mother, I am having the time of my life" (10-31-16). Only once is the European war mentioned in a passing comment: "One of the best players on the [football] team drove an ambulance in France last summer. He just came back last week" (10-21-16).

In high spirits, Carter resumes life at the University in January, 1917: "This is the last of my second evening here and I have written no letters whatever. I have had one glorious good time" (1-1917). The new year inspires him to lay out a strict schedule of daily life into which he builds five hours of study a day, but also two hours and a half in late afternoon for "exercise and bath," as well as an hour after supper "for time with boys in parlor" (1-5-17). He designates nine to ten every morning for letter writing, and still holds to his practice of not studying on Sundays.

Carter, the prankster, is evident when he encounters a malfunctioning water fountain:

> . . . [C]oming home I tried a drinking fountain on East Range and it sent forth a concentrated stream directed about two inches above my left knee [giving me the appearance of having wet my pants] . . . I'm going to catch someone else on it if I live" (1-5-17).

Finally, Carter has a date with a young lady. His cousin, Mary Randolph Catlett, writes him from Gloucester that he must "go to see her friend, Miss Rombaugh." So, with encouragement from his roommate who lectures him about not living like a hermit, he manages to take Miss Rombaugh to an organ recital: "I got through very happily without showing my ignorance of music to its enormous extent and the organist could make some beautiful noises" (1-24-17). Several weeks later Charlie persuades him that they should have a double date with Miss Rombaugh and another girl, the expense of which is met by their sale of several old books. "We got $1.65 and enjoyed ourselves very much" (1-24-17). But Carter "persist[s] in failing to see how . . . [young ladies] can derive any benefit from having me go over and sit around and say something once in a while and play with my hands and look unhappy" (2-23-17).

Midway in his first year, Carter begins to think about work for the coming summer, assessing himself as being practically useless on the farm:

> I'm willing of course to work on the place but I always felt that I was worse than a half-witted negro boy at any piece of jobbing I took up. Of course it would be much nicer to be at home but if I could get a good tutoring job . . . I might make enough to run me through next year with the help of the Ryan Scholarship . . .

> All my life I have had less work to do than boys in families of our means usually have and I feel like it is time for me to show that I am fit for some steady work (1-24- 17).

In addition to the "half-witted negro boy" remark, Carter, speaking the mind-set of his culture, calls St. Paul "the little Jew man" (2-23-17).

But one evening he is shocked at the racial attitudes of most of his housemates. They discuss the "[N]egro question," specifically the education of Negroes, which others think will lead to "race war." Two housemates have "back-woods prejudices," and all of them, he thinks, are "many years behind the educated and enlightened public opinion" of the day. In his indignation about their views, he "waxes eloquent":

> My opponents say that their ground is from the view point of the interest of white America. Mine is based on the best interests of the human race. If Christianity means anything to me it means that my best interests are those of my fellow man . . . [My housemates] know what they have read in the newspapers but have they *known* any of the best types of [N]egroes? Have they ever had a chance to see them in joy and grief, distress and sympathy. Does a [N]egro help me with my ice at Dixondale wharf for hope of reward[?] I think not. I know no white man does it at all and [N]egroes have done so from the time I was old enough to haul anything from the wharf . . .
>
> You see my pen gets warm when I tackle this subject. I feel strongly and let me say I am not dreaming a beautiful dream of an oppressed, ground-down race of martyrs. Negroes sometimes smell bad and they are not Uncle Tom, but they are people (3-6-17).

In discussing his Sundays, Carter twice mentions time spent reading Jacob Riis' book, *How the Other Half Lives,* "a startling picture of the New York tenements and entertaining withal" (2-19-17 and 3-6-17). He also describes the plan he and several housemates have for Sunday evenings to visit all the churches in Charlottesville. He calls it "a

Dixondale wharf on the North River where Carter received help with his ice.

merry party going to a new church every week" (3-6-17). Included in their list of churches to be visited is the Jewish Synagogue.

At intervals he comments on the personalities and interests of his housemates. Billy McIlwaine is particularly beloved. He is a fourth year medical student whom Carter and Charlie admire "above all the men here . . . Besides being kind-hearted and friendly to all, he is the life of the whole boarding house with his life and humor" (1-24-17). Later, he says Billy "could keep me even-tempered at my own funeral" (2-19-17).

Though the threat of U.S. involvement in war is coming ever closer, Carter does not refer to it directly, in contrast to his second year at the Episcopal High School when he mentioned a number of lectures and strong opinions on the subject. Carter's view of this second term is summed up in this comment, which he begins with words from Thomas Gray's "Elegy Written in a Country Church Yard": "I am pursuing the noiseless tenor of my way, attracting less attention than I most frankly confess I should like. My points of contact with [the] outside world are few" (3-6-17).

One month after he pens those words, the United States declares war on Germany, and that outside world breaks in. Only a postcard survives, which infers the change in his daily life:

> [Military] [d]rill is very fatiguing on hot evenings and we have been adding a little baseball to it . . . I killed time to day waiting for the uniforms to arrive. I have the riding pants and a pair of borrowed leggings (4-18-17).

* * *

When he returns in the fall of 1917, Carter finds the University a changed place, and three months of conflicting feelings ensue, progressing from wistful overtones in September to distress he can hardly contain by late November. In his first letter he writes:

> Many things have happened in my short stay here and all go to indicate that this will be a very pleasant year, all the more so for the undercurrent of sadness which pervades the place. Many of the new men this year will be the deans of the place next year and the older men will be in France (9-16-17).

The University has already lost hundreds of men to military service, and he reports more departing or being on the verge of leaving: "Staige Blackford (11 months my junior) is driving an ambulance" (9-16-17). "One fellow is in naval reserve like [Cousin] Powell and is subject to call at any time" (9-16-17). "Mr. Tucker preached a fine sermon . . . He leaves with the hospital unit" (9-18-17).

Writing his mother some weeks later, he describes his own inner turmoil in this time of war:

> Your son feels his shortcomings never so deeply as when he writes home. It seems an age since I wrote last and my letters now seem to tell so little. Never in life was I so changeable, so enthusiastic, so discouraged, so reckless, so well satisfied and so dissatisfied. Each letter mirrors a passing mood and each convinces me more an[d] more of my immaturity of judgment and infirmity of purpose. With days of extra work to be done I seem not to feel any strong driving impulse to grind it out of the way (10-28-17).

At the same time, he is enthusiastic about canvassing for YMCA funds to support its work with soldiers and sailors: "I always wanted to hitch myself to some good movement and speak in favor of it" (10-28-17).

Several weeks later, Carter ruminates on many things in a wide-ranging letter addressed to both parents:

University of Virginia
Nov. 17, 1917

Dear Parents,

. . . I was a good deal worried to know what to do about my own subscription [to the YMCA fund]. I knew that you would give all you could to the work and felt that the burden of my subscription would fall upon you. However, I felt that I might (as many others here are doing) economize some on pleasures and I further bethought me of my military uniform. We are all to have them and I hope they will arrive before Christmas. I can then easily do without my green suit that I bought last spring . . . Can you sell it? It cost me only $13.00 but it is worth fully that much now as a second hand suit . . .

My subscription was $15.00, five payable Dec. 15 and ten Jan. 15. When I write about it, it seems too much but when I gave it, it looked too small . . .

Charlie has an old lady friend in the hospital, with a broken ankle. Knowing my way to the hearts of old ladies he has tried to get me to supplant him. I know his scheme and won't bite the first time. He would have me going every day, puts it on the ground that it is my Christian duty and all that. It may be but I have so many Christian duties now that I feel called upon to take up the rest of my time in unholy loafing. Except for drill I don't often take much exercise on those days.

This evening I took a short walk across the ravine to the west of this place. The hill on the other side was a small oak grove with pretty houses in view on two sides. On the third side there was the railroad cut backed by the mountains and to the east Mrs. Macs. I enjoyed looking at the mountains but I am not a nature poet.

> "Let me live in a house, by the side of the road,
> Where the race of men go by,"
>
> So I turned my eyes back and looked at Mrs. Mac's on one hill and the University on the other and the dingy houses of poor whites in the hollows. All around Charlottesville there are crowds of people who live on very little. They fill in the gaps between beautiful houses such as are so many old homesteads and new edifices in Albermarle [County] . . .
>
> When there is so much of wasted opportunity in the world it seems strange that the human race really does progress. I have never studied heredity and environment but I have my own theories. It seems to me that the world is like a seething caldron. The liquid is always in motion. So too the same family does not stay on the "top of the pot" very long. Success seems to ruin a family like drink. Rich men's sons lack ambition . . .
>
> Hadn't I better be looking for a job of some sort for next summer in case I decide not to go to the wars? . . . How would it suit you if I were offered a place at E.H.S. for next year? This old war is going to give me plenty of time to mature.
>
> With a heart full of love—and sleepy eyes—
>
> Your devoted,
> L. C. Catlett Jr.

Ten days later he is questioning what work he will be prepared for when he graduates from college: "There is nothing I laugh at so as one of my teachers who knows nothing not learned in books . . . Shall I come out of college just such a man?" (11-27-17).

By late fall, he is signaling the end of university life for him:

> . . . I am enjoying this life to the fullest but I don't know how long I can stick it out . . . [T]here is an undercurrent of unrest which keeps sucking men away from the University. Every friend of last year who comes through burns my vitals out with longing. When they tell their anecdotes, they look chiefly at me—because my whole soul is looking at them through my eyes and ears and mouth . . . I may be romantic

but I do not think a young man wastes himself by dying doing his duty. I have in mind something I have been reading:

> But youth's fair form, though fallen, is ever fair,
> And beautiful in death the boy appears,
> The hero boy, that dies in blooming years:
> In man's regret he lives, and woman's tears,
> More sacred than in life, and lovelier far,
> For having perished in the front of war.

Romantic, am I? Here follows realism. There is one branch of service in which a man may be commissioned as young as 18 and will not be accepted if he is over 25. That is the aviation corps and for that I am bound . . . I just must take the [aviation] exams in the spring . . . [They are] difficult but I have hopes of being found unblemished physically . . . When a man practices drill all the time and salutes an imaginary officer at every telephone pole and goes to sleep every night thinking about the army, he is in what you might call a receptive mood . . . If . . . I can get in [the aviation] service, I'm sure you won't stop me. Well, it is after twelve and my enthusiasm is conquered by sleep (letter fragment, late Fall, 1917).

A little later Carter is offered a teaching position at the Episcopal High School. He is not inclined to accept it, though he insists he will if his parents want him to. But he cannot hold to that, for in his next sentence he clearly states the direction he intends to take, what the financial possibilities are, and how he might still be of help with his sisters' education.

I want to leave college . . . but what I want to do is go into aviation . . . The age limits are 18 and 25 and a Virginia alumnus has been commissioned especially to present this matter to Southern colleges. They want me! I want them. If I am not commissioned, I lose three months and get paid $800, out of which I can bring back certainly half. If I am commissioned, I shall carry $10,000 insurance, which will cost about $100 per year, I think. Then if I didn't pull through, Mary and Fanny could go through Stuart Hall and Bryn Mawr any way (12-3-17).

Finally, on Dec. 16:

> . . . I've ceased to care much about being prominent or influential. That doesn't count at a time when everybody who is your friend this month is in the army next. After the war some of us are going to come back and we are going to be looked up to by the younger fry all right . . .
>
> Mother dear, if you haven't already decided to give your consent to my enlisting please send it by special delivery or telegraph. I would hate to disobey my parents but if ordered to return to the university after Christmas, I should either disobey or feel like a whipped dog. I had a presentiment of it when I came back last fall. Now I know it. I will no longer be in a position when I must apologize for the bread I eat. I am ashamed, ashamed, ashamed to be here (12-16-17).

Dear Young College Man,

I'm happily immersed in your first year at the University. You have a roommate you like, an admirably congenial place for bed and board, acquaintances in abundance and several new friends. None of your courses is particularly exciting, but sports, the "Y" and church activities are by turns challenging and satisfying. And I see you stretching your social and religious horizons—reading Jacob Riis' How the Other Half Lives, *visiting a different house of worship every Sunday night, and having your first date.*

It's wonderful how you turned your health around. I think you did a "Teddy Roosevelt." You never let up on regular, demanding exercise, and of course you ate well (because of your never-failing appetite and Granny's coaching—remember all those oranges and the cod liver oil). And, like the rest of the family, you made sure you got enough sleep. You have none of the miserable nose and throat infections that plagued you constantly in your two years at EHS. And there are no words of homesickness. Life is good.

Abruptly, in the middle of these freshman high spirits, comes a letter that brings hallelujahs from me. It's your report to Daddy Catlett about the argument with fellow students concerning "the [N]egro question," an argument during which you get "warm and wax eloquent on the subject." I love your words, which can be summed up in your final statement: "Negroes are people."

In this same letter you attribute "back-woods prejudices" to your fellow students' rejection of Negro education out of fear of a "race war." Aren't you aware that you come out of the same prejudices in your own community? I learned not long ago that Gloucester County refused to establish a public high school for black students until 1921—three years after your argument—and then it had to be called the Gloucester Training School, because so many white citizens opposed publicly-funded secondary education for young black people. How come you didn't succumb to the "back-woods prejudices" in your own community?

I think I know the answer: the words of Jesus came straight through to you, despite the ugly static of the society around you. And your parents' basic attitudes toward other people gave you the foundation for declaring "Negroes are people."

Now I have a little story to tell you that may identify at least a thread in the fabric of your boarding house argument:

> *One hot summer day at Gloucester Court House many years ago, a short, almost roly-poly black man with a crown of white hair was walking toward me on the sidewalk. He was dressed in a most un-summer-like black suit. Having seen him in court, I recognized Lawyer Walker, but was not prepared for his greeting. He asked me if I was Carter Catlett's daughter, and when I said I was, he addressed me with a little speech in praise of you. I was accustomed to an aura of admiration around you, but this was particular and purposeful, even urgent—he personally wanted me to know what a fine man you were, and how much he admired you. Self-conscious teenager that I was, pleased but awkward, I thanked him, but did not ask the connection you and he had. The warmth of his feeling remains with me, but no knowledge of the experiences with you that produced it. I still feel the loss.*

So how did Lawyer Walker know you, and what was your relationship with him? (I am sure he was referred to as "Lawyer Walker" so as to impart some status, but avoid the courtesy title accorded white men.) I expect you were aware that he had been born a slave, and against unbelievable odds had secured an education at Hampton Institute, becoming the first black lawyer in Gloucester, and perhaps the first in the state of Virginia. Gloucester was proud of him, as long as he kept his place. My guess is that you saw him every time you went with Daddy Catlett to the bi-monthly court days to sell produce and catch up on the county news. Mr. Walker's autobiography attests to his great interest in young people, and he probably engaged you in conversation.

Beyond that, I can spin only a gossamer thread between your family and him. Granny mentions that "Tom Walker" purchased cream from them for his wedding reception. I wonder about other contacts, in addition to those on court days. You don't seem to be aware that Mr. Walker worked many long years to establish the public black high school in our county, and was an ardent prohibitionist like your parents.

With your views, they needed the likes of you in Gloucester, Young College Man. As your happy first term at the University closes, I wonder whether you are having thoughts beyond the university years. There's no hint of them.

I don't wonder for long: a month after your argument over "the race question," the U.S. enters World War I. For the remainder of your freshman year, I have only your postcard in mid-April speaking of how "fatiguing" drill is on a hot spring evening.

I read your sophomore fall letters with foreboding. I can see you increasingly drawn by the words of the military recruiters that come to the campus. Already you have friends in the ambulance service overseas, faculty members are leaving, and you are beset with changeable moods—by turns "enthusiastic . . . discouraged . . . reckless." Not only is your strong patriotism engaged, your romantic associations with war and honor come to the fore. I attribute them in part to the southern "Lost Cause" romanticism of the post-Civil War years in which you grew up. That's the only way I can account for your liking this poem:

> *But youth's fair form, though fallen, is ever fair,*
> *And beautiful in death the boy appears,*
> *The hero boy, that dies in blooming years:*
> *In man's regret he lives, and woman's tears,*
> *More sacred than in life, and lovelier far,*
> *For having perished in the front of war.*

I cringe when I read these words. Perhaps your parents did too, for it is clear that they have warned you about your romanticism:

> *Romantic, am I? Here follows realism. There is one branch of service in which a man may be commissioned as young as 18 and will not be accepted if he is over 25. That is the aviation corps and for that I am bound . . .*

Your "realism" doesn't help me—my heart is leaden as aviation enters the scene. Where is that happy young college man I was so much enjoying? I curse what I see as a wicked, wasteful war.

Catharine Carter

4

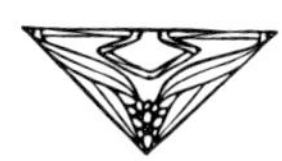

AVIATION

Spring, 1918–Spring, 1919

Carter does not return to the University in January. There is no reference to anguish over disobeying his parents, so it appears they accede to his wish to enter the Army Air Service. He attends to the details of enlisting and having the physical exam, using the YMCA in Richmond as his headquarters during the day and spending nights with the aunts and uncles at The Cedars. He speaks of wearing out shoes "walking on these rocks four miles and more every day" (2-1-18).

While still in Richmond, Carter writes a poignant letter revealing his frustrations—and hopes—for his father as he seeks a new job. His father has asked Carter to intercede on his behalf with Mr. J. S. Bryan whom Carter may be seeing to express gratitude for receiving the Ryan scholarship at the University. Carter tells his father that in the context of his visit to Mr. Bryan, he would be very uncomfortable doing this. In urgent and loving words he encourages his father to see Mr. Bryan himself:

> For me to introduce myself to Mr. Bryan to thank him is one thing and for me to ask him a political favor *after introducing*

> *myself* is another. He knows you. The thing to do is for you to come up here. I'll come home and take charge. Don't think about the lack of clothes. I can furnish you shoes and a gay neck tie or two and if you buy new clothes it will not be wasted money. You can afford to sacrifice something to the chance of getting a place (2-6-18).

Then follows a combination pep-talk and love letter—strong encouragement mixed with deeply serious words of admiration and love—all directed toward moving his father forward to what Carter considers his rightful place. He tries to build his father's confidence:

> . . . [C]ome see Davis, and the Messrs. Bryan yourself. You can see, if you think of it, how easy it will be for people to turn me down who will treat your claims with respect . . . Get your opinion of yourself in line with our opinion of you, do not depreciate yourself, and come after this job. You are the best man out for it until somebody else proves the opposite . . . Don't apologize for your age. It is the same as Woodrow Wilson's—you are a few months younger. I know your high opinion of me, [F]ather. Mine of you is just as high, though I fear I am too reserved to let you know the extent of it. I consider you the ablest public servant that Gloucester has had in a generation, the best educated man in Gloucester and far above all of Gloucester and the surrounding counties in oratory, oratory arising . . . [from] idealism applied to public conduct . . . Such a public conscience as yours is rare (2-6-18).

We do not learn the outcome of Carter's urgent words, or of his father's employment problems. Shortly before this earnest letter to his father, Carter passes the Air Service physical exam, but not without initial dismay over the depth perception section: "I worked on that thing five minutes or more . . . Right there I might have failed if I had gotten panicky" (2-1-18).

Finally on March 9, after several weeks at home, he enters the Cornell School of Military Aeronautics in Ithaca, New York—commonly known as "ground school"—studying there until graduation in late June. At

Cornell, he is one of 600 men sleeping on cots in a huge building, which also has "aisles, shelves[,] a passage way, offices, and then one-half taken up by aeroplanes and apparatus" (3-9-18). After three days he still has received no mail, and has endured "gruesome tales of men flunked out," but "I see an aviator ought to be a man without nerves and try to keep this talk from getting on mine" (3-12-18).

A severe case of mumps lands him in the hospital for several weeks, and he suffers the discouragement of being dropped back to a different squadron, which will graduate about three weeks later than his original outfit. In mid-May he confides, "in the hospital I lost faith in myself but last night I dreamt I got the chance and found flying greatly to my liking" (5-15-18). The next day his optimism returns:

> I'm going to fly yet . . . I passed my equilibrium test this morning. I vomited a little but really wasn't sick much . . . My exam was given by enlisted men and I was quite surprised to find them very considerate, almost tender. My respect for the medical corps was increased (5-16-18).

As his health and strength return, he reports he has "almost been having a good time." He regales his family with anecdotes about two officers who have come up from the ranks after long service as sergeants, one of whom "has the gift of profanity":

> An old sergeant who has been made a first lieutenant came upon a sentry making a noise on the floor with his heels, "walking his post in a military manner." Instead of commending his diligence at 4 A.M. he said, "Couldn't you find any damn place to sit down?" He meant it too . . . (5-18-18).

To give further color to his new military life at Ithaca, Carter quotes as much as he can remember of the songs the men are singing:

> Oh, it's not the pack you carry on your back
> Nor the Springfield on your shoulder
> Nor the five inch crust of Tompkins [County] dust

> That makes you feel that your limbs are growing older.
> Oh, it's not the sox of sister's that raise the blooming blisters
> That drive away your smile.
> (and then another line)
> It's the Last Long Mile (5-30-18)!

He also tells his mother about an especially poignant moment when his old, pre-mumps squadron paid him a "pretty compliment":

> It is not customary to give "Eyes Right!" even for an officer except on parade. But I came to attention as . . . [my] old squadron passed me on its way to class and the squadron marcher gave "Eyes Right" and saluted just as if on parade. It was a very sweet and bitter moment when they passed by. The boys are nice to me all the while (5-15-18).

By June, Carter is feeling strong and well again, and writes both about his concern for his behavior under battle conditions as well as his introduction to the gas mask:

> [My friend Charlie Engard] lacked education but knew engines and loves a fight—which is more than I ever would if I grew to be Goliath of Gath. I hope I am not cowardly but it will take me some time to get used to being bombarded. I feel sure of that (6-4-18).
>
> We have been drilling with gas masks this week . . . I never realized the horrors of gas until I had one of those things on and double timed about fifty yards with a rifle, bayonet, and belt. Your nose is pinched by a rubber clip and you breath[e] air from a chemical strainer . . . with your mouth. When you get hot and perspiring with it on, it is about as hard as a football game. Also you lose a little compression around your piston rings (an engine term) and your eye pieces get steamed up. Then you can't see and you must fight Germans in that fix. Thank goodness I joined the air service. Another thing you can do is to breathe in without holding your lips and teeth tight enough on the rubber mouthpieces. Then the rubber mask puffs in and out and your goggles steam up like window panes. When you breathe out the air escapes through a rubber tube under your

chin. Beginners are always unable to control their flow of saliva on the mouthpiece and consequently after being "gassed" my shirt front looks like the manger of [a] horse with the same complaint. They say all these troubles are conquered by practice. This then is the American gas mask, the best in the world. The Germans offered a reward for the capture of one (6-7-18).

Mid-month, in a jubilant mood, he reports his proficiency with a gun, and gives his views of waging war in the air as opposed to the experience of ground combat. He sees remnants of chivalry in air combat:

Ithaca, N.Y.
June 16, 1918

My dear Father,

Letters from you all overjoyed me and adding the others I have lately received I feel quite overjoyed with life in general.

There are other things, and I will tell the good first. I broke 21 clay pigeons out of 25 shots and before I never got over 7! I have found myself and when fellows come up suddenly like that they generally stay there. And gunnery is the most important thing in aviation. The best gunners get the best planes. You speak of taking human lives. I realize it. I detest it but since it is to be done I had rather take and give in the air where there is some chivalry yet than on earth, where men move like thugs—by night and armed with clubs. I have read that it pained British airmen when the Germans began to bomb hospitals. They said the German airmen were deteriorating—that Boelke, Immelman, and Richtofen would never have done such a thing. They still admire the foes, even as knights of old! . . .

I'm happy as I ever shall be until the treaty of peace is signed . . .

You are surely doing wonders on the place. I should like to get home and see it but we are graduated Saturday noon and report back Monday night . . .

With love to you all Devotedly,

Carter

Upon completing ground school, Carter is assigned to Souther Field, near Americus, Georgia where he will immediately begin flying instruction, as well as see many friends from his old squadron who are already there. He concludes a card to his Aunt Mary Nelson on June 25 with these words: "I'm well and immeasurably happy."

Carter arrives by train at Souther on June 28, after sleeping "two to a berth . . . and two of the three nights in an upper" (6-28-18). With no air conditioning, it is undoubtedly an arduous journey, though he says only that "the trip made me lose a little sleep . . . " (6-28-18). A couple of days later he can report, "The fatigue of the trip has gone and I am feeling fine but it is something of a change to jump from Cornell Tuesday to Americus Friday" where the temperature is over a hundred degrees some days (c. 6-30-18). "It is so hot I enjoy the novelty of it" (7-6-18). He writes his aunt that "kitchen fatigue duty and writing a long letter home have reduced my brain to lard and perspiration" (early July, 1918), but after becoming acclimated to the Georgia summer, he seldom mentions the weather except when cloudy days prevent flying.

In the two weeks before he starts actual flying at Souther, Carter reads novels—available in the YMCA library—and perfects his skill in evading make-work projects imposed by the sergeant:

> . . . I'm getting "fed up" on novels. I shall turn to poetry next. The "Y." has a pretty good library and I mean to enjoy it. I hate this easy life and don't enjoy loafing but what am I to do. The only amusement I have is ducking work which does nobody any good. I get out of shoveling oftener than anybody I know. The work is just given us to keep us out of mischief. I've gotten out of a lot by sitting coolly in the Y.M.C.A. Of course I had a right to go there and sense enough too, for even by our first half-holiday I had learned that our sergeant was "hard-boiled" and put men to work on holidays. A lot of men stayed. They were grown men rather dignified and slow of wit. They did not know the great game of school boy and teacher which I happen to remember.
>
> The other morning we had a half-holiday—there are two a week—and I went off without permission to the "Y." I was

> afraid to ask for fear of refusal. Well, I was reading The Literary Digest, or Motion Pictures when here came my squadron of cadets and halted in front of the door, the hard-boiled sergeant at their head. Well, Carter, my lad, says I, they are going to be paid off and you want your pay. So I put on my hat with its white band and walked right by the sergeant just as though I had a perfect right to step into ranks at Heaven's gate. He never noticed me. But he had called the roll. My friends advised me to try to square it with him but I knew something of military methods and doubted whether he had the list of absentees. Sure enough my name was called and I got my pay—without any kitchen police or tongue lashing. Of course my heart was doing double time when I was waiting for my name and standing three feet from the sergeant, trusting his forgetfulness . . . A bold innocent face, a controlled tongue and watchful waiting keeps me out of trouble in the army. Of course, the best thing is never to offend, but who can do that in this army (7-7-18)?

At last the dream comes true. By early August Carter is flying, and reports he has "taken 15 trips alone . . . and the last one is the best of all. In another week and two days I'll be turned loose entirely except for general instructions as to where to fly and what to do" (8-8-18). By inquiry of other cadets he learns that his grades are right in the

The "Jenny"—Curtiss JN4, the training plane for Carter and other World War I pilots.

middle of what others are averaging. He reports receipt of a new and "proud possession"—his pilot's book in which he can now record "11 hrs 26 min." flying time (8-8-18).

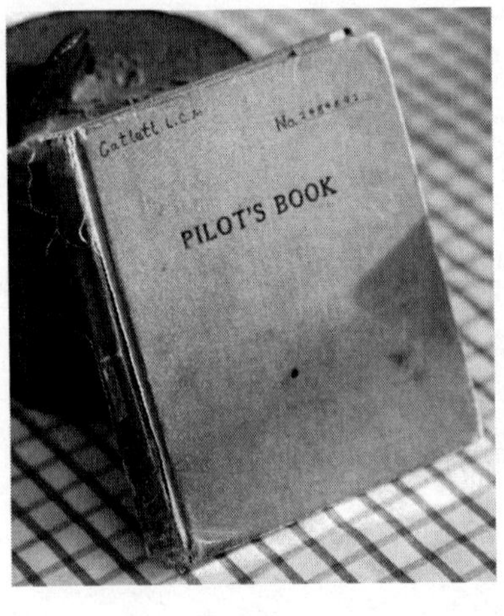

A jitney driver takes him on a wild ride into town, and has a minor accident: "I knew our driver was a fool all the way but I wasn't going to let him say he had scared an aviator . . . " (7-7-18). By mid-August he is describing the next day's schedule as "something like Heaven. Three hours of flying and three on the gunnery range . . . " (8-17-18). At the end of the month he reports, "Flying is all pure delight now. We have one more day in primary solo and each day my work has been pronounced very good—though far from perfect" (8-25-18).

Days at Souther test him in many ways. Using his head, following instructions carefully, building confidence in himself and maintaining his nerve are recurring themes. He is also at pains to underscore to his parents what he considers to be the low risks in what he is doing, as in this description of cross-country flying experiences:

> Anybody can do . . . [cross country] if the engine holds up and nobody can do it if the engine goes dead. The only thing to do then is pick your cotton patch, find out what section of the U.S. you are in, and telephone in to camp. If they think you were justified in landing—if you picked the best cotton patch in the county—you may be exonerated. If not, they may transfer you to a school for bombers or observers. It has happened and nobody could tell why. These trips are 50 or 60 miles and there are a couple of cadets out somewhere now. They never get hurt and almost always get a chicken dinner at some farmhouse. Still it is disconcerting to land in a place where you can't take off. They sometimes land in tree tops and climb down the tree

> unhurt. A fellow can land very well in a treetop if he has to. It is remarkable how badly a machine can get busted up without hurting a man. Lt. Zapp, a very daring fellow, before he came here fell 2000 ft—and cut his lip. Sometimes they say a ship is completely demolished and the pilot picks the splinters out of his clothes, and lets out a blue stream of profanity. In ten minutes he is up again . . . but we've had no . . . fatal or disabling [accidents] so I've gotten over my horror of them—though I'm careful for I'm sure they are uncomfortable and over 90% due to the pilot's fault. But, thank Providence, I have perfect confidence and so perfect safety. Loss of nerve is the one great danger in the air (9-4-18).

Two days later he experiences a very challenging and difficult exercise, but he notes the confidence it gives him:

> I did my radio to day and expect to fly Canuck ships (a little faster), do my acrobatics and photography next week . . . That radio I worked off gave me confidence because I did it in clouds, wind, and rain. The lieut. said my work was better than average in spite of the adverse weather conditions. I was very much surprised as I felt like I was making a mess of it, what with losing my self in the clouds and not knowing what I was sending on account of the roar of the motor. I lost 300 ft of cable with a sinker on it too . . . I was letting it run with my coat sleeve as a brake when suddenly I started into a cloud and my tail-heavy ship started to climb. Just one second I gave to the ship and in that second it ran out the last 100 ft and snapped off. I lost it all but they may find it. I landed and got a new one but, believe me, I was busy in the clouds with ground panels to answer, reeling and unreeling, sending messages and always that ship trying to stand on its tail instead of nosing gently down like a good ship. That trip was more pleasant to look back on than to experience. Now that it is over I wouldn't take a lot for the confidence it gave me. And the lieutenant complimented me on using my head and conquering obstacles. He never mentioned the 300 ft I lost (9-6-18).

During the first week in September, Carter faces a new challenge—learning acrobatics. Initially he reports enjoyment of the new work and is pleased with his performance:

> 7:15.—I come in all smiles and enthusiasm. I got my first hour of acrobatics and enjoyed it immensely. I did numerous Immelman turns and one or two loops and tail spins. Of course the instructor did them first. An Immelman turn beats a loop. It looks the same until the machine is almost on its back. Then it suddenly flips right side up and glides down in the opposite direction. In a loop you end going the same way as when you started. In a tail spin your nose points straight at the ground and the whole ship spins round and round, the tail describing a wide circle. Some tail spins are much faster than others. At the end of the trip the lieut tipped the ship over sideways and cut the gun, holding the nose down slightly. We sideslipped down 1500 ft or more. The way you tell that you are slipping is by the wind coming against the side of your face instead of straight into you. It was a grand ride. I came down pretty weak but that's to be expected for the first time. It is much harder to sit and "experience" acrobatics than to do it yourself because then you know what is coming (9-8-18).

Despite the daily challenges a cadet aviator experiences, Carter is restless in off hours. He confides his discontent to his mother in a letter in which he revisits the knotty question of what he is going to do with his life:

> . . . My old classmates [from ground school] got their commissions yesterday and went home. Of course that reminded me of the mumps again but my bitterness is gone . . .
>
> I have plenty of time and I do nothing but write letters and read novels. You know how I read. It is like smoking opium. Each novel is a spree. I read one, sometimes two in one day and then stop for a day disgusted with myself. I've been unable to find taste for any study to improve my mind. I surely cannot fly in the morning and take recreation in Greek and philosophy in the afternoon. These fellows here don't know anything about politics. Well,

> neither do I, but I know government and they don't . . . None of them but one ever quote[s] poetry. Once in awhile I find a man who admires a sunrise or sunset. The sun and the moon surely do know how to rise here in Georgia. One day I found a fellow who showed me how ants kill flies and once a fellow taught me a little about stars. On the whole, I've gained something of human sympathy and the matter of making friends but nothing mentally. I feel stagnant because my mind isn't sufficiently occupied. At times I believe I could remedy this if I had anything to study. But what? I've had no start in French. I care nothing for aviation except the actual practice of flying and study has apparently little to do with it—save of course, knowledge of the fundamentals we learned at ground school. I have no desire to delve deeper. I once felt attracted by the ministry but if I entered it I should feel always that "for appearances sake" I should or should not do certain things and I do despise theology and doctrine. I want to be of service to the world but not as a minister of the gospel—at least I don't now. I did hope to be a Professor of German but do I want to be now? Really, I am afraid not. Latin, Greek, the German seem such poor things to make a living from, while such a delight to have knowledge of. Still I'm war-mad now and see all this with distorted vision. Please don't show this letter to the general public . . .
>
> At present, I admire the West Pointer very much and I may yet go if the war ends in a year or two. I cannot tell . . . Nobody but me would be worrying about what he is going to do after the war anyway. But I must talk to you about it when I come home (9-1-18).

A respite from long thoughts and daily challenges is provided by "a very remarkable comedian here," who mocks their daily hazards with bold words:

> You would enjoy him singing and dancing a ballet in the center of a host of young soldiers accompanied by a ragtime artist on the piano and by a banjo which never stops . . .
>
> Oh, [M]other, suppose I had stuck to my bargain and finished my session at U. Va! I wouldn't have been able to fly till

> next summer. I had sense enough to know that such a golden opportunity wouldn't stay open forever . . .
>
> And fancy my being subject to draft this fall! Oh, I'm glad I came in when I did all right. I hope that none of my family ever stay out of war except from a strong sense of duty (9-8-18).

Just a week before completing the course at Souther the weather "is so cold we are wearing our leather coats. They are lined with corduroy, fairly warm, and excellent wind protection. I never expected to crave a fire here" (9-21-18). He describes a unique test that he passes:

> The wind was from the northeast all the way yesterday and very cold. I made my last cross country trip and wore woolen sox and helmet, sweater, winter breeches, and leather gauntlets with wool gloves inside, and my issued leather coat and goggles. I didn't suffer but I could feel the cold. I got seasick rolling around in the heavy wind. As usual it was because my breakfast had been very scant and unpalatable. I always wondered if I could drive a ship and vomit at the same time. I did it and felt much relieved (9-21-18).

Formation flying, which reminds him of "a flock of wild geese" (9-4-18), comes at the end of the course, and brings out his spirited—and sole—criticism of a fellow aviator's skill:

> I'm getting along fine and fly fairly well in formation. This is a stage that shows up the imbeciles and weaklings. We've found two. I never imagined that a fellow could enter aviation and be too timid to fly close enough in formation. We had one fellow today who couldn't climb a ship and couldn't come close enough to make a good formation . . . He doesn't know how to fly and in three days he'll be an officer. They ought to make him a mail carrier. He has no brains and no spine, coupled with a gift of exaggeration that approximates a "turosity for lying." All five of us have cussed him out and still he doesn't realize it is his fault. He blames his ship . . . The truth is he couldn't keep it in formation because he lacked sense (9-24-18).

Carter comments that he is "not dashing enough to be a pursuit pilot" (8-22-18), but on completion of the course at Souther, he is recommended for pursuit training, which he considers "the highest recommendation" (9-21-18). In late September, 1918, he receives the treasured silver pilot's wings and his temporary commission as a second lieutenant in the Army Air Service.

Landon Carter Catlett, Jr., after receiving his pilot's wings and his commission as a Second Lieutenant, Souther Field, Georgia, September, 1918.

After a disappointingly brief home leave, Carter arrives at Carlstrom Field, Arcadia, Florida, on October 10. Almost immediately he is flying the faster pursuit planes and stunt instruction begins, accompanied by a rebellious stomach:

> Monday and Tuesday I flew a machine like I was used to and did no stunts. Yesterday the instructor took me up and "stunted" me in a high-powered machine. I got sick as a horse after half an hour. To day I stood three quarters of an hour and lost my lunch just as he landed. After half an hour's rest I took up a Curtiss JN4D (the kind I'm used to) and did stunts alone for 45 minutes. I brought it down, rested three quarters of an hour and did 8's for twenty minutes. The instructors are very considerate . . . [of] me and very encouraging. 65 hours of flying doesn't give every man an acrobatic stomach. But in another week I feel sure there won't be any stunts in the curriculum that I won't do and do right. After flying the 100 mile-an-hour machine my old JN4D seems like a tumble cart, everything happens so slow. But at first the high powered JN4H numbs your muscles, it whips over so fast. However I'll wager that in two months it will seem as slow to me as the D does now.
>
> The D and H have the throttle on the right side and one drives them with the left hand but the Thomas Morse scouts that we drive after a couple of weeks are just the opposite so I am practicing with my right hand. I can drive fairly well that way. I hope Spads are driven left handed. The ambition of all pursuit student officers is to drive a Spad (10-16-18).

A couple of weeks later, his perseverance begins to pay off, and confidence about stunting begins to build in him:

> Another of my class from Souther has transferred to bombing. A lot of them have been sickened by acrobatics but my case encourages them to stick . . . Each new kind of ship whirls me faster than the last and makes me sick. I went at it too fast yesterday but today I flew around some between stunts and didn't get sick. I passed the week's work but the instructor advised me to take an extra week of stunts before going into formation and combat, which finishes the course . . . A number of men are busted on . . . [combat] but believe me, [M]other, if my little stummick learns to behave like I think it will, your little son is going to pass his combat on schedule time. He has confidence in his own grit, which was something he never had before. He always wondered if he would show a

> yellow streak if he were put in a front line trench and now he *knows* he wouldn't . . . Flying with a sick stomach [makes me confident]. I wouldn't take something for the test it has put me to. I've wanted to transfer to easier work but pride has held me up when enjoyment of the work was unhorsed and even when sick I have never ceased saying "I won't quit unless they kick me out." And today I stood it and enjoyed it (11-2-18)!

Sometimes, he writes his mother, he has been afraid of not graduating from Carlstrom, "for all through my course there have been times of almost despair." He also notes that he does not "often write anything confidential because too many people read my letters. Many things I could write to none but you and [F]ather" (11-24-18). By early December he successfully completes the training at Carlstrom and makes the long-hoped-for move to Dorr Field, Florida, for training as a pursuit pilot.

In a mid-December letter to his sister, Mary Mann, he describes some of the work he is doing and mentions the fatal accident of another student pilot at Dorr just before his arrival:

> Last week I shot silhouettes of airplanes, shadows of ships flying over ponds, parachutes, and tow-targets. The silhouettes are made of concrete and covered with water so when the bullet hits you see a splash. You dive at the silhouette until you are two or three hundred feet from the ground and pointed nearly straight down. Then you climb up again. When you are diving you sometimes get a dose of water and oil in the face which makes it like the Germans were shooting at you. One day my shell deflector came loose and all the empty cases came flying by my right ear at 80 miles an hour. All of us have black faces from the oil when we come in. You can imagine how good soap and water feels because the sand blows and sticks to the oil. Not all airplanes throw oil but these "Hissos" (Hispanos, J.N.4. H's) surely give us a dose. But you don't notice it till you get down. Then you feel hot and greasy and the sun is right there to fry you all day long.

> The parachute has an 8-pound bag of sand tied to it. You release it by pulling a string at 5000 feet and shoot 100 times at it before it lands. Of course you can't shoot in the direction of the field. Due to the fact that the war is over I keep away from that 8-pound sand bag. One fellow hit it with his wing the day before Thanksgiving. He left a widow and one child . . . (12-14-18).

Carter goes on to talk about night flying, making no further comment on the fatal accident:

> Last night I did my first night flying. The ship has green lights on the tips of the right wings, red on the left and a white on the tail to keep another ship from running into it. The landing place is lit up by a searchlight. In case of a forced landing the pilot (at bombing fields) can drop light bombs, rockets or parachute flares to see his way down. I just made three landings to get the hang of it. That is all the practice they give us here. It is beautiful, too beautiful for words, to fly on a bright moonlit night (12-14-18).

On December 20, 1918, he graduates from the School of Aerial Gunnery at Dorr Field, and thus completes the course for student officers trained to be pursuit pilots. His was the last group at Dorr, the armistice having been declared six weeks earlier.

Carter's comments on the war's end are sparse, possibly because following the armistice there is a two-week hiatus in the letters saved. On Armistice Day itself he writes:

> The papers say that Germany has surrendered. I am as frankly thankful as any of you. I am entirely happy that it wasn't necessary for me to kill a man. Of course I should have performed the duty pretty cheerfully if necessary . . . (11-11-18).

When thoughts turn to his plans for the future, he tries to sort out further his goals and options, reflecting over and over again on what holds meaning for him:

Souther Field, Ga.,
September 13, 1918

Dear Mother,

[Father's] generation has brought forth prohibition and compulsory education and woman suffrage, which are as great a service to the world as the abolition of slavery—and much better brought to pass. But I hope that my generation will clean up city and state government, save the nation from millions of pork barrel expenditure[s] by a sensible budget system and bring it to pass that an office holder may once more be held in honor and may deserve it. Ah, [M]other if only my heart was in the business of being a minister of the gospel as it is in politics. But could I be a good minister and be bored to death? If I were a minister I would be a missionary to Alaska but can I convert heathen when I am not sure of myself? On the other hand I love the business of government, the least respected of all professions and I can't enter it because I would never make an honest living at it and would fail, being not the man to appeal to the American voter. Should I study the law then? God forbid, for the science of government is the only part of it I care for, the least remunerative and uncertain for an honest man. I should be in the worst company in the world if I became that sort of lawyer. No, [M]other, at present I see plenty of ways to make a life, several to make a living, but it is not easy to pick the best combination . . .

With a heart full of love to you all, living in hopes of seeing you

Devotedly your son,
L. C. Catlett Jr.

When Carter is anticipating the armistice, he writes his father that he has decided to apply for an appointment to West Point, even though it means he will have to resign his commission:

> . . . there is a career of usefulness and honor for a Pointer both in the army and out of it. It is the only service I know of that gives the man a chance to serve his government honestly without toadying politicians—and I always wanted to serve the public

> good . . . I fear that after being in the service a professorship looks rather tame for one so young. Besides there are plenty of teachers in the army. I had rather teach . . . say aeronautics, than the German language, which I had intended to study in Germany, etc., in my old college dreams . . . How many dreams I have dreamed, but I have prayed God many times to make of me what he wills (11-3-18).

Carter acknowledges that army service will not be very lucrative, but thinks it suits his feelings about money. As to the army overall, he claims to have no illusions about it:

> I know something about the army. I know it harbors laziness, snobbishness, and selfishness, as do other professions. Still, though these are not civil war times, it means something to be a "Pointer" . . . [The army] offers a good living and not great wealth, which is the argument these Yankees give me. "You can make more money (with your brains) in business for yourself," they say. I do so hate the striving after money that a fixed salary and ultimate pension with an opportunity for holding responsible position[s] looks good to me (11-3-18).

But the matter of West Point remains unsettled as he argues back and forth with himself:

> I've decided to stop trying for West Point but I shall strive to keep a permanent commission and try by hard work to get a military education while serving as a flier. Besides flying is going to be a big thing and I want to stay in the business till I am a top-notcher. If the field in the army doesn't promise much, I can cut loose and I'll still be young . . . (11-24-18).

At year's end there is still no final resolution about his career plans. During January, Carter does more hard thinking about why he favors the regular army despite the fact that others think that it's foolish for him to stay in the service:

> [A]side from . . . [my expectation that army pay will be raised] and aside from the fact that I like to fly, I have a big reason

> for staying in. I don't know anything else I want to do and I would hate to be out of a job at 40 years old because I chose a poor kind of work and grew dissatisfied. The army is a sure thing—sure as human affairs go. If I stay in till the age of retirement I am retired on ¾ pay and so for my whole life it is a good living, neither poverty or riches. It is an opportunity for an active life out doors and a life of real service. An officer can do much to make men happy or miserable. He can have moral influence for good or for evil.
>
> Of course you know how I love to be a soldier. That is probably the root of the matter . . . (1-12-19).

He complains about attitudes of others toward the hazards of flying, and in the course of refuting their dire predictions, throws new light on his flight training experiences:

> I dislike to say hard things of people but the people who go around saying that aviation will get anybody sooner or later make it rather hard for us by giving our dear ones anxiety . . . There are some flying fields who have never had a casualty. Souther Field had only one. The work at Carlstrom and here was difficult, carried on under high pressure, and some of the men we had feared neither God or devil. Most of the accidents happened to students, inexperienced as I was at the start. I had some lucky chances and close shaves but by Providence of God I came through without a scratch or nervous shock and some of my instructors (this is secret) said they had never seen my beat for nerve[,] that I had a complete self-sufficiency of nerve or something of the kind. But it wasn't a brilliant stunt. It was merely a grin and a laugh when I had a right to a little nervousness and was determined not to think about it. I never have and my friends still talk about my serenity (1-12-19).

A little later, he characterizes himself as a "family man," and reflects on the somewhat difficult and aimless social environment of life at Carlstrom Field:

> I am a "family man," with all my life plans made, except the lady that will be my wife, who is not decided upon. So you

> see I have omitted what some might call the most important thing of all, but that doesn't matter. I find that it is easier to do right and life is happier, when I look on every action of my own from the point of view of a "family man". Do you see what I mean? While all around is reckless pleasure seeking in ways that do not attract me and the camp is quarantined from flu and religious services, when you find no man to give you spiritual counsel and very few who care to discuss such topics, then thoughts from home and letters from home are the strongest moral support we soldiers have (1-18-19).

On February 11, his twenty-first birthday, a bombshell drops and puts an end to his ruminating: he is offered an appointment to West Point, and is catapulted into decision-making. He considers the implications of his decision not only for himself but for other family members as well:

> [Feb. 12, 1919]
>
> My darling Mother,
>
> Yesterday I became of age and yesterday I had to make what is probably the most momentous decision of my life—one that I could not make alone. At first my decision was to refuse the appointment but after talking to the Commanding Officer (who would not advise me) and to some of my best friend[s] among the officers, I saw clearly that West Point was the only thing. I realize that I shall be of no help in starting Mary Mann's education but I couldn't do much any how if I was discharged from the army and had to finish my own course. Even staying in the army, I should always regret my lack of technical education and for the mere aerial chauffeur there is little or no future. Of course West Point will be a grind for me. But if I get in I shall stick.
>
> What worries me is the mental exams on history, geography, geometry, and other high school subjects. I have lost my freshness in those branches and see very little opportunity of polishing up. I have no books here. But my fund of general information will help me and maybe my University certificate will get me excused from the mental examinations.

> Colonel Duncan recommends a 30 day leave beginning March 1 and it is about to start on its way to the Southeastern Department. If it is granted, I shall [have] 15 days at least at home and with relations and I can spend some time in preparation for the exams. During that month I shall not receive any flying pay . . .
>
> With a heart full of love for each and all,
> Your devoted son,
> L.C. Catlett, Jr. (2-12-19)

Others are enthusiastic about his appointment, but his ambivalence remains:

> About 51% of me wants to go to West Point and 49% has no stomach for it. But 101% of me wants to get that 30 day leave and come home. Nothing else matters much. West Point is a great opportunity for education but to accept it I am giving up a good deal in position and immediate prospects. Which will prove wisest in the long run, no man can tell . . . I should enjoy studying and playing football again but cadet life will be pretty hard after being an officer for eight months. I don't like to hear about all the stuff that the cadets have to stand their first year because I feel somewhat like a grown man and rather above the continual hopping to attention and moving at double time. My swelled head is the natural result of my army life. I hope I shall be able to keep it to myself if I do go to the Academy. Going up in officer's uniform will probably get me unfavorable notice among older cadets but I certainly won't buy civilian clothes for the occasion (2-21-19).

The quick turn of events requiring immediate decision, the farewells to friends, as well as his eagerness to be home for a while, leave him in a state of decidedly mixed emotions: "I feel like a lad graduating . . . [from] college only more so. I feel like a bride and groom. I can laugh and cry at the same time" (2-21-19).

Carter finally gets the longed-for leave in April, and after his visit home, returns once again to Carlstrom to await his discharge, hoping to have a month in Virginia before he enters West Point in June. A final frustration faces him. Because of bureaucratic bungling, a good part of the precious time he had expected to spend with family and friends is passed at Camp Hill in middle Virginia waiting for his discharge papers. His letter home on May 16 expresses his dismay and anger, which is so great that he uses a word that has never before appeared in his letters:

> I am sick at heart. Carelessness and delay in the Personnel Office here has tied my discharge up in an awful snarl . . . After putting my papers in two weeks ago, I found out yesterday that they had not gone to Washington! If ever I get into a position of importance in the army I'm going to slash red tape.
>
> I enjoyed Fanny's letter immensely and would answer it if I were not in such a raging humor that every word is a labor. When I get home I'll be there [only] 2 ½ weeks. Damn.

In mid-June, 1919, after his greatly reduced home leave, Carter travels to New York to enter the United States Military Academy at West Point high above the Hudson, and to endure a three-year hiatus in flying.

To my father, Landon Carter Catlett, Jr.:

You beguile me with your mischievous avoidance of the make-work sergeant, your accounts of surmounting the challenges of the primitive "ships" you are learning to fly, and the anxiety about your longed-for home leave. I am impressed with your abiding interest in politics and government, and touched by your yearning for poetry—in the decidedly unpoetic surroundings of a raw flying field.

Then how on earth can it be possible that you, with your inquiring mind and appetite for life, will confine yourself to flying airplanes and waste yourself in the army? You reject college teaching, law, the ministry, politics, and, of course, you don't even mention farming, having long ago made it quite clear that agriculture is not for you. Business does not interest you in the least; in fact, it appears distasteful. But isn't military service antithetical to much that you enjoy and value? Where is choice and decision-making in the army—isn't it in the chain of command and the bureaucracy rather than the individual? And do you really want to give your life over to studying war?

It's clearly your love of flying that is leading you into a military career. I understand the attractions of neither the military nor the flying. A friend gives me Antoine de Saint Exupery's Wind, Sand and Stars, *thinking it will help me have sympathy for your love affair with flight, but even it does not reach me. I have to force myself to read it. Aviation means loss to me. Can you understand that? Listen to your two sentence report on the death of a student pilot: "One fellow hit . . . [the sandbag] with his wing the day before Thanksgiving. He left a widow and one child . . . "*

Did you pause even for a moment to think what leaving "a widow and one child" meant? Did you ever consider that you might do exactly that? Patriotism and honor and duty—well larded with your love of romantic adventure—let you avoid looking into the face of suffering.

You write Granny that you will not send a letter of condolence to the family's aged family doctor whose wife has died: "I can pity a man who has felt such a loss but not sympathize because sympathy can come only from experience in suffering, which I have not had . . . "

So where is your (self-proclaimed) prodigious imagination? Had you no means of picturing to yourself the heartbreak of your fellow student's wife, and the bewilderment of the abandoned child who, life-long, will live with emptiness where her father's love once lodged?

I know what happened to that child.

"He left a widow and one child." The grown child of our story speaks now, but the one who is "the widow" died years ago, having lived sixty-one years after her love crashed on the shores of Ft. Kamehameha. I never, ever, heard a word of reproach from her about your unwavering commitment to flying. You had the security of her full acceptance, but you don't have mine.

If you could have glimpsed the loneliness and hardship of her life without you, would it have made a difference to you? Remember, that though she had a child to support, she had no education to equip her to make a living. Most of all, you must know that your love gave her life, a life of warmth and acceptance and appreciation that she had never known before and was never to know again. She had different interests from the rest of her family, and without a facility for sharing her feelings, she suffered periods of depression. The memory, though dim, lingers: she is lying in bed early on a summer morning, her face sad and her thoughts far away, and on her bureau, the pictures of her dead husband and his planes and the framed verse beside them: "I cannot say, I will not say, that he is dead—he is just away."

And what of the struggles of the little girl as she grew into adolescence and the bewilderment of relating to boys? Having no sisters or brothers, and knowing no positive model of husband-wife relationships, that child had a hard time knowing what it should be and realistically, what it could be. Despite two sets of grandparents, the child had no fathering. She has no memory of snuggling into a protective father's arms, or sitting on anyone's lap except her mother's and your mother's.

You think only in terms of your own attitude toward death:

> *While I am not a daring flier I do not allow myself to be frightened off by a few accidents and the prospect of a military funeral. I*

> *really don't think I am afraid to die, if I can die in the course of duty . . . But I am thinking precious little about dying. I am learning to fly so fast that it makes my head swim and while I am a graduate pursuit pilot I regret like Alexander that there are not more worlds to conquer (12-20-18).*

Mastering flight seems to have taken hold of you, and you can't get enough of the exhilaration of facing—and overcoming—danger. But later your 23-month-old daughter could not understand any of this. She knew only that you waved good-bye one morning, and never came back.

* * *

Even in the midst of my anger, I cannot shut out the joy you take in flight: "I'm in primary solo now, flying over an hour a day. It is heavenly . . . ," and later, "It is beautiful, too beautiful for words, to fly on a bright moonlit night."

So I think of you now on that night of December 13 eighty-four years ago—in leather coat, helmet and goggles, heavy gauntlets on your hands—piloting the fragile wooden plane. Reluctantly, I acknowledge the joy in your heart as your skill, and the wonder and beauty of the night, satisfy your deep longing for both the physical and poetic in life. Your joy confronts the bitterness in my heart.

* * *

Words of our cousin, Sally Catlett, spoken back in the early 1950s when Franklin and I were soon to be married, come back to me. She told us that when someone challenged you about the hazards of aviation and the questionable wisdom of pursuing it when you were about to marry, you replied firmly that Catharine knew and accepted that flying was a part of your marriage.

There's no room for compromise in these direct and honest words. I know what it would have done to you to turn your back on this adventure of flight that fired your spirit. When you wrote your mother that you would "feel like a whipped dog" if you could not apply for the Air Service, you used a metaphor for a broken spirit.

But did you realize the price you asked Catharine to pay—to make promises to an unknown life fraught with mortal danger? Did you consider the children you surely looked forward to having? My bet is that possibility was anticipated only in the rosy glow of being in love, not for a moment in terms of what would happen to them in the event of your death. For Catharine, you spoke of the life insurance you carried, with no further attention to how she would support herself and her child in the event of your death. I suppose you thought the government pension would suffice, but the thirty dollars she received monthly for herself, and five for me, were far from adequate.

Overcoming fear, uncertainty, and troublesome physical reactions while learning to fly gave you hard-won confidence and determination. You made yourself almost impervious to doubt, which to you would mean loss of nerve. You wrote Granny that some of your "instructors . . . said they had never seen my beat for nerve . . . It was merely a grin and a laugh when I had a right to a little nervousness and was determined not to think about it. I never have . . . "

You had found your bliss. Because she loved you, Catharine was in an impossible position, unless she was brave and committed. She was both, and courageously hitched her star to yours. Loving you, Catharine could want nothing less for you. There was no other course for her to take.

For your daughter, it was a matter of being born into decisions already made.

Now in my third age, I ponder the silence with which I greeted our cousin's recollections. Think of the opportunity I had: Cousin Sally had known you since birth, was often in your home—would ride her horse the ten miles from Timberneck to visit or help out in time of sickness—even helped to bake your birthday cakes and supply you with your favorite sweet pickles at Episcopal High School. She could have given me immediate reflections on you in love and your talk about flying. But I made no comment and asked no questions.

I try to understand my unresponsiveness, to name the feeling that lay behind it. I know that a sense of remoteness shrouded you. Paradoxically, talk of you might have taken me to a place too personal, too unknown—it would have put me in a foreign land where I was a stranger. I didn't even know what to call you. I had no experience in talking about you and no language to use.

My mind goes to another experience that I now see as related to this one: my sudden rush of tears as I smoothed your uniform before returning it to the attic. There was no passage of time, no seconds ticking by. Touching the uniform, I was touching you. Smoothing out wrinkles in the cloth, I was stroking your broken body. Straight to the heart of your death I went, so close, intimate, immediate, shocking, and overwhelming, I couldn't tolerate it. I said nothing to anyone about it, not then or later. To know you in your woundedness, in the hour of your destruction, was too much. I had never before thought about the relationship we must have had, and for the first time I consciously grieved the loss of you.

Now I see for certain that somewhere deep inside is the experience of your love for me, and mine for you. It's been stored and waiting, but there was no trigger to activate it—until I touched your uniform. Sixty-three years passed, without an inkling of this buried treasure. But Connie, my therapist, had an idea of it in asking me from whom I got my warmth. When I suggested my aunt and my Catlett family, she shocked me with this statement: "I think the source of your warmth was your father."

"How could that possibly be?" I said. "I never knew my father—I have absolutely no memory of him!" Connie then spoke of the significance and importance of relationships in the first years of life, of how a baby absorbs feelings, attitudes, and ways of relating from those closest to her. I knew that this was well-established knowledge about infancy, but it astounded me when applied to myself. I think that having no conscious memory of you, I had not pictured myself as having a father in everyday experience. For me, no memory of experience was equal to no experience.

But your letters could tell me. So I chose an afternoon to read all of them beginning with September 2, 1923, the day of my birth. I closed the door to the bedroom, turned off the phone and settled into the armchair, with all your letters written after my birth beside me.

I read all thirty-three straight through, tears streaming—so copiously at times I couldn't read the words on the page. For there was both the wonder of your love, and the loss of it. And I cried in happiness—and in anguish.

You were interested in every detail about me and my care, ready to do anything that was needed, from answering my cry in the early morning to changing a soiled diaper. Now I know my own baby stories, and they are life-giving. Mother didn't tell them to me—in that era there was no understanding that a child needs to hear them, and it may have been too painful, as well, for her to recall those happy days. But now you have written amply on the blank slate of my early childhood.

* * *

I think of the little, little girl whose Daddy didn't come home one day, and who, a few weeks later, after traveling across a third of the Pacific Ocean and all the way across the continent, found herself in a strange household of big people, with her sad mother being the only one she knew. The lovely life of the little girl with her young parents was ended forever, without a shred of memory remaining. She now lived in Toddsbury a very old house, on a very old farm, on the shores of the North River, in Gloucester County, Virginia, with her mother, maternal grandparents, aunt and great aunt, and the latter's companion-caregiver. She was the only child in the household and there were no neighbors within walking distance. On this farm the earth was tilled in age-old ways with horse-drawn ploughs, disks and cultivators. Animals were raised for eggs, milk and meat, and a quarter-acre garden was tended to provide vegetables and fruits to feed family, guests and boarders.

* * *

On a cold and windy winter morning, I snuggle under the covers of my warm bed while Mother builds the fire in the air-tight stove that will soon warm the back bedroom that we share. I follow the ritual by ear—the scrunching of the newspaper, laying on of light kindling with a couple of heavy sticks on top, then the lighted match and the momentary whiff of sulfur when it's extinguished, a rattle signifying the final adjustment of the draft, and

Toddsbury, drive entrance in the 1920s.

Toddsbury, the view from North River.

soon the comforting pop and crackle of a good fire. Mother is dressing quickly, and admonishing me not to get up till it's warmer. As yet, there's no bathroom in the house, so our morning preparations take place behind the screen in the corner of our room.

When I reach school age, I catch the bus each morning at the head of our mile-long lane. When I get home on a winter's afternoon, Mother takes from the still-warm wood stove a plate of food from the family's one o'clock

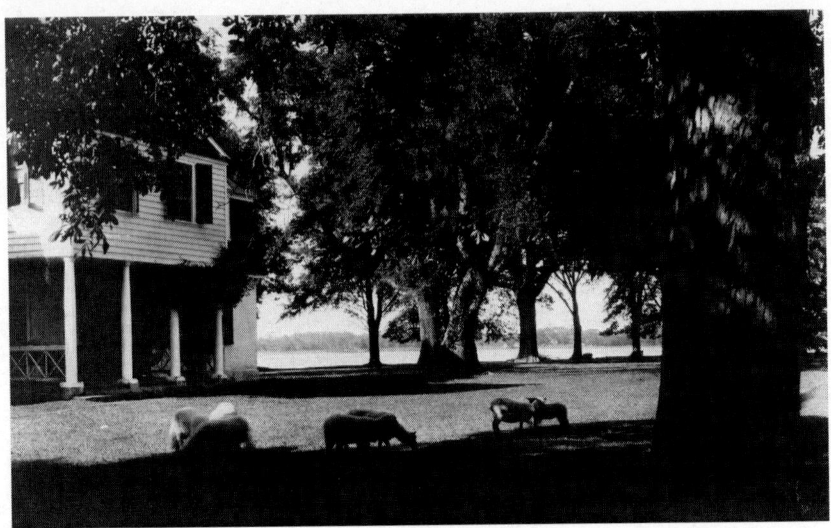

Sheep grazing the Toddsbury yard in the long shadows of a late summer afternoon.

dinner. Warm sweet potatoes glow in a moat of butter as the low rays of the winter sun stream in the kitchen's west window.

I sit at this same kitchen table on waning summer afternoons and talk to Lena Banks, the "colored" woman who helps in the kitchen when we have boarders. I hear Mother and my aunt, "Eddie", talking about her wages—five dollars a week. Even on that amount she can order a new dress for the church "Big Meetings" coming up in August. Together we pore over the Montgomery Ward catalogue, with Lena discussing the pros and cons of different styles. She favors a dress with a wide white collar. I think it's pretty too. I like these quiet times with Lena. She hums and sings in a high, plaintive voice a hymn I do not know—something about a telephone line to God.

When I'm a freshman in high school, I sit at the kitchen table while Rachel, who has succeeded Lena Banks, helps me with my Latin. The family think it a joke that "the colored girl" is doing this. None of them can help me with Latin, and I resent their ridiculing Rachel.

Sunday is the only day we heat the dining room. One Sunday Mother, the cook in the family, has pan-fried a T-bone steak, a cut she likes rare.

Grandfather starts to carve it, throws down his knife with a gesture of disgust, and says loudly that he is not going to eat raw meat, elaborating on the monstrosity that is before him and the insult it is to be presented with such a dish. Mother leaves the table in tears and silence reigns for the rest of the meal. I never hear words of apology or remorse from Grandfather, nor do we ever speak of the incident.

For summer meals we are always in the dining room, with Grandfather presiding at one end of the table, and Eddie, the eldest daughter, at the other. Mother, Grandmother, Miss Boykins (Great Aunt Janie's companion) and I sit on the sides, along with varying numbers of boarders, sometimes as many as four or five. Just-picked English peas from Grandfather's garden, and butterbeans and corn—both Golden Bantam and pearl-white Country Gentleman—are among my favorites, along with the abundant tomatoes and cucumbers. The latter are on the supper table almost every summer night, along with homemade cottage cheese. Sometimes we have clabber from a crock in the dairy house, delicious when served with liberal amounts of sugar and nutmeg.

There is lively conversation during some mid-day dinners, such as the running argument between Grandfather and Miss Boykins about the Prince of Wales and Mrs. Simpson. Miss Boykins is all for romance, while Grandfather is relentlessly critical of the Prince's behavior. I take this all in but am not drawn into the conversation, not being addressed except for inquiries about second servings.

There are only a few foods I do not enjoy, such as fried eggplant and our home-cured ham after eating it all winter, and there is much that I love. I especially anticipate supper on the summer days when Mr. Hudgins' fox-horn announces his arrival in the rickety small truck with the melting ice dripping from the tailgate. His early morning catch lies buried in that ice and promises a supper of golden-brown fried butterfish, with a freshness that sets the standard for how fish should taste.

Grandfather, Eddie, Mother and me, about 1929.

Summer mornings I am usually outdoors, often trailing Mr. Emerson, "the colored man," whom I call Arthur as everyone else does. He is kind and patient, looking out for me as he would his own daughter. I often ride the dump-cart with him, and in haying season he tolerates me riding to the field and coming home on top of the piled-high hay wagon. He stops the team at the front of the barn, then warns me not to come around back where they will be working with their pitchforks and the big fork that will be lowered from the barn peak to lift masses of hay into the loft. One day, hanging around the side of the barn, not quite daring to go to the back, I step on a rusty nail. It's a nasty puncture and Mother soaks my foot a couple of times a day and binds it with salt fat bacon, with the idea that the salt will draw out infection. It heals, and I don't get lockjaw.

Sometimes I trail Grandfather. He tolerates my presence but does not talk to me except for an occasional caution. "Stand back!" he says impatiently as I move in for a closer view of his skillful butchering of the lamb that has just been killed. He uses his knife with great precision, and I am fascinated with the lacy veil of fat he carefully wraps around each leg.

Mother, Eddie and Miss Boykins are devoted gardeners, and they're proud of my knowledge of the flowers when I'm just seven years old. I feel important when they have me take people around the garden, naming each flower.

As the Great Depression deepens, there is much talk at the table about "Nolting Brothers" failing. I don't know what Nolting Brothers is, but I do understand that some people have lost money because of its failure, and that maybe some in the family are among them. I also get a sense from bits of conversation between Mother and Eddie that Grandfather and Uncle Jim don't manage money well.

There is a dark undertone about men in Mother's words too. It is mixed up with poor management of money, and lack of consideration of women's work in the family. Mother and Eddie complain about Grandfather bringing a bushel or two of ripe peaches for canning, without warning. Or failing to work out a system to avoid overflowing the water tank, which is above our bedroom. Or by going out hunting on Christmas Day for so long a time that the much labored over, very special dinner for the whole family has to wait an extra hour.

I'm sick every winter. Mother nurses me through ear infections, chicken pox, measles and whooping cough in successive years, and several colds and at least one bout of flu annually. I love her baked custards when I am sick, but hate the milk toast she sees as the perfect simple and nourishing food for my suppers. Propped up in her bed, I chase the limp, soppy bread around the bowl of hot milk and wish for something else.

One cold and rainy evening, I tag along when Mother and Eddie go to watch Grandfather pull cars out of the mud. It is after dark and it has rained all day. One of our neighbors has given a party (to which we were not invited, Eddie notes), and the departing guests are sinking into the mud. Grandfather harnesses the team of horses and goes up the lane to rescue them.

As we come upon the scene, the horses, shining with sweat, are straining to pull a car out of its deep rut. The car does not budge. Grandfather cracks the whip on the horses and they strain again. The whip comes down again. The horses struggle, eyes bulging, sweat dripping. And again comes the whip. I cannot stand it and cringe behind Mother, who walks me back to Toddsbury, with that scene indelibly imprinted on my mind.

Though Eddie is four years older than Mother, she has an adventurous spirit, and sometimes we're not very considerate of Mother—we are having too much fun to heed her sensible cautions. A storm is brewing after a fearfully hot day. The river is gray-green, trees are thrashing in the rising wind, and Eddie calls to me, "Put on your bathing suit and we'll get the ducks up!" Out we go to the two duck coops in the east yard, taking some wet corn meal to entice the mother ducks inside, and the game begins. The addled mothers go round and round their coops. Eddie works one and I the other, with fuzzy ducklings—who will easily drown in a downpour if we don't get them under cover—trailing after them. Finally, we get one mother inside with her little flock, and working together, we quickly get the remaining "deedles" in with their witless mother. All the while, Mother is on the porch worrying and cautioning us about the falling limbs and trees which are all too common in heavy wind and lightning.

Eddie is the one who finally gets me over my fear of swimming in deep water. One afternoon when everybody else is swimming from the row boat, she simply throws me in, and of course I swim—even better than I could in shallow water.

Grandfather has long conversations with his hunting dog, an English setter. With the dog's head between his knees, he goes on and on, but Grandfather and Grandmother do not really have conversations. Grandmother asks him questions with which he is invariably impatient. Once or twice, maybe, I hear him say "Annie girl" with tenderness. I think it's when she is having one of her occasional "attacks", the nature of which we never understand but which cause me to be quickly dispatched to get Grandfather.

We all attend services at Ware Episcopal Church every Sunday and people always sit in the same pews. Mother has chosen a pew on the Catlett side, with her in-laws sitting several rows ahead of us. The Motts are across the aisle—Grandfather, Grandmother when she is well enough, Uncle Jim and Eddie.

There are few other children in sight, and I have a great preference for Morning Prayer over the monthly communion service, because of the comparative brevity of the former. Still, I wiggle and squirm and study the crack in the seat, which pinches me if I lean on it the wrong way. But the views from the great arched windows—twelve in all—surround us with dogwoods, red bud, and maples that are glorious in the changing seasons, and provide distraction even for an impatient child.

Everybody knows everyone else in this congregation and as soon as the service concludes there is a buzz of conversation in and outside the building, with people often lingering at the back door. We are always dressed up for church, and more than once I am complimented on my looks, but Mother immediately cautions, "Pretty is as pretty does."

I am with my Catlett grandparents quite regularly, as well as my two young aunts when they're not away at college. Mother and I have many Sunday dinners with them, and independently I go for week-long visits from time to time. Botetourt Grammar School is next door to their house, so even in the winter I can visit on my own.

During one of those visits, Granny Catlett has her feet propped up on the dining room stove, her favorite spot in cold weather, and Daddy Catlett is at his big roll-top desk. I am at the table writing "I will not talk in class" five hundred times. (I've learned to hold three pencils at once to speed the task.) The black and gold clock tick-tocks peacefully on the mantel above the stove, soon to sound its soft chime. Neither grandparent admonishes me about my misbehavior in class.

Between desk and stove hangs a calendar that quotes Shakespeare every month. Daddy Catlett has me read a selection and asks me, age seven or eight, what it means. Something about the reading or my hesitant explanation is unsatisfactory, and I am uncomfortable. I hope he never asks

Newington, the Catlett home at Gloucester Court House, about 1933.

me again to read from that calendar. On the whole Daddy Catlett is not very communicative, but his habit of sighing loudly—a sort of groaning—is audible throughout the house.

On one occasion in this same room, Aunt Fanny dresses me for a Hallowe'en party at the public school next door. My costume is gaudy and deemed appropriate for the "fat old colored woman" I am portraying. Perhaps I go to the party in black face—I am not sure about that, but I am having the fun of ropes of beads around my neck and down across my ample bosom. My only worry is that I may not be able to keep the pillow-padding in place.

I love to be in my aunts' bedroom where the white iron twin beds are set on either side of the bureau whose top drawers—with their powder puffs, rouge and lotions—are so alluring. I loll on the bed while they dress to go out. Even then they may be saying verses to me. "The Walrus and the Carpenter" is rendered in exaggerated tragic tones, or lines from Winnie the Pooh.

Granny teaches me how to hold the washcloth on the diagonal so that I can wash my back by myself. I do not linger long in the big old bathtub in the drafty bathroom heated by a temperamental kerosene stove. I like to be in the kitchen when she makes batter-bread muffins. I wait for that moment when, with a few deft swipes of her finger, she scrapes all the batter into the black iron muffin pans.

Quite often there are boarders at the table with us. Miss Brooke Byrd, of piercing eye and caustic opinion, is hardly inviting company—especially to children whom she is known to have scared out of the public library where she holds sway. Her black dress smells old and stale, but all are welcome at this table, and Granny's gentle manner defuses her boarder's caustic comments.

Other, altogether delightful boarders are Major and Mrs. Montague, recently back from the Philippines and newly retired. The Major entrances me with his funny stories, and his declarations on the evils of cigarette smoking. As he lights up, he warns, "It's a dirty, poisonous, and expensive habit." On one of those hot Virginia summer days, he instructs me in the language to be used in describing the body's response to all-encompassing heat: "Horses sweat, men perspire, and ladies glow!"

* * *

Daddy Catlett, Aunt Fanny and Granny Catlett in Newington yard, about 1932.

In many ways, it was a rich childhood, but there was a vacancy at the heart of it. Almost three-quarters of a century later, I am trying to conjure life with my father—with you. I yearn to know what it was like to sit on your lap, to feel your rough uniform next to my cheek and your arms around me. What was your scent, the timbre of your voice? Was your body relaxed and comforting as you held me? I watch your great granddaughter snuggle into the curve of her father's neck and think how I must have known that exquisite comfort and security. I close my eyes and try to feel myself riding your strong back as we play in the water, remembering my own children's delight playing with their father.

The more I read your letters, the more love and loss tear me up. I can't get a good night's sleep. I'm enervated, snapping at Franklin, and weeping at the drop of a hat. One rainy afternoon I lie on the bed all afternoon, unable to get myself together.

Tears dampen the board as I try to iron, and I awaken in sadness and cry in the middle of the night. Grief is exhausting me. Two forces push and pull inside me: one is the irresistible pull toward you, the other the awful push out into the cold where you are not present.

Through all this time, many layers of commitment are taking up my days, taking me away from your letters. I'm longing to get back to them, to you. One night I have a dream:

> *I had lost someone very important to me—why didn't Franklin and everyone else realize that? Why had they expected me to live as though nothing had happened? This person very dear to me was both dead and not dead. He was off on a long and dangerous journey, and I was not thinking about him or trying to find out how he was or planning to go to him. Instead, I was constantly pursuing my own interests. How could I have neglected him, this special person who should have meant everything to me?*
>
> *I'm drowning in sadness. I'm sinking, lost, overwhelmed. I can't*

> *seem to come to the surface. I can't shake the feeling that I've failed this person whom I love, this most important person in my life on whom all my attention should be focused. I have betrayed him, and I can't get to him to make things right. All is dark and heavy and the heaviness is weighing me down. No way to get through the murk to reach him, to loudly acclaim him and say here I am and I love you—that's what I want to say and that's what I want to hear him say.*

It's hard to climb up out of this dream.

Catharine Carter

5

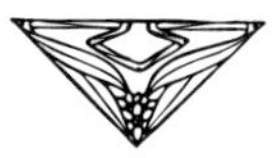

THE WEST POINT YEARS

PART I
Plebe

June, 1919—June, 1920

Periods of despair and discouragement mark Carter's first year at West Point, but initially he writes in good humor:

> I am writing now with white gloves on while waiting for inspection. Pretty soon I shall change my dress and turn out for bath. We have ten minutes to undress, bathe, dress, then four flights of stairs . . . I generally have time to powder my precious feet and open a standing blister on my right heel. My feet are getting well, but they have more work to do than any part of me. I love the work when I get along like I have to day. The worst of the officers are off on leave or something. Mother's long letter helped brighten things too . . .
>
> I wish I could give you some idea of my second week of "beast barracks." It has included inspections of every kind of equipment and in different uniforms, pack-rolling, tent-pitching, and plenty of close and extended order drill . . . Generally I do pretty well but I am by no means up to the West Point standard. Once or twice a day some command catches me wool-gathering and once or twice it has meant

> some double time. But on the whole, I am enjoying my self and learning neatness, speed, and precision (6-23-19).

In early July, the plebe summer camp begins, first on the grounds of the Academy, and then for a period in the countryside practicing war games. Carter writes home at the beginning of camp, telling of his relief to be away from "beast barracks" and conveying a sense of the relationships that characterize plebe year:

> Well, I feel like I had lived ten years in the past three days. Already I like camp better than barracks but it has been fearfully hard work.
>
> We don't salute any cadet officers except when we are on guard but we stand at attention and say "sir" to them. They take up a lot of our time asking us who we are and where we come from and who they are and where they come from and if we guess wrong they are highly disgusted. If we are asked if we know someone in the corps we have to say "No" unless the upper classman in question has "recognized" you. My "pred" [predecessor], Downing, has recognized me and I sit and chat with him without saying "Mr." or "sir". Some of the other Virginia men will recognize me before the summer is over. If being known is a step to being recognized I am on my way . . . I was late getting ready for chapel, needed a shave, had my collar badly fixed, and my shoes unshined. I pulled in my chin and gave no excuses. That's part of the game. But having to report made me miss communion and I hated that . . . (7-6-19).

Carter is introduced to the cadet practice of supplementing camp rations with "boodle" (sweets and other food) and, though this is against the rules, on several occasions he requests small amounts of money from home for that purpose. Similar requests in the fall bring questions from his mother about this practice, and result in Carter explaining his attitude toward rule-breaking:

> But first let me try to answer for myself in the matter of corrupting a government employee, namely, my janitor. There are about 20 janitors here and all of them buy the

> boys cigarettes and bring in packages . . . Jim Coffey is one of the oldest of all. He is very fond of the boys and always comes in to see if by chance we have forgotten to empty our slop bucket. Whenever the boys tip him, he always says "too much, won't take it" and returns half of it or all . . .
>
> The system doesn't fill me with any great horror. I don't defend it, but all my life I have broken school rules and taken my punishments like a man (12-5-19).

Carter enjoys the second phase of camp when the plebes practice war games:

> We skirmished with enemy cavalry all morning. It was lots of fun. I was killed twice but before that it was hard work. I was in the very first squad of the advanced guard. We have boodle in plenty now and I'm happy . . . .Well, I am enjoying it to the full and wish it could last a long time (8-19-19).

While at camp, Carter receives a letter from his old friend, Charlie Wilson, his University roommate at Mrs. MacIlherney's boarding house. Charlie gives a glimpse of a maturing Carter through the eyes of a warm and earnest friend:

> What may surprise you of all people is the fact that I have always considered "you" my ideal male from every angle. It might embarrass you even in writing if I began to elucidate too freely but suffice it to say that I am positive that I know you from A to Z and I rate you about as high as the Ivory Soap advertising force do their product that is *99&44/100% pure. When we roomed together at college I used to watch you very closely...I was horribly jealous of your brains and terribly conscious of your mental, moral and physical superiority . . . and I concluded that you had one main fault . . . just as you told me when we first met each other . . . CONCEIT . . . Well . . . when you returned from your flying with that [Second Lieutenant's] Commission I naturally expected it to go to your head something awful. Let me tell you I got the biggest surprise of my life when I found that not only had you not become more conceited but that you had lost all of your former bit . . . it sure was a great pleasure to mark the improvement there

> and in one other direction . . . you had acquired a certain bit of gracefulness that old Gloucester county had till then failed to produce . . . 7-15-19).

By late August, Carter is back in cadet barracks. Just before classes begin, he writes that "[i]t is time that I should mention some of the upper classmen by name":

> First comes Mr. Dance, from Louisiana, who marches next to me. He is a happy-go-lucky fellow, a V.M.I. and Princeton man, "hivey" (bright in studies), but given to pranks. He was "busted" from his corporalship for smoking a cigarette while on guard. For the same offense he walked the area twenty-two hours and stayed in confinement one month . . . Well, this Mr. Dance is a rich man's son, lovable and irresponsible. He stands high without studying. He treats me handsomely, has given me second-hand uniforms (all upper classmen do) and promises me an overcoat, so I can keep my own for nice . . . (8-31-19).

Classes begin September 1st, with Carter giving no more particulars than reporting courses in "Math . . . English and History . . . and drawing on Saturdays." He adds that they have "gymnasium and drill and parade every day, all in different uniform. It means some tall hustling" (8-31-19).

He is conflicted about making special efforts to excel in his academic work:

> Sometimes I kick myself for coming here. To stand well would mean no especial honor, not to do so would be disgraceful. Well, I didn't come here so much for academic work as for West Point training (9-2-19).

In mid-October, Carter, in a letter to his father, mentions his "dread [of] meeting girls" and expresses his regard for non-commissioned officers:

> Jim Daniel has Miss Betty Valentine here . . . She is a very attractive looking girl . . . I should be glad to back out and not

> meet her, but there is no reason why I shouldn't enjoy myself. I hope some day I shall cease to dread meeting girls . . .
>
> I believe with all my heart that before becoming an officer every man should serve a year as a private of infantry. It gives a man a sympathy and bond of fellowship with enlisted . . . [men] that nothing else can equal. It gives a man a conception of what a soldier can be depended upon to do. One of the most disheartening things in the world is to be ordered to attempt the impossible and to be reprimanded for not doing it and to keep silence. A man who has been a private will never commit such a blunder . . . (10-11-19).

To his father, also, Carter makes the off-hand—and sole—reference to his own "royal" ancestry, Virginia style:

> The historical records I am sending [are] wrapped in a page of the Washington Post that may prove interesting. It shows "Rosewell," "Westover," and "Sabin Hall," home of Col. Landon Carter. I never knew before that "King" Carter had a son by that name (10-30-19).

To his mother he gives details about nursing a sick roommate and reassurances about his own health:

> The sore throat is epidemic here and maybe it is tonsillitis. [My roommate] Gruver has it and 200 have been confined to their rooms yesterday and to day . . . Gruver . . . [had] temperature 103 yesterday, but I kept feeding him his quinine and gargle (Dobell's) and gave him a couple of good sponge baths for his face and arms and he has slept the best part of 24 hours and feels like a new man. They've now moved everybody into improvised hospital wards and he'll be quarantined for a while. I supplemented his rations with an apple and a butter-and-hard-egg sandwich and he ate with much relish, which shows his improvement over yesterday. All the food the hospital has thus far put forth is dry bread and milk, rather monotonous (10-18-19).

By late October, life in cadet barracks gets to him. He "hate[s] this plebe system with an abiding hatred," and reports feeling "too blue to place my reflections in writing" at the time of his parents' twenty-sixth wedding anniversary (10-30-19). A little later he sends a grumpy message via his mother to Mrs. Lee, neighbor, friend and wife of his church rector: "Tell Mrs. Lee I shan't graduate 1st. I don't even care whether I do or not. All I can see in this place is the leaving of it" (11-15-19).

By Thanksgiving, with home leave more than a year away, Carter is still in low spirits:

> I can't tell you how longingly I dream of home and what a dark brown taste I have when I realize how far away it is. Why and how and wherefore I am away, I cannot understand (11-30-19).

This sadness persists despite a visit several days earlier by two good friends from University and Flight School days, Billy MacIlwaine and William Hutchinson, who are on hand for the Army-Navy football game. They take Carter into the city for dinner and the theater after the game, giving him his first experience of "high class theater" (11-30-19). Though disappointed over Army's loss of the football game, it is heart's-ease for Carter to see his friends, and he gladly soaks up their attention:

> Of course Hutch and Billy took to each other more than men ordinarily do before I joined them and I was the center of their thoughts and conversation. It is very sweet to be made so much of for a day as they did of me . . .
>
> I have many and true friends, many gifted friends, but Billy is the chief and most gifted of all. His gift is a sunny disposition. His work now is largely among drug addicts and very saddening. He says he will feel as lonely after this day as I will. It seems ridiculous, yet pitiful, that Billy should ever . . . be lonely, when he cures so much loneliness everywhere (11-30-19).

A week or so after his friends' visit, Carter is heartened by a letter from his mother, and in addressing its theme of the "burden of the valley of vision," shows what fellow spirits mother and son are:

> I read your "burden of the valley of vision". Of course, your meaning and mine had nothing to do with Isaiah's. He was talking of a real valley where he saw his vision. But you and I are always in that valley of vision. I could no more live on everyday, matter-of-fact lines than I could build a steel bridge. Even though I were a galley slave, I should spend a large part of my time dreaming of past and future. I have purposely chosen a vigorous, active life to keep from becoming a mere day-dreamer, but I don't cease to dream, even though this routine keeps me very busy. Maybe I shall do something big some day. You know Kipling promises great things, "If you can dream and not make dreams your master." And if I do then, dear mother, your valley of dreams will have born fruit and it will be your accomplishment and not mine. And if I never do anything . . . I may teach my bright dreams to another and he may have the power of accomplishment which I lack. Surely good dreams are responsible for most that is good in the world. One of the brightest prophecies to Israel is "Your young men shall see visions and your old men shall dream dreams" (12-5-19).

Carter's yearning to fly continues, and his flight experience sometimes causes attention, as it did earlier in summer camp:

> I have come in for a wave of popularity to day. This morning I gave an exhibition flight with a stick, a basin, a nail brush, and a mandolin for controls. I have had nearly a dozen callers who asked me questions about it . . . (7-6-19).

At other times he turns to his Pilot's Book: "A year ago to day I was flying formation with a wireless telephone. I flew 2 hrs. 50 min." (10-25-19).

And in November, contributing to his low spirits, another aviator talks to him:

> Rasche seeks me out on Saturday and rouses the old restlessness with his talk of the Air Force. There is the most elegant bill in Congress to establish a separate Air Force with an "Air Academy" and a combination of the air forces of the land, navy and Marine Corps . . .

> If this bill of Senator New's went through, I'd apply for a commission at once and resign from here to accept it. I'd shake off the dust of my feet against this place and leave . . .
>
> This is the effect Rasche's visit had on me, just when I was becoming reconciled to the life. If I could just forget that I ever flew, I should be much happier. (11-15-19)

Carter spends Christmas at the Academy with the rest of his class, and the long haul of winter on the Hudson sets in along with more gloomy feelings. He fears he has lost his "taste for games," and declares he is not even eager to start baseball practice (2-2-20). In academics, the new year starts with 100 plebes being "found," i.e., flunked out of the Academy. Twelve of them are from his own company: "Among them was Jim Daniel and I surely hated to see him go. He's in the hospital now. I guess it is a nervous breakdown . . . " (1-9-20).

His chief interest in his courses lies in the eccentric qualities of his instructors:

> I have Capt. Grant in English. The boys call him "Slimy Joe". He is exceedingly sarcastic and I enjoy seeing him slash one of my military or business letters all to pieces. I'm not afraid of him and after all, what difference whether I stand 10 or 20 in English, so long as I get entertained? . . .
>
> In History, I have Capt. King. He marks worse than Slimy Joe and isn't even entertaining (1-13-20).

Carter has two roommates, Earl Gruver, whom he discovers during summer camp "is the champion snoring machine of the world" (8-18-19), and Kenner Hertford:

> [Kenner] . . . is a wonderful boy. He and I depend on each other to supply each other all deficiencies of knowledge. He knows business, stocks, and science, not to mention music, but has no great knowledge of government, religion or church history, history [in general] or country life (1-13-20).

The plebe system continues, and Carter's gratitude for the "Paradise" of a short stay in the hospital shows again the harshness of the fourth class experience:

> Now I know what people like about West Point. It is the hospital . . . Monday night I had a slight chill and fever but wasn't too sick to study. I learned my Math and came to the Hospital just after breakfast. I had temperature 100 8/10 so I broke in and the past three days have been an unalloyed delight. Lots of sleep and no work, good food, pajamas furnished free and pleasant nurses and orderlies, about a dozen equally happy cadets in the ward, only one or two slightly sick— why it is just like Paradise . . . (2-5-20).

A few weeks later, Carter reports with relief and satisfaction, that, from now on, beast barracks, the cause of so much plebe misery, is to be ended:

> . . . [Beast barracks] has been abolished. I went through the last beast barracks conducted by cadets. Next year new cadet barracks will be conducted entirely by officers and under the present plan the old bracing methods will go out of existence. I'm proud to . . . see it go (2-2-20).

Until baseball season begins, Carter speaks little of sports except to comment in the fall that he is giving up the effort to play football that he began five years earlier when he entered Episcopal High School:

> I'm through with football for life. I am too small to be any thing but a door mat at it here and I enjoy the time more watching the big team and engaging in literary work (11-12-19).

But his spirits rise when he goes out for baseball in late February:

> I am physically fine and seem to be making good at baseball. I surely would like to get on the squad of 40 men, who are excused from afternoon drills and eat at training table. That's heavenly for plebes because they sit at ease and get extra desserts sometimes, lots of milk and rolls too (2-21-20).
>
> I batted for a fellow in the game to day. If I die the next minute I can say I've played in a college game. The left fielder caught my fly, but I hit the ball anyway. May be Hans will find more use for me next year. I shall work my hardest this summer. We'll begin playing games as soon as we hit Camp Dix and I have hopes of making the team there . . . I just

> believe that when I do get a start, I'll tear things loose on the baseball field (6-2-20).

A "beautiful spring Sunday" in April turns Carter's thoughts to spring at home. He thinks "the yard must be green" and tells his mother that the violets she sent him "brought quite a breath of spring." Mind's eye pictures of home in the springtime contrast with the scene at West Point: "There is very little green around here" (4-11-20).

In June, Carter chooses the option of the three—rather than four—year course at the Academy. His is the last class to have such an opportunity which is a holdover from the World War I years when a compressed curriculum was in effect. He explains his decision to his parents:

> My age and education are exceptional here. My college mates are already taking places in the world and I cannot but be impatient for the struggle for which I already feel equipped. If my three years at E.H.S. and U. of Va. do not overbalance the fourth year at West Point, the fault is in me, not my training . . .
>
> This is not the first important decision I have made without hesitation . . .
>
> What makes it easy for me to decide is the beautiful trust that you, my parents, have always placed in me. You have taught me to trust my self and not to hesitate for chance to make the decision (6-11-20).

My dear Father,

Your first year at West Point has me on a roller coaster. You are enduring the ugly plebe system and the heartache of long separation from home and family. Your lament at Thanksgiving wrenches me—and introduces me to a new metaphor for homesickness and longing—"what a dark brown taste I have when I realize how far away . . . [home] is." But of course there is summer camp and the great pleasure you take in it, as well as those precious hours spent with old friends. At times you are satisfied with your West Point "training," despite the harshness of plebe life. I swing from sadness to delight, as you do, each time your spirits plummet or soar.

I notice in one thought sequence, that you connect home with matters of the spirit: " . . . we find little time for spiritual things. It seems like I haven't had any home life since March 9, 1918, when I entered Cornell." Your foundation in home and family, those nurturers of your strong spirit, carry you through the miseries and discouragements of plebe year, and enable your empathy for others, such as your sick roommate. There's tenderness in your sponge-bathing Gruver and scrounging for food that appeals to him.

Intimations of spring high above the Hudson also send your thoughts homeward, picturing how the yard must be green now that it's April. Those greening yards at Toddsbury and Newington are in my mind's eye, too. We both know the delight of the first soft days of spring in Virginia after the raw winter—and oh, the flowers! I drink in the scent of the violets when you open the box from Granny—in those days, violets could make you drunk with their purple fragrance.

Along with you, I relish the seasons and the special glories each brings, and I know the connection between weather and the yields of the land, the back-breaking work of seed-time and harvest, and the culture shared by those who work so intimately with land and beast, on whom they are dependent.

Mother knew all this too, and did some of that back-breaking work herself. She raised daffodils—jonquils to us—but by whatever name, they were a sight to behold, five or six acres making patterns of gold and white in the springtime. Grandfather loaned her the land and she did the work, which fell mainly in the spring of the year. During the winters, she ordered and made up many five-foot-long cardboard shipping boxes. As the first buds appeared, she was watching the weather, worrying about when to pick, recruiting and transporting pickers, bringing flowers in from the field—often by means of a horse-drawn dirt sled, and giving them a "drink" for at least several hours. Then she packed them, fifty dozen to a box, working against the two p.m. deadline when the boxes had to be at the head of the lane for the truck that would deliver them early next morning to the New York wholesale market. Her hard work made my years at St. Catherine's and Wellesley possible.

You never mention working with flowers, though Daddy Catlett and Granny were among the early daffodil growers in the County. Perhaps they didn't start till after you went off to school. Aunt Mary Mann wrote that she worried about her father picking flowers hour after hour, and when she asked about his back, he replied, "I have no back."

You are perfectly open about breaking rules and taking your "punishments like a man" at West Point. You make a clear distinction between rules and those things that are a "matter of honor." Would you have nurtured me in such a way that I could have made those distinctions, instead of acting out in my school life an overweening response to all rules? I was always trying to be "good," which was what I understood Mother, and the church, wanted of me: behave yourself and comport yourself so there is no blame to be found in you. This was reinforced by what came through to me in weekly worship. I heard those words, "God loves you," but their meaning was not plumbed, and I had no sense that love, rather than judgment, was the first attribute of our faith.

Would your love and nurturing and joy in life have freed me up to a sense of mischief and zest for life, along with your fundamental integrity?

I notice the terms you apply to visits from friends—words of the heart that spring from loneliness and love: " . . . Sunday Billy Mac paid me his long anticipated visit. I enjoyed every minute of it but it left me with a heartache which isn't gone yet." And later, after Thanksgiving: "[Billy] says he will feel as lonely after this day as I will. It seems ridiculous, yet pitiful, that Billy should ever . . . be lonely, when he cures so much loneliness everywhere." In the midst of hundreds of men, you are lonely for those few with whom you have a real relationship. You don't try to mask your pain.

Alone with Mother, I did not learn to express pain, but to repress it, especially if it had to do with losing you. I expect she expressed it indirectly in her depressed moods. But there was one time when she gave way to open feeling. I was about sixteen, and we were in the midst of a West Point hops weekend, arranged by her and a Gloucester friend whose son was a cadet. She and I were alone in the West Point chapel—no service in progress, no friends present. While sitting high up in a choir stall, with the sun and stained glass bathing us in color, she wept softly, but said nothing. I was aware that the chapel must bring back memories of being with you at West Point, but at the time I couldn't go to those feelings. I didn't know what to say, and we sat in silence. Why couldn't we speak about you and about your death? Why couldn't I put my arms around my lonely, grieving mother?

Once, many years later, I overheard her commenting on my shortcomings as a parent, and during my hurt and anger, Franklin, your son-in-law, asked her to tell me that she loved me. Tearfully, she demurred, saying she felt "all frozen up inside," that her family "didn't talk about feelings."

Would we have both learned from you?

Of course, you have your high times, but they are mostly ones I can't enter. I'm speaking now of your delight in the skirmishes and war maneuvers carried out in summer camp. I wonder what you think of today's air warfare in which pilots at high speeds swoop down on their targets and then roar away. During the air show here in Rochester this summer, three such planes flying in formation bore down on our part of the city. I was picking flowers, and thought that I was going to be crushed by the sound before being bombed. I was cowering in my own backyard, feeling kinship with people in Afghanistan where war rages and our bombers sometimes mistakenly target civilians.

It's hard for me to put your comments in perspective: "We skirmished with enemy cavalry all morning. It was lots of fun. I was killed twice . . . " I admit, as a friend points out, that this is a game for you, like cops and robbers. But there does seem to be a most remarkable disassociation from the feeling you expressed less than a year ago on reading a realistic account of World War I in the book, Backwash of War: *"It nearly makes me vomit yet I believe it pictures war more truly than any [other] book we read"* (12-22-18). *I've read that book now, and I know the truth of your words.*

* * *

Now I muster strength to spend time with you in your last letter of 1919—your letter to Granny in response to hers about Isaiah's "burden of the valley of vision." While I can't reconstruct what she said, I can see the companionable spirits that you and she are, and it's clear that part of your closeness is expressed in the sharing of your dreams. You write:

> *I have purposely chosen a vigorous, active life to keep from becoming a mere day-dreamer, but I don't cease to dream, even though this routine keeps me very busy. Maybe I shall do something big some day . . . And if I do, then, dear mother, your valley of dreams will have born fruit and it will be your accomplishment and not mine. And if I never do anything big . . . , I may teach my bright dreams to another and he may have the power of accomplishment which I lack.*

When I first transcribed these words, I made a mental note to find the passage in Isaiah to which they refer, and continued on with my work. But recently, when I returned to your letter, my mind stood aside, and my heart read your words: "I may teach my bright dreams to another and [s]he may have the power of accomplishment which I lack."

Recognition pierced me. I stopped writing, and sat in silence. I opened my eyes to see you. I was so certain of your presence it was hard to believe that you were not physically with me.

Have you been with me all along?

For I, too, have been possessed by dreams—dreams of freedom and equality. Those were my dreams when I walked in the blazing sun of mid-summer North Carolina with hundreds of others demanding that all public accommodations—hotels and motels, restaurants and soda fountains, and filling station rest rooms—be open to all people regardless of race. This freedom dream caused me to keep the picket line going at a segregated restaurant for months on end, and to join others in picketing a segregated motel where delegates to our church convention, including the bishop, chose to stay, despite offers by several families to take them into their homes. They crossed our picket line without a glance in our direction.

During that long, hot summer, I was at many meetings in black churches. Sometimes it seemed the very rafters shook with the fervor of the freedom songs:

> *Go tell it on the mountain*
>
> *Oh Freedom, oh freedom, oh freedom over me*
>
> *We shall overcome, we shall overcome some day*

On those hot nights, how the dream—and our spirits—soared!

Later, it was the misery of people tied to their beds and chairs in nursing homes that took hold of me, guided by the words of a man in a vest restraint: "It's a terrible thing to lose your freedom." After I saw in the Swedish nursing home an approach to elders that excluded the practice of physical restraint, I was compelled to tell as many people as I could about it. A new dream was born when out of that work grew another, carried on with many others, to change the whole culture of nursing homes. The goal is to transform them into places of mutual respect and inclusiveness, where relationships flourish, rather than an atmosphere in which distancing and hierarchy prevail. The work goes on, shouldered by others now, but to have been a part of this dream work is satisfaction to my soul—and surely an expression of your legacy of bright dreams.

So, my dear Father, I see now that I've been close to you my whole life, you who describe yourself as a "theoretical socialist" and claim that Blacks and Whites are all part of the same human race in a time when this claim of brotherhood was unthinkable to many. I rejoice now that I come from a dreamer of bright dreams—one who dreams even in the grayness and loneliness of plebe year at West Point, and who hands on his bright dreaming to his daughter.

My love,
Catharine Carter

PART II
Yearling

June, 1920—May, 1921

The summer of 1920, spent at Camp Dix, New Jersey, is the high point of Carter's first two years at the Academy. It lacks the rigid social discipline that governs life at The Point, and offers opportunities for Carter to grow into a leadership role. He sums up this summer to his mother as "the biggest lot of crowded and pleasant experience that I have ever had" (8-16-20). He gets to know the families of his roommates—Earl Gruver's Pennsylvania Dutch family whom he contrasts with Kenner Hertford's East Coast family—and learns to dance so he can attend hops. Canoe trips and riding instruction are firsts for him, too. Through it all, he learns artillery skills in the mornings, including the firing of cannons and howitzers, and plays as many baseball games in the afternoons as possible.

Reluctantly, Carter leaves camp after the first several days to attend a long-planned YMCA conference at Silver Bay, New York. The conference turns out to be an inspiring experience, with welcome time to talk with other students on matters close to his heart and spirit, and to make new friends—in his case, with the only Chinese cadet at the Academy. In a lengthy letter to his parents, he reflects on his conference experience and breaks the news that he has invited his new friend to visit him in Gloucester:

> I have invited Wong, the Chinese cadet to come home with me for Christmas or a week next summer. I thought a long time over the race prejudices in our country neighborhood but I think that you and the other people interested in mission will not show any misgivings at meeting one of the finest types of a great nation. Wong is the brainiest and best educated cadet at West Point and his morals and ideals are as noble as any I ever saw. He is not yet a professing Christian but he accepts

> all the Christian principles and is glad to see his countrymen, especially the wretched uneducated classes converted. He attends church regularly even when not at West Point. I am anxious that a man who will some day be one of the leading men of China may see some of American home life and I want him to see a Christian father and mother, my own. His own parents raised him very strictly but he had grandparents to humor him when they could . . . He is more than my match but I can tell him some things about history and religion. Another Chinese is entering next year. Don't be uneasy. I'm not going to bring him along . . .
>
> We lost sleep talking over things with the chaplain and others. One night a few of us told what we were failing in willfully and got encouragement and help from each other. I feel much calmer and happier since I told thing[s] that I had always felt ashamed of and I think the others feel the same. It was in the nature of a revival but we needed it. I hope I am going to get back to the habit of Bible reading that the pressure of war broke me of. Now that my plebe year is over I think it will be easier if I can keep this inspiration . . . (7-6-20).

Upon his return to camp, Carter is plunged back into artillery work and is hard-pressed to find time to write:

> I have now taken steadily to the typewriter in headquarters and have move[d] my letters down to refer to but I am no end of busy I can tell you and even to-night I hope to wash some clothes in both gasoline and water to get the artillery grease off them. We are through artillery now. We fired every morning for five days, different kinds of big guns every day and different jobs about the gun every little while. We should be pretty fair cannoniers from just actual experience with very little tedious standing gun drill. Of course we shall get our share of caring for guns and horses going home on the hike (7-22-20).

A chance to take a canoe trip arises, and "since I've never been in a canoe . . . I'm borrowing the money to go" (7-9-20). Two days later he reports the adventure to his mother, with an added note about card-playing:

> I am just through telling all my friends about the best week end I ever had and now I am anxious to write all about it. We took two men to each of five canoes and paddled about 20 miles down a beautiful stream. Canoeing is about the prettiest sport in the world. We left Saturday afternoon and spent the night at Pemberton, a town between Browns Mills and Mt. Holly where we bought ice cream and fresh milk. Gruver was our cook and our happiness was largely due to him of course. But the country is really beautiful and all along we saw canoes on pleasure bent, some playing phonographs to maidens reclining on piles of pillows . . . Gruver is planning to take the second stage of the journey with some girls from his home town some Sunday and he wishes me to take the second canoe . . .
>
> The mess sergeant gave us provisions for the trip and he gave us more than we could eat so on my motion we gave quite a lot to the lady from whom we borrowed the water bucket. Of course we carried our packs and they contained our tents and blankets, so we lacked for nothing in the world. We also had citronella and mosquito bars and we paddled in bathing suits and old trou, carrying our drill uniforms for the towns. We had the materials for lemonade and coffee, radishes, onions, cucumbers, a tomato, pickle (the vinegar made excellent dressing), salt, pepper, bread, canned milk, peaches and pineapple, jam, maple syrup, sausage, cold beef, bacon, and three dozen eggs for ten men. They feed us the best in the world down here . . .
>
> You asked me once if I ever played cards and I forgot to answer the question. I have played once since I came to Camp Dix and three times during the winter. It is not forbidden but there are generally too many more interesting occupations. My personal objection to cards is the waste of time. Of course I am thinking of bridge as it is played, not poker . . . (7-11-20).

Despite the mornings spent in hard, greasy work, the weeks at Camp Dix launch Carter socially, as his own desires to dance and become more sociable converge with appropriate opportunities. When he begins dancing lessons (supplied by the Academy), he discovers he is severely challenged both musically and rhythmically:

> I wish I could express to you just how hard it has been for me to go out and make a show of myself before my classmates, even though nobody was making fun of me. I am painfully aware of my limitations and keeping time is a hard labor above the hardness of all the physical and mental efforts of my life . . . (8-2-20).
>
> I am just getting so I can tell a fox trot from a waltz or a one step. It is still largely a matter of guess work but I am able to recognize some of the latest popular songs as fox trot tunes and that helps some. They say they have them written up on a card at the hops and that I couldn't go wrong but I am still afraid to try it. I am getting really interested in learning to dance well though, because an officer should dance and should do everything he does well (8-5-20).
>
> A dance floor covered with girls and cadets in full dress [is an eyeful]—46 brass buttons on each cadet . . . I danced all but about three dances out of sixteen and melted two sets of collars and cuffs . . . The dance was over at twelve and I was a tired human but not at all bored. I enjoy a ball game more but there is a certain satisfaction, now that I don't have to worry about getting out of time with the music (8-16-20).

Carter's reports on his dancing efforts are often accompanied by comments about the kind of girl that interests him:

> Brains count with me so don't be afraid of my falling for on[e] of these finishing school girls (7-6-20).
>
> [I]f I ever carry a femme canoeing she is going to sit up and paddle and if she is the kind of girl I want to take out she will prefer that to the other (7-11-20).
>
> Both [of Earl's next door neighbors] are nice girls and very pleasing to look upon . . . [J]udging by estimate only I should say they weigh about 125 or 130 pounds apiece and they are strong as most young men. That is no drawback in my eyes as

> I like to see a girl [be] a good baseball and basketball player . . . (8-2-20).
>
> I danced my first hop with . . . [Kenner's sister] Friday and she was very sweet about teaching me . . . She is a tiny little thing. I like rather more to tie to when I'm dancing, but those that know say she's a wonder (8-9-20).

He notes the social "drawing power of the corps" (7-22-20). Hertford's mother rents a house nearby for the summer, and Gruver's mother visits frequently, bringing home-town girls to the dances: "They come here from afar and we are the only attraction. Everybody has one or more invitations for every week end . . . " (7-22-20).

One of Carter's invitations is from Earl, to visit his family in Easton, Pennsylvania. He is already much taken with the Gruvers, and describes the experience of meeting them at Camp Dix by comparing the Pennsylvania Dutch culture with that of Virginia, even before he goes to Easton:

> [Earl] is delighted that I like his people. They are different from us in not looking back on a tradition of gentility and aristocracy. They don't speak as pure English. But they suit me a lot better than Kenner's people with the blood of the Dukes of Hertforshire in their veins, though the latter are just as nice as can be to me and would be nicer if I could dance and talk socially. They have never known what it is to have servants in these Pennsylvania families and they haven't had time to polish up the delicate social arts. Cards and dancing they care comparatively little about and church is their social center just as it is ours . . . (7-24-20).

A report on a weekend visit to Earl and his family, which he speaks of as a "broadening experience," follows:

> I had about the best time yet in Easton meeting Earl's PD [Pennsylvania Dutch] connection . . . Sunday afternoon they took me riding through the neighboring towns of Bethlehem and Allentown. Bethlehem is where the big steel works are and we saw them stretching over many acres across the valley and

> up the mountain side. On Sunday morning we both made talks in chapel to the junior branch of the Sunday School . . . [T]hey seemed to enjoy my description of stunts in flying and then a few words about the West Point honor system. I spoke on subjects near my heart and tried to mingle fun and interesting description with high ideals . . . Later on in the evening we went to see two femmes next door, the same two that we had on the canoe trip a week ago . . . [They] had refreshments [for us and] music and dancing (lessons for me) so that I stayed later than I ever have before and enjoyed the society if not the dancing . . . [B]etween times [on Sunday] I played with a host of little children and told them the first Uncle Remus that they had ever heard . . . I was crawled over and petted and worshipped to my heart's content . . . [T]hey all like to hear Southerner's talk up here. I am getting so I don't mind Dutch, I've heard such nice people talk it. These are prosperous and well educated people though they don't think the same of manners before all that I think characterizes Virginia society (8-2-20).
>
> [Kenner and his sister] . . . are delightful chums and very bright mentally but may the Lord deliver my family from such popular people. I am very fond of both but that is not where I am in danger of getting engaged. The Pennsylvania Dutch are more nearly my style, though of course there are some things about Virginia I don't find anywhere else. For instance, the Dutch don't have any corn bread and that is a handicap, no matter how well they cook . . . Of course they have funny localisms of their own and they are all a colony like Virginians, though they don't trace kinship so far . . .
>
> Earl . . . is no mixer. His people don't possess the gift. You have to go to them to know them (8-16-20).

Along with his new socializing, Carter remains very much his own person—still nurturing hopes for greater equality among people, still struggling with a lack of money, and, as always, deeply bonded to his family and his Virginia upbringing:

> The chaplain has picked me to act as scout leader next fall . . . I think boys work is a very fine thing to introduce in

> any army post and would be a good influence to bridge the social gap between officers and enlisted men in the army. Their children first and then their wives to an interest and neighborly intercourse with each other. It is a big idea to me (7-6-20).

His egalitarian leanings are also evident in his comments about the automat:

> I went to Philadelphia to a movie and a . . . meal in the automat, a place where you drop nickels in the slot and pull out clean and delicious food. I had rather eat that way than be served by a waiter and it is twice as cheap and you can take what ever suits your eye (7-22-20).

Several times Carter writes home for money, after borrowing earlier from the chaplain. He regrets these requests, and explains his situation at some length:

> I am writing home for money again and I surely hate to do it but I get hooked up for things in the line of sociability that cost more than I expect or that I feel I ought not to miss and so I am spending more for pleasure than I ever did before. Well, to make a long story short I am asking for $15.00 or the nearest convenient amount . . . But this has been such a summer that I really don't see how I could have done otherwise and have gained the fullest extent of education . . . I shall probably get a considerable sum for furlough next summer and maybe I can get some work to make me independent for the next winter. Then I graduate (7-24-02).

Except for the arduous dancing lessons and his great reluctance to make "a show" of himself on the dance floor, there is little suffering in this wonderful summer, in contrast to the previous months at West Point. He even works enthusiastically:

> Friday I marched out on an infantry problem, routed the enemy, got rained on, came in and got a skin full of lemonade, went out for cavalry and bounced up and down a bit, got wet again, came in to dinner, attended to . . . [some] routine

> business connected with my not arduous office, played a ball game and hurried back to dress for parade. I acted as adjutant and was complimented by the C.O. on my marked improvement. Then came supper and some of the fellows went to a hop that night. I was glad to lay off. This life is so full of athletic opportunities that anybody with blood must get too much exercise to get into mischief . . . I play a ball game to-morrow and Tuesday throw the javelin, football and put the 16-pound shot, besides playing on the medicine ball race team for the third squad of the second platoon of the second company . . .
>
> It surely is nice to wear a uniform and talk Southern and be in love and Charity with your neighbors and go abroad in the land meeting people. Everybody expects you to be a gentleman and is ready and anxious to be friendly. It makes one forget that there is so much suffering in the world and so great a need of men to make the waste places blossom. I am glad that I went to Silver Bay and also that I am seeing this beautiful Jersey water and the people and holding a place of honor in this little corps of ours. Our officers anticipate our desires down here—so different from West Point last year that it hurts . . . (7-11-20).

Several weeks later the friendliness he enjoys on all sides results in this news to his mother:

> This night I have been elected Class President for the ensuing year. It came as a surprise and disappointment to me because I had hoped they would pick the man that would be Class President permanently and not have a political stirup later but I suppose that I am too old for the honor to turn my head and if it is given in good will I should be thankful (8-5-20).

By the time the cadets break camp in mid-August, and start the long march back to West Point, Carter is enjoying his standing, and writes his feelings openly to his parents, including his views on "managing men":

> Of course you realize that I am a bigger man in the eyes of my associates this summer than I have ever been before in my

> life and than I shall be again until I attain the rank of captain at least in the army. For I shall not be a West Point Adjutant, aviator, president, and ball player in one breath as long as I may live. I am usually introduced by one title or the other and I am known by name to all the officers and employees and am treated with the greatest respect and consideration by all. Perhaps you had better not read all this out of the home circle. It sounds like a lot of brag, but it really is the truth and I am telling you that you may rejoice with me just as you will sympathize with me when my trials come. The best thing of all is the comradeship of the cadets . . . And they give me cheerful obedience to all commands . . . And I am a regular public service man as far as my office goes. I am always ready to investigate anything or make any reasonable recommendation to the major and that does a lot to keep the command contented and trustful of their officers. I've really made my office amount to something more than a parade figure this summer . . .
>
> Well I have given you all of the philosophy of managing men that I have learned this summer and it is all summed up in the two qualities of comradeship and firm, polite, decisive commands. It is dead easy for anyone with Virginia manners. The more I travel the more I appreciate my raising. There is a little compliment to you that slipped in quite unawares, [M]other (8-16-20).

On August 18, the cadets begin their hard march back to West Point, covering close to two hundred miles in eleven days, with one Sunday off. Along the way, Carter sends details to his father:

> Talk about Sunday morning chores, we are having a taste of it to day. I'm ranking member of a gang of forty who are taking over the motorized artillery, 7 tractors (caterpillar drive, like tanks), 1 Dodge, 1 Dodge truck, 3 big trucks, 1 repair truck, 2 medium sized trucks, 2 155 Howitzers, and 2 4.7 inch guns. Guns and Howitzers have nearly the same sized bores but guns have long barrels and are fired with small elevations . . .
>
> . . . All along the march the movie men have been taking pictures of us. We must be quite the most popular part of the government at present . . . (8-22-20).

Earlier in the summer, Carter is apprehensive about his return to the Academy. Nevertheless, he has hope that the changes made in beast barracks for the current plebes will improve daily life for all:

> My conversation has a different tone from what it had at West Point, eh? Yes, and it will be different again from what it is now. Everybody is different here from there. I am wondering how much they will change the rules for the better this year. They have already put in some athletics twice a week instead of drills . . . (7-24-20).

Dear Daddy,

It's a joy to hear of your good times in summer camp after your hard winter. And about the Chinese cadet you so much admired—did he ever make the visit to Gloucester? If not, I completed your wish: I had a Chinese visitor at Toddsbury in 1945. He was a beau, Wu Wai Chao, from mainland China, whom I'd met at a college mixer. He always had his camera with him so I have a lot of snapshots taken during his Gloucester visit.

And Daddy, guess what? Many of Franklin's forbears were good Pennsylvania Dutch, for whom you express such fondness. His strand probably came down the Great Wagon Road from Pennsylvania to North Carolina before the Civil War—never were slave owners, and usually not employers of servants, as you note in your discussions of the Gruver family and their community.

I understand so well your struggles with dancing, because I have many of the same. I'm never able to get my body to be at one with the music, the way others do. And your first times in a canoe remind me of my wonder and delight when Franklin introduced me to hiking and camping in the Great Smokies—the trees and ferns and flowers and streams and the hard-earned vistas across waves of distant mountains were all magical.

As a family, we—you, Mother and I—could have had good times canoeing and camping. Once introduced to the experience by you, I believe Mother would have enjoyed it too. She taught me to row, so I can see her paddling a canoe—just the kind of girl you like.

You are mulling over ideas about class and culture and race in these summer months—matters that I'm always working on in my mind and heart. I'm too serious, I suppose, as I have been told more than once. But that's the way it is for me.

You are interested in bridging the gap between officers and enlisted men. Your vision is that if they meet as people, first through their children and "then their wives . . . [they would develop] an interest and neighborly intercourse with each other." You add, "It is a big idea to me."

I've had this same "big idea," not in the army setting, of course, but in everyday civilian community life. Here I am again—to my amazement—finding your vision in my life. My first opportunity for this bridging was in Chapel Hill in the four year span of Tom's and Mary's preschool experiences in the early sixties. It was a cooperative preschool, and, to our knowledge, the first integrated preschool in the South. Because the parents ran the school, we came to know each other across all the social divisions—race, class, culture, occupation, education, income. Just as you envisioned, we were drawn together through our children and our hopes for them.

It was through the school that Mrs. Gaither Lassiter and I became friends. There were distances between us—created by the prevailing culture—of race and education, but Sister Gaither, as I came to call her, simply didn't see such divisions between people. She welcomed me to her home, and I was there often.

The early sixties were tense years in Chapel Hill, with almost constant demonstrations and sit-ins for open public accommodations. Though Sister Gaither's arthritis kept her from marching, she brought countless people to her table, and I was privileged to be one among many. I recall one such occasion when the movie Porgy and Bess *had come to town. She gathered round her table potential participants in an action to break the segregation policy of the movie theater. Though the theater's barriers didn't fall till later, this and other gatherings in her home contributed to the momentum of the movement in Chapel Hill.*

Sister Gaither's formal education had been slight, but her mind and spirit weren't in any way limited. I deeply admired her resolve for freedom and equality, born out of the hard circumstances of her life and her Christian faith. She told me how, as a young woman, she and her husband regularly drove a wagon many miles from their farm home in Chatham County to Durham, where they went from door to door selling vegetables. Out of regret for the lack of educational opportunity for herself and her generation, she was a devoted supporter of Livingston College in Salisbury, North

Carolina, which had been founded by her denomination, the African Methodist Episcopal Zion Church (AME-Zion).

From 1960 to the passage of the Civil Rights Act of 1964, tension was high in Chapel Hill. With children and job obligations, Franklin and I didn't engage in sit-ins, but we took turns marching in demonstrations, and I regularly was part of a group of four women, two white and two black, who sought service (unsuccessfully) at segregated lunch counters, and access to segregated rest rooms. (We garnered a description of ourselves as "a bunch of garbage" from a lunch counter operator when he called the chief of police. Chief Blake told me, "And I come to find out it was you ladies." After that, we let the chief know ahead of time where we would be seeking service.)

There were a few times when I was scared. Once when Franklin was out of town, the phone beside our bed rang about one o'clock in the morning. No voice responded to my hello, only heavy breathing. I hung up, and when I'd just got back to sleep, it rang again, and again there was the heavy breathing. A third time it rang, and the performance was repeated. Mary and Tom, about 7 and 4, were not awakened, but by then I was feeling very alone and frightened, with my imagination in full gear. The Ku Klux Klan was present in Chapel Hill at intervals in 1963-64, holding an occasional rally and cross burning. I'd not seen any of it, but a young man staying with us had, and now I was having trouble keeping my uncertainty and fear under control. After considerable hesitation, I called Charlie Jones, the minister of the nearby Community Church where Tom was attending pre-school.

It was probably two or three o'clock in the morning by that time, but Charlie answered. Immediately his calm voice drew me back out of incipient panic. He reassured me that this was a familiar tactic. How about taking the phone off the hook? I was loath to do this because there was such emphasis in our home on being accessible by phone in case a patient needed Franklin. In retrospect, this would have been just the right time to give a strong blow on a referee's whistle, but I wasn't seasoned enough to be prepared with a whistle. The person at the other end of the line was unlikely to present himself bodily; still, it was scary. Where was he, and why did he single me out, and how did he get my phone number? A sense of vulnerability unnerved me. I passionately believed in the civil rights cause—but where was my courage?

The other time I worried about the Klan was a night when they were holding a rally just outside Chapel Hill and Franklin had gone to a Town Board meeting. By 10:30 he had not come home, so I called our close friend Walter Hollander who had attended the same meeting, and learned that Franklin was arguing with the editor of the local paper at meeting's end about the weak stance of recent editorials. Walt suspected they were still at it. To my relief, Franklin arrived home about a half hour later, confirming Walt's report, and frustrated that he could not move the editor to stronger support of social change in Chapel Hill.

During this period, our church—the Episcopal Chapel of the Cross—did not engage in any meaningful way in the civil rights struggle, and worse yet, sent out a list of segregated hotels for delegates attending the diocesan convention. As my anguish grew, Sister Gaither invited me to come to evening services at her small A.M.E.-Zion church a few blocks from her home. There I found welcome and solace, and after a discussion with her brother, the Rev. Lonnie Horton, who served the small congregation, I was received as an associate member of that denomination on Trinity Sunday 1963, as the small congregation sang, "On Christ, the solid Rock I stand, All other ground is sinking sand . . . " The beautiful voice of the young woman who sometimes sang at services, the straightforward messages of Rev. Horton's sermons, and the extemporaneous prayers of an elderly church member—"Oh Lord, thank you for being able to get up this day and get dressed . . . " put things in a right perspective, and made the tiny church an anchor for me in that time when much of the Episcopal Church in the South seemed bent on avoiding the message of love and justice that was Jesus' life.

Later, during Sister Gaither's visit to us in Rochester, we attended Frederick Douglass' own A.M.E.-Zion Church, and one wet afternoon she and I wandered around Mt. Hope Cemetery until, to our great satisfaction, we found Douglass' grave. After that, I had several good visits with her on brief returns to Chapel Hill, and loved seeing her drive her own car and do salaried outreach work from the senior center—with white and black elders. We kept in touch with occasional telephone calls, but there was much too much time between calls. When word came suddenly that she had died, I had a deep sense of loss. Sadness wells up in me now as I remember her and feel the hand and heart of friendship she gave me.

I don't share your straightforward pleasure in being a Virginian. Our differences partly lie in the consciousness-raising about racial oppression and inequalities that I have lived.

To begin with, my years at Wellesley opened up new opportunities and experiences. Though I had only three black classmates, I accompanied one the summer of 1944 to an internship in Washington DC, and enjoyed the novel freedom of unsegregated rail travel, because south of Washington, such travel was governed by Jim Crow laws.

Ironically, in July of that same summer an event occurred in our own Gloucester County that had the potential for removing racial barriers from all interstate travel, but I didn't learn about it until almost sixty years later. That summer a black woman in Gloucester, Irene Morgan, refused to move to the back of an interstate bus, and was arrested. Her case was carried all the way to the Supreme Court where it was argued and won by Thurgood Marshall and William Hastie in 1946. Her historic action, eleven years before Rosa Parks refused to move to the back of the city bus in Montgomery, Alabama, is now claimed with pride in a Gloucester brochure that guides visitors to "Selected African American Historic Sites." But, in the forties, so complete was the exclusion of news about equal rights for citizens and so great was the fear of equal rights in the white community, that I never heard anything about Mrs. Morgan's historic action.

All of this is related to my struggles with our Virginia ancestry. As I became more and more sensitized and aware of racial oppression, I increasingly viewed with sorrow, and then with shame, the role of our Southern forbears in the oppression of a whole race of people. How can one be proud of ancestral slave owners?

In recent years, Colonial Williamsburg has begun acknowledging the role of black slaves in producing the beautiful homes and enabling the luxurious way of life of the white planters. The credit is long overdue, but I'm doubtful it has spread to the general consciousness. There is almost a sense of shrine worship in the attitudes of many sightseers. All that is seen and marveled at—and perhaps envied a bit—is the "gracious" life style of the white plantation families. There's no doubt it was high living. One has only to read the diary of Philip Vickers Fifthian, the young Presbyterian seminarian who came down from Princeton in 1773 to tutor the children of Robert Carter III, grandson of "King" Carter and first cousin of your great-grandmother, to get an idea of the constant hospitality, frequent balls and regular visiting back and forth that characterized that society.

Robert Carter III was your first cousin several degrees removed and his uncle was Landon Carter, the first holder of your name.

In the late 1980's, a neighbor gave me a copy of a paper written by his graduate-student son about Robert Carter III, who had freed his slaves during his lifetime. Was I a relative? I was too busy to pay much attention. A few years later, just as we were about to leave Washington and return to Rochester, I opened the Washington Post *one day to find a Gainsborough-like portrait of an elegant young man who turned out to be the young Robert Carter III during a two-year stay in England. He was in the news because the 200th anniversary of his freeing of his slaves was being commemorated. I didn't get to that occasion, but your granddaughter Mary did, and I still have the program she brought me here in my study. I hung it from a book shelf and went on with my nursing home advocacy work, but made time to read a range of recent books dealing with the South.*

The more history I read, the greater my despair. Everywhere I turn, it seems, I absorb more details of the horrors of slavery, and our forbears' prominence in the system. Virginia Cavalcade, *the state's historical quarterly, featured a cover picture on its 1998 summer issue that embodies the myths and delusions Virginians—along with other southerners—lived by, the myths they generated to disguise the horror, scandal and depravity of one human being making property of another. The cover picture is an oil portrait of two boys around 1710. Both are dressed in fine clothing and one wears a silver collar around his neck. He is positioned—possibly in a kneeling posture—so that he looks up to the first boy and offers a bird he has retrieved for him. The silver collar, says the picture's caption, is "symbolic of his servitude," for this boy is black and the other is white. So the pronged iron collar placed on the apprehended runaway slave is converted to the gleaming beauty of polished silver, and the picture of bondage is gilded.*

In the very same issue of the quarterly, the ungilded truth is contained in an article entitled, "Slavery at Carter's Grove in the Early Eighteenth Century." It reports a scholar's research into the management of slaves by your great-great-great grandfather, Robert ("King") Carter. When a slave persisted in running away, Carter ordered the man's toes cut off, saying "nothing less than dismembering will reclaim him," and adding that, "I have cured many a Negro of running away by this means."

*Do you understand now my joy in your fervent support of education for "the Negro" in your argument with fellow students at the University? To take that stand, you broke through a heavy thicket of wicked myths, including those perpetuated by Thomas Dixon, who during your childhood actually wrote his best-selling scandalous novels—*The Clansman *and* The Leopard's Spots*—right there in Gloucester County at Elmington, not far from Toddsbury. Those two books were the basis for Dixon's script of the movie,* Birth of a Nation. *In his introduction to* The Clansman, *Dixon proclaimed the Ku Klux Klan the savior of the "Aryan race." I had thought that word and concept belonged to the Nazis, not my own society.*

Your fondness for Uncle Remus tales makes me uncomfortable, because these stories by Joel Chandler Harris, as well as those of Thomas Nelson Page, converted the days of slavery into times of sweet nostalgia. They assuaged the souls of white people, not those of black people, the only ones qualified to tell their own stories. The results of this myth-making are hideous. Do you realize that lynchings averaged 62 a year between 1910 and 1919? And the horror continues today in the sense of imminent danger that envelops a person of color in any possible police encounter.

Such have been my thoughts, as I have read more American and Virginia history in recent years. I have tried to make some peace with my heritage, but my gloom has only deepened. In our family, we have many Colonial leaders, but all were slave owners—and professing Christians. (Robert (King) Carter, owner of more slaves than anyone else in Virginia, even built a church.) How can slavery and Christianity go together? The young seminarian tutoring Robert Carter III's children, recounted some of the treatment of slaves by owners and overseers and exclaimed, "Good God! Are these Christians?"

As I study your letters of this 1920 summer, it's clear to me that you pay no attention whatever to forbears. I marvel at how heritage doesn't even figure in your consciousness. You could have matched Kenner's Dukes of Hertforshire by strutting out a bunch of prominent ancestors, but they never even enter your mind. Genealogy and family networks unto the seventh cousin and beyond are your mother's enthusiasm, not your interest. You are a free man.

But you did not have the gift of long life, and you never reached that stage of development in old age in which you survey the vistas of many years, look again to see where you came from and try to get a sense of where you are now. I have the experience of returning several times a year to Gloucester—the very place you and I grew up. I am as bound to Gloucester in certain ways as you are in your thoughts. But the culture we came out of remains a huge stumbling block for me.

And increasingly I have yearned to discover one hero in our background—one person of whom we can be truly proud.

About two years ago, Robert Carter III came to me for the third time, and this time I paid attention. At a friend's home, I saw an article in The American Scholar *entitled, "The Anti-Jefferson" by Andrew Levy. Thinking I would scan it for the latest revisionist history of Jefferson, I took it to my room, expecting to have a nap after a quick read, but the subtitle made me forget napping: "Why Robert Carter III Freed His Slaves (And Why We Couldn't Care Less)".*

Professor Levy writes:

> *In the long history of antebellum America, no one . . . [other than Robert Carter III], while living, freed that many slaves [more than five hundred]; no one even came close. No one walked away from slaveholding and slavery with as much to lose, simply gave up the plantation and moved on. And no other Virginian of the Revolutionary era—including those, like Jefferson and Washington, who spoke out passionately against slavery—managed to reconcile freedom in theory and freedom in practice with such transparent simplicity.*
>
> *While those men [others of the Virginia gentry] got their religion from the aristocratic, undemanding, and pure white Anglican church . . . Carter was sure he met Jesus one May day in 1778, and asked him, "Lord, what wilt thou have me do?"*

It took Professor Levy's words to jolt me into awareness that this cousin was the hero I'd been looking for.

So why had I never heard about him? Why had you never heard of him? Why wasn't the story of his great deed handed down with pride to future generations of our family? Was he an embarrassment that other family members tried to hide? Was the "transparent simplicity" of his action too threatening to his generation? Was this radical quality in him simply unacceptable in a society that abhorred any disturbance, any wave-making? I feel cheated out of what should have been part of my inheritance in the pervasive pride of family.

But now, I proudly claim our kinship with the remarkable Robert Carter III.

Your loving daughter,

Catharine Carter

PART II continued

Once back at the Point, Carter feels oppressed as he anticipates the winter's work. Incidental comments convey the tiresome sameness and endless details of which the daily life of a cadet consists:

> My English grade is better because I have an easier teacher, Captain McEwan instead of "Slimy Joe" Grant . . . He is humorous to an infinite degree and asks only necessary questions on the lesson . . . he isn't hard to please. It is a change for me and at West Point, changes are always a relief . . . (10-11-20).
>
> I lost .3 on one Math lesson last week for forgetting to put my problem number under my name. Nobody can remember everything around here (10-11-20).

Living conditions are trying also:

> Things are not so comfortable this year. We are in crowded quarters, the laundry is swamped with work and jumbles it, the meals are not quite so good, the cadet store has no time to repair clothes, and 150 goat plebes don't get new overcoats (9-18-20).

He branches out socially, inviting a girl from Bryn Mawr College for a hops weekend, and reports he and Gruver enjoyed "our company immensely" (10-18-20). But after several blind dates, he decides to cut out the dance weekends, because, while often fun, they are tiring, the hardest part being "to show strangers around the place all day Sunday, when I need sleep and a day of rest" (10-11-20). By late October, he is cutting them out completely for "a good rest up" (10-27-20), but drifts into a brief discussion of marriage and the present state of his heart:

> . . . [M]y number of feminine acquaintances has increased tenfold and nowadays I have almost enough girls to keep my heart safely from any one. I'm afraid this may disappoint you, but it is even too true. I don't know whether I shall be married at thirty-three or not. I have certainly no immediate prospects and no desire to surrender my single state for a long time.

> I've never been able to live with any roommate without quarreling save Gruver. When the break comes, he humors me. But Hertford, Charlie, and John Scott could all drive me insane with teasing, even though I smiled it off for a long time. What could a sharp woman's tongue do to me? It makes me shudder (10-29-20).

He even begins to appreciate the beauty of the Academy, nudged into acknowledging it by the comments of visitors: "Every body thinks this place is so beautiful that I'm beginning to notice it myself" (10-18-20). Later he writes that on "a brisk walk in the crisp evening . . . the Hudson looks beautiful in the twilight and mist" (12-12-20). But what he is most enthusiastic about is the change in plebe life. The administration of the Academy, led by General Douglas MacArthur, is determined to wipe out hazing and with it the evils of "beast barracks." He wishes the plebes realized fully what they are being saved from:

> We grumble a little at the way the plebes take for granted liberties we never had, but I am as happy as can be at the way the new system is working and I am proud to be the leader of my class in it. Some day when it is far enough in the past for me to see it as a whole I shall tell it all to you and [F]ather and I think you will be proud of the duties that your son has seen and obeyed during his yearling year at West Point (9-24-20).
>
> The plebes have an easier time than we, but they have to work. I inspected seven of them yesterday who had to work one hour on cleaning their rooms, or until they satisfied me. I made them all do a lot more at the end of the hour when I inspected. There's a lot they don't know about cleaning rooms (10-3-20).

Along with other yearlings he is called on to intervene with plebes at times:

> I've just been trying to persuade a plebe that he should write home. He hasn't written for four weeks and says in effect that it is a personal, private affair. There are some of us who look on it as a disgrace to the Corps of Cadets. His mother asked

> Hertford's mother to find out why he hadn't written. I must confess I can hardly have patience with such selfishness. He's a big handsome lad and says he's enjoying life here. I'm going to speak to the tactical officer about it to morrow (9-18-20).

> I got that plebe started writing home and I hope his mother's broken heart will heal. Kenner just got two pounds of candy from a lady whose son he persuaded not to resign. The Colonel and his wife ought to send me a fruit cake for making their spoilt young hopeful break his five weeks silence (9-24-20).

But leadership has its down side for him too, and when in the thick of responding to classmates in "all their joys and griefs," conferring with administrative officers and persuading recalcitrant correspondents to write home, he has a longing for a lower profile and less responsibility:

> I pray that I may rarely in my life be compelled to lead as conspicuous a life as I lead here. Sometimes I long for a long stay at home to be treated more as a boy and less as a leader (9-24-20).

In his last letter before the trip home he warns that he will be unable to bring gifts, except two articles of used clothing for his father:

> I have . . . had a pair of good shoes provided with very thick soles such as we wear to drill. These are for [F]ather and also the Stetson hat that I used to wear in the Army. It is still pretty good and I've been wearing it all fall. Otherwise I have no Christmas presents, I am sorry to say. But these are our lean years. Times will be easier in less than two years now (12-12-20).

By taking the Chesapeake Bay steamer from Baltimore, he expects to arrive at Clay Bank wharf in Gloucester on Christmas Eve—his first time home since his departure for West Point a year and a half earlier.

* * *

Major events occur at the opening and closing of this semester: in the first month, a tragedy involving a classmate, and in late May,

Carter with his parents and two sisters, Mary Mann and Fanny, Christmas 1920.

Carter's action—sharply criticized by some—in doing "right against prudence" (5-25-21).

In the first week back at the Academy, a classmate is missing:

> A man of my class has disappeared and nobody has any idea what has become of him . . . I hope he has not had a fatal accident. We have searching parties out in the neighborhood (1-7-21).

This news is followed the next day with word of the cadet's suicide, and Carter comments that though "he was of a gloomy disposition . . . so many of us have gloomy dispositions that nobody thinks anything of a despondent person" (1-8-21). He makes no further reference to the tragedy.

In mid-January he details the ordinary things that occupy his time and thoughts:

> I shall adopt the usual program this week, movies to-night, a little fresh air tomorrow, and the Y.M.C.A. tomorrow night.

> There are a great . . . [many] matters of interest now hanging over us . . . I . . . am greatly interested in the class standings for the last term, my balance with the cadet store, this week's grades . . . , the basket ball team, my table's education, and the coming of spring and baseball.
>
> I no longer doubt that I did right in coming to West Point now. As things . . . stand in civil life, the best money I could make would do little more than support me. It seems too good to be true, being paid $97.40 per month for board, clothes, expenses, and $14.00 per month compulsory saving. Counting quarters, my pay is equivalent to $110.00 per month. That was small six months ago but it is getting bigger all the time now (1-15-21).

Hospitalized in March for treatment of a painful carbuncle on his neck, Carter heads straight for the baseball diamond upon discharge, and plays ball that very afternoon, saying that he would "give anything I possess to develop into a first class baseball player this year. A fellow can get deadly tired of these perpetual intellectual pursuits . . . and baseball comes as a great relief" (3-27-21). But, by late May he is giving a sober assessment of his skill, saying that his "best work is in steadying the team. I'm not wonderful as a player myself" (5-24-21).

One glorious, redeeming victory comes at the end of the baseball season:

> May 28, 1921
>
> Dear Mother,
>
> We won a Navy game at last! I'm almost crazy over it. We won 8 to 7 in the last inning. We swarmed on the field and did an eternal snake dance. I have seen five defeats and this one victory in my two years. It surely does us good . . .
>
> Sunday morning—Such a time as we have had. Singing, shouting, and speech making in the mess hall with the officer in charge yelling like the rest of us. Last night we got up at 2 o'clock and paraded around in fantastic undress costumes. It was like an Indian war dance around the big bonfire and the cadet band playing as though their lungs would split. I

> carried a blazing broom in the torchlight procession. Capt. McEwan addressed us with his thrilling eloquence and ridicule and was cheered to the echo. Finally we broke up and went quietly home . . .
>
> Everything is bright and gay from now on.
>
> With best love,
>
> Your hysterical son,
>
> Carter

Always dependent on family letters, Carter often re-reads them to the annoyance of his roommates:

> I have thoroughly enjoyed all the letters from home and from Mary Mann, which have been long and frequent. I disgust my roommates by chuckling constantly while reading home letters. I often read them through twice and the first time with yours, [Mother], takes quite a while, which leads Kenner to remark that if I did not get so many letters, I might get my math a bit better (5-13-21).

A week later, worried that his mother might reduce her writing because of Kenner's remark, he hastens to correct any such tendency: " . . . I hope you won't pay any foolish attention to what I quoted from Kenner. Your letters can never be too long or too frequent" (5-20-21). He adds that he no longer enjoys Kenner as a roommate.

From time to time, warning messages from others about the hazards of flight draw a strong response from Carter. He writes his father:

> Aunt Mary J. writes me that she hopes Warner's accident will be a lesson to me never to fly again. My answer is, "Wist ye not that I must be about my country's business?" When a real man sees an opportunity of great service, of high honor, of glorious adventure, he seizes it. Only the sluggard lives painfully in accord with the great law of self-preservation. My greatest contempt is reserved for men who take up the ministry, law, medicine or any profession and refuse to pay the price of discomfort, unselfishness, complete self-surrender, which has made their professions illustrious. And it is foolish

> or thoughtless women who breed the ease-loving men of the world. Well, those people are all right in their way but I am glad that my mother was one of those whose eyes burned when she spoke of [Generals] Jackson and Lee (1-30-21).

In a lighter vein, he speaks of his tendency to be distracted from his studies when he is looking forward to a gala weekend:

> My lessons are getting along fairly well, but I do not study as hard when I have a big frolic ahead of me. I never did and never will. It must be a family failing not to be able to mix pleasure and business . . . [Cousin B.] solves the problem by never taking any pleasure (2-16-21).

The highlight of the semester's social life is the visit of several Gloucester girls for a hops weekend in May. After they come, chaperoned by Mrs. Dimock, a kind Gloucester lady of means who brings her daughter and a few of her friends, Carter writes happily to his mother:

> I had a most delightful week-end, the best I have ever had here. They all seemed to enjoy themselves, promised to come again and to give you a most favorable account of me. I am all

The girls from Gloucester at West Point for a hops weekend: Catharine Mott, Eliza Cary, Emily Dimock, and Mrs. Dimock. The two cadets are not identified.

> spoiled for dragging Northern femmes after this. All my plans for them worked out wonderfully, aided by wonderful spring weather and their delightful tact.
>
> Mrs. Dimock promises to bring up more Gloucester girls next year. I told her to bring them in flocks and singly, as many and often as possible (5-16-21).

At the end of May, a situation arises involving prohibition, which is the law of the land, and in Carter's view, cadets are on their honor to uphold those laws. He writes his parents about the incident:

> . . . The other day (yesterday) I got a letter addressed to Furlough Banquet Committee, Class of 1923, soliciting trade in "wet goods" from members of the class. I decided that as Class President, I would dispose of the letter according to my lights, so I mailed it to the District Attorney, Manhattan, Special Delivery. Kenner and I had hot words over it . . . and he told it outside. I never saw anything spread as quickly in my life. To all inquiries, I replied by an explanation of what I did, why, and said I was sorry to disagree, but would do the same again. After one or two explanations everything quieted down. The friends I have lost appear to be the ones I didn't value much.
>
> Of course, the maddest man in the Corps was my old friend Dupre Dance. He'd like to see anything happen to me. There'll be quite a bit of bitterness if the guy gets a jail term. These cadets said they wouldn't be able to buy liquor anywhere in New York this summer, that the fellow was a friend of theirs, that he meant the letter for them . . .
>
> I am afraid that all this will not come to pass. The fellow undoubtedly has police protection and the district attorney is already swamped with cases. However it may teach the bootleggers not to depend implicitly on the cooperation of the Army in breaking the law . . .
>
> I don't even guess what the result may be. I am exalted with the belief that for once I did right against prudence . . .
>
> . . . I don't think I'll ever be a social outcast, even if I do lose a bit of that humbug, popularity, for which we are prone to

> sacrifice our consciences . . . Of course [some cadets] warned the wet goods man, thanks to Kenner (5-25-21)!

Six days later, Carter writes his father, “My action has not produced more than a ruffle on the waters” (5-31-21).

As furlough time comes closer, he is ever more eager to be at home. After the initial disappointment that there will be no flying in the summer as earlier hoped for, he declares, “I am going home, home, and that is a great blessing. I . . . [will not have been] at home so much since 1917” (5-20-21).

Dear Daddy,

Here I am 83 years after your Yearling winter at The Point, with snow falling and blowing outside my Upstate New York window, north and west of West Point-on-the-Hudson. I like snow, so I revel in this white winter. But the oppression you feel doesn't have to do with weather. It is the "grind" of courses of little interest to you (other than your French studies), the grind of endless and sometimes mindless details and of the pressure of many obligations beyond your academic work. Gone are the bright days of summer at Camp Dix.

The one redeeming element of these days—other than the knowledge that you are inching closer to the end of your West Point years—is the change in the lives of the plebes. It's a drastic change aimed at eliminating the West Point brand of hazing, and you are tremendously pleased to be participating in it. As you did at Episcopal High School, you write that after time passes—probably during a visit home—you will describe the frightful things that went on, as though they and the pain they caused are too fearful to commit to paper. I am left to imagine what you and others endured.

I don't really understand your relationships with roommates. I remember how mad you got with Scotty at EHS when he teased you about writing home so much. You had an actual physical fight with him. And here again you identify teasing as the means of roommates getting under your skin. I wonder what they teased about, and what you did and said when you couldn't take it any longer.

At Christmas you have no gifts to take home, except clothing issued to you. That's an eloquent statement of the moneyless life you led.

I laughed out loud when you said that Cousin B. has solved the problem of mixing work with pleasure—which you find hard to do—"by never taking any pleasure." You conjure in a flash the perpetually somber expression of our cousin. I never saw him smile. Do you understand my delight when you and I share an observation and a good laugh?

But there's something in your first two letters of the new year I don't understand at all, and that's your reaction to the suicide of a classmate. In three lines you dismiss it, never to return to it again. With your care for your classmates, this seems an uncharacteristically terse comment. But it has a familiar ring, too. At Dorr Field, two-and-a-half years ago, you also spoke in brief, cut-and-dried fashion about the death of another student pilot. Maybe steeling yourself against loss of nerve as a student pilot, when you had a close call, made you seal off death in a box by itself, and you don't want to visit that box (as for years I didn't want to open the box of your letters). You dealt with death in practical terms by making sure you carried life insurance, anticipating it could help your parents see your sisters through college, if need be, but loss and grieving—the emotions that have to be lived—you avoided.

It shocks me when you say "so many of us have gloomy dispositions that nobody thinks anything of a despondent person." That says all too much about the quality of student days at West Point. How much good can come from living and studying in such an atmosphere as this?

Those are strong words you use in responding to a warning from Aunt Mary Armistead about the dangers of flying—words about service, honor and "glorious adventure." You find contemptible those men who abuse their high professional calling by not paying "the price of discomfort, unselfishness [and] complete self-surrender, which has made their professions illustrious."

I see in your words the fruits of your immersion in the Idylls of the King, *your love of adventure, your respect for the honor afforded by others for work well done and principles adhered to, and the deep need to be of service, all reinforced by the atmosphere in which you grew up—of hero-worship for the southern military leaders who stood so valiantly for such a wrongful cause. You know how I feel about that atmosphere, and I know you surmounted it in many wonderful ways. But oh, how I wish it had not stoked the fires of romanticism that burned so brightly in you.*

I'll bet there was a flap about your action on the bootlegger letter. I expect you downplayed it, not wanting your parents to worry about you having a bad time. I have a memory—but only of the vaguest kind—that the family was proud of something you did in support of prohibition, at the expense, they thought, of losing status with your class. In your opinion, this was not the case, and the clarity of your action is deeply satisfying to you—and to me.

In your first fall at the Episcopal High School, you confessed to your parents that you had been trying to "cultivate popularity," and that you very much wanted to be elected to some school office. Well, you enjoy a very sound popularity at West Point, as your election as class president demonstrates. Now, you view yourself as having had your fling with that experience, and refer to popularity as "that humbug." But I still like it that you had that recognition from your classmates.

One more note: for the first time you mention "Catherine Mott." Since you spell her name incorrectly, it's pretty clear the two of you have not even had so much as an exchange of letters. I'm getting anxious about whether there is time to accomplish a successful courtship, though my almost eighty years of life reassures me that you do!

With warm love,

Catharine Carter

P. S. Day before yesterday, just after I wrote you the above, the Columbia Space Shuttle disintegrated as it re-entered the earth's atmosphere. All seven crew members died, with body and vehicle pieces spread over two states.

At intervals throughout the long day, we listened to the radio as bits of information began to filter out. Between times there were interviews with former astronauts. One was asked, "Why did you want to become an astronaut?" Prominent in his answer was the chance for great adventure—perhaps the greatest remaining to humankind, and his sad voice took on a momentary warmth as he talked about it.

Your words—so many of them deeply engraved in me, Daddy—melded with his words and feelings. You speak of " . . . an opportunity of great service, of high honor, of glorious adventure . . . " and my heart knows that flying is for you as space travel is for some young men, and women, today. I heard you in the words of that astronaut, and my understanding grows about your complete engagement with flying. To deny it would be to deny yourself, to be something less, to live always with regret.

That leaves me with the question of the astronauts' families, and our family. I've lashed out at you in anger for your apparent disregard of what your risk-taking might mean for those most dear to you.

It won't surprise you that I think now about the children of the astronauts, especially the little ones, who lost their fathers—and in one instance—their mother, in the Columbia disaster.

C. C.

PART III
First Classman

June, 1921–June, 1922

The sole letter of the summer furlough shows Carter filling the vital role of head housekeeper in the absence of his mother, who is likely staying with her sisters at The Cedars during another bout of poor health. He takes the job in stride:

July 2, 1921

Dear Mother,

Things have been moving smoothly since you left. We know that you will suffer with all that medical attention but hope you will be permanently improved by it . . .

[Aunt Molly] professes to miss you greatly, but has come every day. There never was such a boiling [to sterilize things] as Mary Mann has carried on. Fanny and I would much prefer to eat germs . . .

The girls both continue to act like angels (of the sprightliest kind, however) and seem to enjoy housekeeping. [In Latin w]e are finishing the Caesar to day. Fanny is making good progress in French too . . .

We sold 50 cents worth of milk, whole and skimmed this morning, and Fanny has been making very fair butter, considering the lack of ice. The man can't get as much ice as he has orders for . . .

Monday morning.—Sunday is a very hard day around here, with church, Sunday School, and social duties . . .

Father is busy in the office and the children hope to join three cars from Newport News in a picnic at Timberneck. If that doesn't come off, we'll all try to go swimming this evening.

Devotedly,
Carter

Upon completion of the long summer furlough and his return to the Point, the end of Carter's time at the Academy is clearly in view. For a few months he suffers what he says are his usual low spirits in the fall season, but all is redeemed at the end of the term by the "perfectly wonderful time" he has when the Gloucester girls come for a big hops weekend in late November. He writes two letters four days after their departure, a matter-of-fact one to his mother, and a less guarded one to Mary Mann, who is emerging as something of a confidante. His letter to Mary Mann is rich in detail:

> I hardly know how to tell you about our week of festivities, but I can promise you it lived up to all expectations. No higher praise could be given it. The girls got here on Wednesday and I went straight over and delivered the photographs for them to take home to [M]other and for them to flatter me about them of course. But I kept one for you so [M]other could not forget and give it to someone else. I am just delighted I am to have one of yours. If it is as good as your friends think it shall be one of my most valued possessions.
>
> Well we had a dance till one o'clock Wednesday night . . . I took Catharine [Mott] . . . I do not know whether Catharine was the prettiest girl there, because I looked at so few of them.
>
> Thursday I had to play in the championship game in lacrosse and we won, 3 to 1 . . . Friday we had classes so the girls had to entertain themselves . . . All of them, but Catharine[,] seemed not to care much for sightseeing. Let me give you a tip. If you come to a place like this, always be interested in seeing everything that is going on. Not only is it the best and most courteous thing to do but it is the way to have a good trip and carry away something to remember—and to get invited again, for the most satisfactory thing in the world is to entertain company that always takes an interest in everything that goes on around and likes everything good to eat. Ask any housekeeper . . .
>
> Catharine was right up to the minute in every respect and seemed to enjoy herself all the time, which of course doubled my pleasure in the occasion . . .

Catharine Mott, during a visit to West Point, c. 1921.

Friday night we danced till twelve and then bade the party good-bye till after the game, when we met in time for supper at the Hotel Gotham, at 55th Street and 5th Ave. For supper we had planked steak and ice cream molded in funny shapes, and oysters on the half-shell—not in that order, of course,—and some other trifles. In case you don't know what they mean by planked steak, as I did not until about three years ago, it is a nice thick juicy steak with gravy around and a lot of vegetables on top, browned creamed potatoes in a ruffle around the outside as a retaining wall and peas and carrots and other things within. It is good. I did not eat such a big dinner as you might expect, because I was so happy that my sense of taste was impaired. The party was very merry in spite of the defeat [in

> the football game with Navy] and then we went to see George Arliss in The Green Goddess, which was splendid. Here again I enjoyed the intermissions as much as the play. Minutes get precious so near the end of such a pleasant holiday. There was such a jam around the theater that we did not take a taxi after the show, but walked home, along 5th Ave., just like we owned the town. And I was so interested in talking to Catharine that I walked two blocks by the Hotel . . .
>
> After a little while at the hotel we said good-bye and went to the station. There the boys insisted on eating some more and I joined them. At 3:30 we got in bed at West Point and got up at 8. For the next two days I was busy making up sleep (11-30-21).

Until that big November weekend, Carter's letters concern familiar topics—roommates, studies, sports, family matters and occasionally politics. He is happier with his roommates than in the previous year. Kenner has moved out, and John Pitzer, a football player and boxer, joins Carter and Earl Gruver. Carter reports the efforts of the three of them to be economical, and expresses his appreciation for Pitzer's honesty:

> We are all making the most remarkable economies this year. My roommates tore a shirt off me the other day because it was so perforated with holes that they did not approve of my wearing it. They are surely a jolly pair and keep up my spirits at all times. Everything is much nicer than last year (10-29-21).
>
> Pitzer is assistant manager of boxing. That means that if he behaves himself he will be the manager next year. He is all for honor and glory so that makes him very happy. He says that it is not for his sake but because his father likes to hear about it and tell all the neighbors. John is a simple hearted cuss. He never gives you a false motive for his actions (12-10-21).

In one area of cadet life, however, Carter's roommates cannot help him, and he pours out to his father his regret that he cannot enter into the popular music scene of the day:

> I don't get so much done yet I never find time to enjoy life, as most of those around me seem to do. I suppose it is because I'm not interested in the same things. I surely wish I could enjoy music as they seem to. It's all a mystery to me how any one can find relaxation or pleasure in playing ragtime on a victrola. They all say I miss a lot, but I have to sit around like a sphinx when they start to sing. Well I have no right to quarrel with fate, because it gave me my share of accomplishments and I should make the best of them instead of wishing for more. But I do lack the gift of enjoying the routine here... (11-13-21).

References to his studies are less frequent than in the past, though he comments that Spanish, his fifth language, "looks easy" (9-23-21). He reports other bits and pieces of interest: the significance of having a class ring, more drunkenness in the Corps, the boredom of being reviewed by numerous overseas leaders of World War I, and, as always, his delight in exercise and sports. He is enthusiastic about lacrosse, a game new to him, and his D Company intramural team does so well he hopes for the intramural championship.

Concern about his family continues, with his father having lost an acting county postmaster position because the Republican party is now in power, and his mother undertaking her usual duties which he fears make too great "demands on her strength" (9-23-21). In his next letter to her, he is "reply[ing] promptly . . . if possible [to] cheer you up a little" (10-4-21).

He is a bit testy with his father when writing about his class standing:

> This letter will clearly and accurately set forth my class standing. Preserve it for reference and don't tell me [at] Christmas that I never explain anything.
>
> The important thing is that for the two years my rank is *8*, class of 298. Remember that *8* if you forget all the rest . . . [A]mong the three year men . . . it will be a pretty race for

> first place, but the odds are on Beadle. I think I can slip in second (10-15-21).

Finances are problematic as usual, and in October a split in his pants requiring an expenditure of $14 for a new pair is a setback. That he has a loan from the Gloucester bank in order to pay his life insurance premiums also comes to light, for he requests his father's help in arranging a continuation of the loan, which he hopes to pay off by midsummer (10-29-21).

One possible political development having to do with disarmament is of great interest to him. He writes his father:

> After reading the account of Hughes proposition on Naval Disarmament, I am thrilled . . . There surely has never been any such colossal plan offered in the history of the world. I am proud of my country, because though she has once sacrificed ideals to politics, she is again facing the light. Why, this disarmament would put us in the League of Nations before the ten years was up . . .
>
> I suppose the army will be decreased too. If necessary, I shall be proud and happy to change my profession for the cause of peace. But I do feel sorry for the officers and men of middle age in both services who are proud of their profession, have families, and no other way of earning a living (11-13-21).

As the time of the Christmas holiday draws near, Carter warns that he has a few social engagements that will take him away from home: "I hope I won't be on the go too much, but I must confess there are two or three little trips I hope to take and one is to the dance at Elmington [which Mrs. Dimock is giving] the day after Christmas" (12-14-21). So the fall term ends, with Carter sounding as happy as a lark as he heads home for Christmas and, clearly, more time with Catharine.

* * *

Two major life-course decisions dominate Carter's final months at West Point. Both come from the heart. "Crazy" about Catharine Mott, he writes Mary Mann in mid-February:

> I had better warn you . . . that I shall probably not help much teaching Fanny French [this summer]. I shall have some other fish to fry. There is no use trying to keep the secret from you any longer. I can not keep secrets. I am going to be courting Catharine like smoke next summer and I am writing to her every day this last month and it is a wonder I can study as much as I have and be so crazy about her at the same time. And now she is every bit as fond of me, so the matter is all settled except the date. We won't get married next summer, but I think I shall be at Fort Monroe and when I see my way clear I'll cross the river and grab her and take her off to the Philippines or Panama or Hawaii or California for a four year honey-moon. And by the time that is over, you and Fanny will be grown ladies and we will come back east and have you to visit us at some swell post and introduce you to some of the sweetest young beaux that you ever tasted. Won't that be nice? Of course I can't tell whether I'll be able to support a wife for two or three years until the new pay bill goes through, but I am not worrying. It is lots of fun just to be courting and I know that my pay will be going up every few years, so if I can get started safely there is nothing to worry about . . . Catharine took all of January to come around, but neither of us has any doubt now and we shall announce it in June. In the mean time nobody but our respective parents know . . . , so do not mention it in letters to anyone please . . . (2-14-22).

Once Catharine "come[s] around," Carter is much occupied with figuring out how he can manage marriage financially, and arrange a wedding date before he heads for his first post assignment, so he will not "spend another year away from the girl I love" (5-3-22).

These matters depend upon Carter's second big decision: the branch of service he chooses to enter upon graduation from the Academy. He continues to regard aviation as his "heart's choice," though he is constantly aware that this is a decision that his parents are very reluctant to have him make. He rejects scholarly pursuits, and embraces the adventure that lies ahead in the pioneering days of aviation. This decision has to be his own, so his parents—or others—can say whatever they "feel on the subject without fear of intruding." On April 1, he pours out his thoughts to his father in one long passionate paragraph:

> I have just read up on the new pay bill and it seems that it will go through this month. I do not know positively how it will affect me but at present I find in it ample cause to justify my heart's choice and go into the Air Service. I know that it is hard on my family and I am not disregarding their wishes entirely. Still it is my judgment that must decide what my life work is to be. I believe that the Air is the coming branch and I am fitted to get a fine start in it from previous training . . . There is something in me that makes me respect the Air Service men more than most other mortals and I hate to think of giving up what I worked so hard to earn, the right to fly. And while admitting there is danger I do not see it as so far beyond what men undertake the world over to gain a living. The old sailors of England and France used to run just as much risk as the modern aviator in their sail vessels that crossed the ocean and their efforts have not been in vain, seeing that they discovered this country and made it a great nation. Had I lived then I should have been a sailor and not a tonsured monk, I care not how much of Latin and Greek they crammed me with. And I do not feel that I ought to miss the biggest venture of this age, the conquest of the air. The machines that we use now will doubtless be considered flimsy sail vessels by the generations that come after, but we will be the first in the field and that is a big honor. Of course the every day part of life has a strong hold on me. I love my family as much as any boy and do not think of myself as compelled by the lust of adventure to take this work up, but I do think that a little bit of the spice of life is to be desired while you are young. Then when you are old, if you attain unto that honor, you will have somewhat to talk about by the open fire. And I have the feeling that if I let myself be persuaded out of flying now that I would always have a little lower opinion of myself. Of course you and [M]other have not tried to persuade me, but almost everybody else has (4-1-22).

By the end of April, Carter makes his final decision, and—probably to the surprise of no one—he commits himself to aviation. He asks his family to keep the decision a private matter for the present, and tries to help his parents consider aviation not to be such a dangerous pursuit after all. Again he dwells on the opportunity to be a part of "the most thrilling discovery of my century":

> Private for family! April 30, 1922
>
> Dearest Mother,
>
> I am going into aviation. I am sorry for your sake, but my mind is made up. I'd always regret it if I didn't and I am not interested in any other work. It won't be so hard if you trust God and my cautiousness and won't listen to overkind friends who try to sympathize. I have thought over the risks very carefully and I don't think they are great, save in case of war. In that case, I shall go out not expecting to come back, but I hope that time is far off and I'll probably be too old to fly at the front if it does come. Flying is getting steadily safer and I may live to see daily passenger service across the oceans by air! I am sure that the thing is in its infancy now. It is not twenty years old in all! It is the most thrilling discovery of my century and I want to be with it all the way. And it carries with it an honorable name among men, untold admiration among young ladies and boys and girls, and a very sizeable income for one of my tastes and habits. I feel like I have not an ailment or nerve in the world. My hand and eye have never been as steady and I am eager to take off once more . . .
>
> With a heart full of love once more,
> Your son,
> Carter

Carter's plans progress to his satisfaction as more information comes through about pay and the post assignment he can expect. He declares his intention to contribute to the costs of his sisters' college expenses even after his marriage, and addresses the matter of Catharine's health, a subject raised by his mother. It now appears that a double wedding is expected in September, as Libby, Catharine's younger sister, is also engaged to be married:

May 3, 1922

My darling Mother,

. . . In the first place, my finances. I have bought all the equipment I need, calculated my expenses minutely for the whole summer, including several little things for June week. I shall find my self, on Sept. 1st with no debts, engagement ring paid for, $20,000 insurance paid up to October, and all the clothes I need for winter but an overcoat, and with *$550 in cash,* probably a little more if I figure right . . .

I love . . . [aviation], and it is the only work I do love. It is a big, new field and when I see Moseley, [a visiting army Air Service test pilot], wearing the wings and hear his modest speech, I know I have done the only thing . . . When I had decided, I felt the same sort of happiness as when I decided to join the Church and when I decided to propose to Catharine. Each of the three decisions I put off long after I felt there was no use in delaying, so each time I know my decision will not waver . . .

With all the other . . . [men going into aviation], it is a new thing, but for me it is living again . . .

[With] 50% extra pay while . . . flying . . . [t]hat makes a second lieut's. pay almost equal to a captain in anything else . . . So you see, I shall be able not only to marry, but also to help Mary Mann and Fanny, carry the present insurance for father, and the government policy for Catharine. I will expect to pay part for Mary in cash in Sept. and I can endorse father's note for the rest, with my insurance (for him) as security, so the place won't be tied up. I expect to be clear of that by Christmas getting $250.00 per month!! Catharine is in on my plans, approves them, and we are both used to economy.

Now the question of health. Both of us are entitled to medical aid from the Gov't, so we can never be ruined by doctor's bills in case of illness like people in civil life. But I realize that Catharine hasn't a strong inheritance. I am prepared to care for her as gently as I can. I may be overconfident, but I think that, in spite of the demands of married life, I can give her an easier, less strength-straining life than being mistress of Toddsbury, as she has been since recovering from the operation. With all her frailness, do you realize she has been the only girl in the house for several years? Both the others were in school or working. Libby did keep house awhile—and broke down . . . Haven't they always got company there, in spite of Mrs. Mott's health and Mr. Mott's financial condition (which must be serious, I should think, though I know nothing)?

Another thing. When I go as far as Texas, I'll have to stay at least a year before being entitled to a leave. Do you think it possible for me to spend another year away from the girl I love?

I am the one who suggested marriage in Sept. They are all willing. Everybody gains but poor [older sister] Ellen, who gives up her work and goes home to take care of her mother, who may have another heart attack at any time. That would depress me, I know. But Mr. Mott gains, because one wedding stir-up costs just half as much as two. The rest of us gain the same way, and it is less work for everyone. And I gain, by not feeling quite so conspicuous, when there are two grooms!! . . .

Have I forgotten anything important, [M]other dear? Almost nothing else has been in my mind since Christmas. Do my plans seem wild or unreal? They all seem as reasonably sure to me as anything in this uncertain world can be. Pray for us all that God in his Providence may direct and I will do so too.

Devotedly your son,
Carter

Carter writes Catharine's father and in May receives a reply which he says "was very fine in tone," adding, " I surely have been treated kindly by the whole [Mott] family" (5-10-22). He is now quite certain he will be sent to Texas, and this gives him an idea for a honeymoon:

> I plan to get married in Sept. and take a steamer from Baltimore to New Orleans and Galveston. That will give me a pleasant honey moon and the government mileage (computed by rail) will cover the cost. I'll be $500 ahead by then and drawing from $215 to $250 or more a month, so it isn't a leap in the dark. Of course insurance costs about $20 a month, but I get quarters furnished too. You see, going into flying puts me at least ten years ahead financially, so I expect to be fully able to help the girls even though I am embarking on the seas of matrimony (5-10-22).

Carter's father writes his children in a rare moment of jubilation. He is sympathetic with his son's desire to marry in September before going to his Texas post, and calls himself "a poor man" when he married:

> May 14, 1922
>
> My dear Children:
>
> Wedding bells are in the air. What a world of merriment their melody foretells . . . I have written [M]other that she is to be the grand dame at a double wedding in Sept and that even I will borrow or buy some clothes and make a fair appearance for the sake of the Lieutenant. I do not blame the boy a bit. If I was in his place I would not want to go away off to Texas and leave my sweetheart behind. Mother may have written what the Negroes term "a lone gospel". I do not know what she wrote. Of course one can easily be very practical for others. If it were proper to use the argumentum ad hominem one could remind [M]other that she married a poor man who had neither property, profession or business ability and whose salary was $37.50 a month. I am not counseling anyone to follow her example, but you will observe the vast difference between the conditions that surrounded that marriage and the one we are so much interested in now. I believe the Lieutenant will make good and he certainly has my blessing in whatever he may undertake. Should he attempt to reach the moon I will sympathize with him . . .
>
> I hope my boy will begin his married life . . . [with family prayers]. I was brought up with both whiskey and cards. I

> long since concluded that it was best to cut out both. I know well enough there need be no harm in cards, but I know just as well that there is constantly harm in them. I know most people would be horrified at the bare suggestion that an army officer should not have cards in his house and should never play. They would harp on the old string about being different &c. I should hate for my boy to go into the army if he were not going to be different from the ordinary run of officers. In stead of being a handy cap it would be found to be a helpful and good thing for an officer and his wife to be different to the extent of not touching cards. I see I have not written handicap properly. Well we will not argue any of these things . . .
>
> Things seem to be running powerfully smooth for a case of really true love. I hope this is one of the exceptions that but proves the rule. I hope you will not know from experience the truth of the saying iras amantium amoris interratio est [Lovers' quarrels are the renewal of love]. Good night. Sweet rest and pleasant dreams . . .
>
> Your father,
> L. C. Catlett

Carter responds warmly to his father's letter, addressing the subjects of family prayers and card playing raised by him:

> Thank you from my heart for so many kind words of encouragement. Mother too seems quite pleased with my plans and as I passed the Air Service exam yesterday I think we may consider the matter as settled . . .
>
> Yes, both of us are heartily in favor of family prayers and planned to have them long ago. But though we shall have precious little time to waste on cards we can't go so far as to forbid them. We have not seen any of these great misfortunes through card playing that we have heard about . . . I do always draw the line at gambling and at playing on Sunday, but when you tell a lot of people "Thou shalt not do this", you must give them another occupation to take the place of it, one that will prove as interesting. And for people who don't shine

> in music, letters, conversation, or dancing and who haven't thoughts enough to entertain them alone, cards are valuable to keep *them out of mischief* or insanity . . . I should be likely to lose what influence I had and be classified a curiosity, not a strong man, if I inveighed against such comparatively harmless things as social bridge playing (5-17-22).

Academic work recedes into the background, but Carter's pleasure in sports, and exercise in general, continues. In January he describes his running experience in frigid weather and gives more details about lacrosse:

> This morning the temperature was 9 below zero and it hasn't warmed up much yet. I don't see how it can be good for a man who breathes through his mouth, but fortunately my nose is so large I don't have to. Some men with small nostrils can't run at all with their mouths closed. We grease our limbs with goose grease to keep from taking cold. It is smelly stuff . . . I have had only one chance to skate and three to go coasting. Running takes up my outdoor time (1-26-22).

He pictures the lacrosse team for his parents, to whom the game may be unfamiliar:

> You ought to see the padding I'll wear in Lacrosse—big gauntlets with pads on the knuckles, arms sheathed in felt, a padded cap with ear pieces . . . [T]he ball is white and of hard rubber. I believe I can throw it as far with my stick as well as by hand. The latter is not allowed.
>
> I just came in from practice and bathed. My blood is still coursing with the lust and joy of battle. I don't believe I'll ever get too tired to enjoy playing it . . . It was clear and cold to day and I enjoyed the game and showed up to good advantage for a new man. It looks like I am sure to make the squad all right. Now I must aim for the team. But I never yet have made a first team in anything, so I am afraid now it is too late (3-18-22).

Also part of Cadet Corps life are occasional trips in order for cadets to march in parades. In April Carter has such a trip to Washington, which he describes in a letter to his mother, including the spectacle of veteran admirals and Civil War generals bedecked in the finery of earlier days:

> We [cadets] left at 8 AM Wednesday and took the Pullman down to Washington. I had to sleep with a flanker, so didn't have much room or much sleep. We got into Washington about four [AM] and I lay awake from then on making plans. One of the chief attractions of the trip was the opportunity to buy clothing from the Q. M. . . . By the time I got back from shopping it was time to go back and gird on my sabre for the parade. We fell in back of the White House at 11:15 and after much delay marched down Pennsylvania Avenue to the Capitol and turned to the right towards the Grant Memorial hard by. Then more delays and speeches till 4:30, so I was on my feet for five hours and without food for ten. . . .
>
> The Vice-President spoke, and Mr. Hughes [and others] . . . But I was standing up and off to one side where I couldn't see or hear them. The feature of the day was an old-time Confederate reunion speech by Gen. Julian Carr, of North Carolina, Commander of the United Confederate Veterans. He had a voice as of many waters and he alone put any humor into the ceremonies. Among his flights were "I come from the Land of the Long-Leaf Pine, where the weak grow strong and the strong grow big." "Grant was a friend to the Confederate soldier when he needed a friend." "Then we beat our swords into plowshares and our plowshares into pruning hooks." Gen. Carr made a great hit with the tired cadets and all the crowd. You never saw the like of the old epaulettes of Admirals and Generals, who were youngsters in the Civil War and hardy men in '98. I never want to live that long and totter about in battered gold lace, cocked hat, plume and all (4-30-22).

Though Carter speaks little of daily life at the Point, except for his pleasure at having two congenial roommates, he does return to a matter of enduring interest to him—relationships of upper classmen with plebes:

> I had a compliment that surely puffed me up to night. One of the men who was a plebe last year said that then he made up his mind to treat plebes exactly as I treated them, and that he could truthfully say that he pulled his shoulders back harder for my quiet word of command than for anybody else's crawling. So the new leaven is leavening the whole lump! I've seen lots of signs of it before (4-9-22).
>
> . . . I'm pretty sure . . . [the plebes] work as hard for my quiet instructions as for anybody's driving—maybe harder (5-21-22).

Meanwhile, in Gloucester, preparations for the June graduation trip—made possible again by the generous Mrs. Dimock—are proceeding, with Catharine, Fanny and Carter's mother assembling their wardrobes for the festivities, as well as an evening of theater in New York. Two letters from Catharine to her future mother-in-law indicate a developing relationship:

> Toddsbury
> [Dixondale, Gloucester Co.]
> Thursday night
>
> Dear Mrs. Catlett—
>
> You don't know how very happy it made me—when I received your lovely letter last evening. I haven't the words to express my appreciation of the splendid things you said—and oh, I am so proud to have Carter's love—it is the finest and noblest.
>
> How delighted I am that we are all going to have the trip to-gether in June—and I can tell you of all our hopes and plans. I felt as though it would be so lovely to have Carter here when we tell all our friends—that's why we are waiting until June—before we make it "public property." As for the trip we needn't keep that—for it will be so nice to talk about it all—and we are going to have such a good time. Tell Fanny she and I will have to let all our *thrills out* on each other!
>
> Thanking you again, with all my heart—and with love for all of you.
>
> Catharine Mott

In June, while the rest of the family makes the trip to West Point for the graduation festivities, Mary Mann and Carter's father remain in Virginia, Mary Mann to graduate from Stuart Hall and take entrance exams for Wellesley College, and her father to tend the farm.

Carter at graduation from West Point, 1922.

* * *

The letters of this pre-wedding summer reveal that Carter is at a boy's camp in New Hampshire, doubtless to earn money to pay off his bank loan as well as meet his and Catharine's initial expenses. He ends one letter by saying "I continue to gain weight and entertain a cheery disposition" (8-11-22).

In mid-summer, jolting news comes about the outcome of Mary Mann's examinations for admission to Wellesley—she fails to pass three of them. Circumstances were against her in that all nine examinations were administered in one day, and, in Carter's estimation, the school had not given her the extra preparation she deserved. He is at pains to express confidence in her and does not want her to be discouraged. He also boldly states that he does not "listen to college officials":

> Tell Mary not to be discouraged by this. The greatest characters have been strengthened by their early failures, and her course will be the more valuable and enjoyable for being hard-earned (7-24-22).

Even at a distance, he is mulling over other details of the wedding, and is particularly anxious that he and his bride not be the brunt of wedding jokes:

> We can arrange later where the brides change their clothes. As you say, best keep it rather quiet. I shall try to be good-natured but I have little patience with wedding jokers. It is a darned serious matter to me. I've been six months planning to make things go through without a hitch, and I don't want my tires flat to start with or something like that (8-11-22).

Mindful of his mother's interest in the flora of other regions, he sends her, not long before leaving camp, "five varieties of ferns," and responds to the news from Catharine about his parents' wedding gift:

> I just heard from Catharine and it is mighty sweet of you all to give us the gilded china [ice cream set]. I surely do hate to take it, but it was my earliest admiration as a young man of three years and upwards and I'm sure we both shall prize it above every thing (8-17-22).

Dear Daddy,

There's a lot for us to talk about in these fall letters, but for me other matters pale beside your words about Mother, which I pore over, trying to catch every nuance. Having coped with our unusual spelling of "Catharine" all my life, I notice right away that, contrary to late April, you are now spelling it correctly. Did Mother point this out during the "Gloucester girls'" May visit, or did you see each other during your summer furlough, and correspond in the fall?

Letters between you must have gone back and forth, because you can hardly wait to see her. You go over to the hotel the minute she arrives, ostensibly to give her pictures that she will deliver to Granny, but that's hardly a matter of urgency, since she will be there another three days. I think the relationship between you two has been developing long distance.

(I recall, now, that Mother once said that you had a habit of correcting the spelling in her letters—not a very romantic practice. But to me it indicates you had already taken her into the family, since all of you were very spelling conscious, except for Granny, who blithely went her own illegible way so no one could tell whether she misspelled or not.)

The long awaited Navy-game festivities finally arrive, and you have the better part of three and a half days together—along with the rest of the sizeable party, which includes Mother's sister Libby, another friend from Gloucester and of course the chaperone. I suppose you and Mother had no time alone together, unless you contrived to have a few moments during walks, as in your wonderful promenade down New York City's 5th Ave.—arm-in-arm as I picture it—"just like we owned the town." You overshot the hotel by two blocks because the two of you were so engrossed in conversation.

I love the ways you express your delight in being with her: "I do not know whether Catharine was the prettiest girl there, because I looked at so few of them," and at the elegant hotel dinner you were "so happy my sense of taste was impaired." I note, too, that you "enjoyed the intermissions [when you could talk to Catharine] as much as the play." And then you add, rather wistfully, "Minutes get precious so near the end of such a pleasant holiday."

The pleasure you take in talking to Mother tells me she was a good listener and responder. I can imagine that she was indeed beautiful (as I grew up hearing from elders in Gloucester who let me know my looks were a cut below my mother's), and that her face was often wreathed in the broad smile I see in one of the snapshots made on a West Point visit.

I bask not only in your happiness, but also very much in hers. You see, I can't remember any of the happy days she shared with you. Later in her life she had some pleasure, particularly in the planning and building of her own small home and garden, but I did not know her in any time of deep happiness. Try as I may, I can't conjure an actual glimpse of the two of you together. Surely as a toddler I saw you embrace many times, but these images are entombed in unreachable memory. So to know a little of your courting days, and the enchantment of your early love brings me joy—and hot tears.

Mother once told a friend of mine that she had had "the love of one good man," and that sufficed. Though she received attention from a few other men (there weren't many eligible ones in Gloucester), she responded almost with indifference. She wore her wedding and engagement rings until she died.

Just one more note. In writing about your "perfectly wonderful time," there's a big contrast between your letters to Granny and to Aunt Mary Mann. You are shielding your tender feelings toward Mother from parental discussion and their habit of circulating your letters. I think this is the first time you have held something back from your mother and father. I understand so well.

And now I go to your last term at the Point. You do a lot of serious wrestling with the money aspects of marrying, and how to maintain your contributions to your sisters' education expenses. I feel your growing satisfaction as you become quite certain you can meet your new obligations.

I marvel at your certainty about marrying Mother. You wrote her every day in January until she "[came] around." It didn't take her very long, though it seems to me you two hadn't had much time together except on those hops weekends at West Point. I envy both of you your certainty. It took me a long time to commit to marriage. So I look at your courtship a little wistfully, thinking that if I had grown up with both parents, commitment might not have been such a high mountain for me to climb.

My wistfulness is soon dissipated by a bunch of delightful details: honeymoon plans, the buzz of gossip in Gloucester, Mother's health and your "rescue" of her from the "strength-straining" life at Toddsbury.

Oh my, did you ever have it right about "the swirl of old Virginia society and the drudgery of an old Virginia kitchen." Both were amply present at Toddsbury. I can testify to that personally, because that is exactly what Mother returned to after your death. I can remember her complaint that "Ellen and Mother want company all the time." So your question, "Haven't they always got company there . . . ?" is right on the mark. And you are right to add, "in spite of Mrs. Mott's health and Mr. Mott's financial condition . . . " because neither seemed to prevent Toddsbury from being crammed with people, especially in the summer. They were mostly boarders, but friends and relatives were frequently at the big dining table too. All of that added up to a lot of hard work, despite the presence in the summer of a helper in the kitchen. And, of course, there were the upheavals of canning season—vegetables from the garden, apples and pears from the orchard and bushels of peaches that Grandfather brought in, or fish to be salted and hams to be cured. Hog-slaughtering time was particularly arduous, with all parts of the hog being utilized one way or another. The work of farm and kitchen was unending and "strength-straining" in a big way.

Well, you rescued Mother from this for almost three years.

I'm interested that Granny raised questions about Mother's health. You say you "realize that Catharine hasn't a strong inheritance." I suppose that must be a reference to her mother's poor health—my sad, semi-invalid Grandmother Mott. She had a hard life—seven pregnancies and four living children, and a difficult family situation, because her mother-in-law remained mistress of Toddsbury for the first twenty-three years of Grandmother's marriage. The after-effects of "Bright's Disease" (acute kidney disease) which had brought her to death's door, was the cause of Grandmother's semi-invalidism, as well as what was thought to be heart disease, though she outlived Grandfather by a number of years.

I suppose the awareness of Mother's surgery, the nature of which I never knew except vaguely as some "female problem," made Granny worry about her future daughter-in-law's health. Lovely words frame your response, "I am prepared to care for her as gently as I can."

You stagger me with your certainty about what your life's work must be. Your conviction about it is so complete and it is so clear to you that you alone must make the choice that, "When I do make it I shall make it regardless of what anyone else may say to me, so you can say whatever you feel on the subject without fear of intruding."

I've been able to read your sentiments over and over again in the letters from these months, taking a fairly intellectual approach. But now that we are in coversation Daddy, your presence enfolds me. Your strong, warm spirit, your passion and conviction, your clear sense that you have to respond to what calls you—pervade your daughter's heart.

You are not pleading; you are simply yourself.

A warm embrace, and dear love for you,

Catharine Carter

P.S. I grew up with snapshots of you sitting in an airplane and standing beside one—just everyday kinds of pictures Mother always kept on her bureau. Nothing made them outstanding, so far as I was concerned, but I see something new in them now. I see Mother's understanding of you, her recognition that aviation was at the center of you. This is the way she always remembered you—in and beside your airplane, rather than as a handsome officer all dressed up for a formal portrait, such as those for your West Point graduation.

I think you received love's chief gift, that of being truly and completely accepted. She went off with you to Texas to learn and to share the life of early aviation. Her courage awes me. And her unquestioning acceptance of your calling makes her my hero. I've been too long in coming to see this.

Mother and Aunt Libby, brides in the double wedding September 7, 1922.

My father, the groom.

Wedding guests outside Ware Episcopal Church, the site of the wedding.

6

FAMILY AND FLYING

1922-1925

PART I

Newlyweds
Fall, 1922

Carter and Catharine are boarders for their first several weeks in San Antonio, until early October when they move into "half of a pretty little bungalow" (9-19-22). Their days are filled with acknowledging wedding presents and furnishing their new home, as well as meeting a remarkable number of people who have relatives or friends in Gloucester. Carter is stationed at nearby Brooks Field and initially is placed in ground school, from which he hopes soon to be freed by passing exemption examinations. He is eager to be flying.

The first surviving letter of their new life is written September 19 by Carter to Catharine's great aunt and uncle in Albany, New York:

> Dear Uncle Will and Aunt Kitty,
>
> Catharine wants me to say that she will write as soon as ever she can get her little house in order and her presents thanked

for. She still has about thirty of the latter and we spend part of each day with our pens, she thanking people and I trying to keep our two poor mothers from getting too homesick for us. My mother is sending one girl to college and one to boarding school, both going to strange places, so my mother has no children at home and Mother Mott has one only with her.

Everyone has been lovely to us and substantial presents, yours especially, gave us a fine start in life. Besides that, we have been very fortunate in being sent to San Antonio, a pleasant place to live, a winter health resort, and a place where living is cheap, especially since we do not have to use coal.

My work has not really begun yet. I am a student officer and my classes begin Thursday. The work will be somewhat in the nature of a review for me, because I went through similar courses during the war. That will give me time to keep my little wife from getting homesick and extend our honey moon through the winter. We have decided that it shall never end any how. We feel just like t[wo] children playing at housekeeping together.

Thus far we are boarding but by the first of the month we shall take possession of our dining room, living room, kitchen, sleeping porch and bath. We have half of a pretty little bungalow that is just being finished and it has a pretty fireplace and glassed-in sleeping porch.

With thanks and much love from us both,

Your new nephew,
Carter Catlett

A letter to his mother is eloquent in its simple heading:

Home,
Oct. 12, 1922

Dearest Mother,

As you can imagine, moving has kept us busy . . . All our furniture fits in by inches and we have just all the room we need. The only thing we have still to buy is a serving table, to keep silver and things on. Our living room is complete, down to a cute little bronze Japanese pagoda with incense to burn in it. It came from Mrs. Meem in Seattle. Who is she? I've heard but I've forgotten . . .

It is blazing hot [here] from 10 to 4 and then cools off till by seven it is quite cool and it stays so all night. They never have any dew . . .

We went to a dance last Friday, moved in Saturday, went on an auto trip Sunday and swam, and have been straightening out ever since. That sounds strenuous, but really we have gotten a long night's sleep every night, usually retiring at nine o'clock. Catharine doesn't want to leave the house. She's like a sitting hen. When I get home she just wants to sit and gloat over the house and tell me what she is going to make and do. We've paid our duty calls, but soon we must have the Montagues . . . and maybe others to supper. [They] have been so especially good to us, keeping us from feeling forsaken at first.

Catharine will write the details of the dining room and living room next week. The best she can do tonight is to lie down and stop planning aloud for me to write . . .

You wouldn't approve of all the funny bugs, lizards, horned toads and scorpions that this country grows. Nothing has bitten us, but a scorpion I killed makes me feel a little crawly. They are not dangerous, but quite painful and they usually occur in pairs. I killed but *one* in our kitchen . . .

With a heart full of love for you all,
Your devoted son,
L. C. Catlett Jr.

In a note the next day to Mary Mann, Carter drops the "sitting hen" image of his wife:

> I never saw . . . [Catharine] look so plump and well and she coos with delight every time she looks at her furniture. We have lots of fun laughing at each other. Right now she is hurrying me so we can spoon till she has to get supper and dress for the dance. We have not had a single quarrel and we spend so much time spooning we never get to movies or such things (10-13-22).

For the present, the financial picture is a good one for the young couple, and they are further encouraged by "a most complimentary letter" from Catharine's aunt, Nora Moore, who works in the War Department in Washington (10-16-22). Aunt Nora reports that Carter was put on flying status Sept. 20, which means his monthly pay check will be a little over $260 after deductions for the government life insurance. Carter is unaccustomed to having this much money, and he and Catharine watch their numerous first-month expenses carefully:

> It is rather bewildering to handle so much [more] money than you have ever been used to . . . My check for last month was deposited this morning and such a large day as I have spent paying bills. Among other things I paid for my wedding ring, two rugs, a walnut serving table, a half dozen coffee cups and saucers, a cream pitcher and soup plates, the water bill, officers' club expenses ($5 for dues and dances), a week's groceries, a bread box, curtains and rods, a month's rent (in advance), gas and light, and government grocery bills. And we have about $90 left to run three weeks . . . Well, we calculate on having enough to run us till the first and get a hat and skirt for Catharine too. And when the first of next month comes, there will be just rent, water, gas and electricity to pay, all of which won't be but about $40. It surely is fine to come to the end of the month and find you can pay for things in advance instead of lagging a month (11-4-22).

PART II

Flying and Fathering
1923

Life unfolds at a rapid pace for Carter and Catharine in 1923. By early March they purchase a car, and their social life becomes even more active. But the matter of greatest moment is Catharine's pregnancy—not an easy one in the early months. Laced through Carter's reports of her progress, are his comments on flying, beginning with these words to his father in mid-January:

> I am sublimely happy. I fly alone every day and work on motors in the afternoon. In a month more I hope to be done with my flying tests and to take my own time and fly when I please (1-17-23).

The matter of the car purchase is one Carter takes seriously, writing his father detailed comparisons of Fords, Stars and Grays. He finally settles on a Star, to be delivered March 1, stating that they are ready to pay "over half the price down" (undated letter, early 1923). In addition, he encloses a check to his parents for $100.00, which he has "no doubt will be as water upon a thirsty land." He and Catharine are able to do this because they practice economy in all aspects of their lives, and feel that they come out better than others:

> I have ordered peanut gallery tickets to hear Farrar and Schuman-Heink. I am a week ahead for one and longer for the other, so hope to get something fairly good. We always take cheap seats, so we can afford more things. And if while we are young we climb stairs, may be when we are old, we won't have to. We always sit in the balcony at movies, which saves nearly half the price. Now a lot of our friends won't practice such parsimony, but they talk about not being able to "afford" this or that (3-1-23).

But in one area they spend without reservation or regret. They eat often at the officers' club and arrange for help for Catharine at home as she experiences prolonged morning sickness, and nauseous reactions to food generally. Early in the year, Catharine wrote Carter's parents about her pregnancy, and reassured them about the Army medical care available to her:

> [We hope] . . . Grandmothers and Grandfathers will be very pleased and happy with us . . . [about the baby].
>
> I must stop & write to Mother too, as I haven't written her a word about our little secret either, for I didn't want her to worry. The Army hospital here is one of the very best, & I will keep under the dr.'s care, & take the best care of my-self possible, so please don't any one worry (undated letter, 1923).

Early in February, Carter writes Mary Mann about the miserable time Catharine is having:

> . . . Catharine has been unwell ever since Jan 1st and I have done nearly all the cooking for a month! You'd be amazed at how easy I find [it]. I cook well too. But I surely will be glad when she takes it up again . . . Catharine suffers from nausea everyday and can't bear the sight or smell of food. She eats just enough to keep alive on and loses part of that. I tell you, getting married is no easy job for any woman . . . I just hate to see Catharine feel so miserable (2-2-23).

But a month later he can report improvement:

> Catharine is better than she was and seldom has an upheaval, but she is far from comfortable, poor child. Lizzie cooks her breakfast and dinner and we have been going out to the Club for supper this week. Having so many people around and not knowing what is to be set before her helps. Going to a restaurant does not help because the menu card brings up so many unhallowed associations! From what they say these symptoms should be leaving her soon. The doctor has named September 2 [for the baby's birth]. That comes near being our anniversary, doesn't it (3-1-23).

He goes on to describe a particularly big outing that Catharine, to his surprise, feels like making. They pay two calls, eat supper at an Italian restaurant, and then attend a "big Methodist revival":

> Either I had forgotten what they [revivals] are like or this one was extreme. The preacher surely did have the most capacious grate for roasting sinners in hell that I ever heard. I was almost afraid to fly the next day, for he damned me on nearly every count . . . And he quoted from . . . [Sam Jones], as well as on his own hook, the most gruesome details of the agonized sufferings of people who had put off repentance till too late . . . As was to be expected Catharine was quite amazed, not having ever attended any but colored revivals (3-1-23).

By mid-March Catharine is out and about a good deal:

> Thursday morning Catharine sewed with the Army Guild at Fort Sam [Houston]. Saturday afternoon we went shopping and saw Robin Hood and ate a Mexican supper, the hottest I ever struck. Catharine hated it last fall and now she loves it! I like it very well indeed, but some of it is too hot for comfort . . .
>
> Yesterday we were invited to dinner by my classmates of the 15th artillery Mess. We hated to go because of the raw wind, but had no way of phoning them, so we went. When we got there, it was not a dinner but a hunting breakfast, of which they could not warn us. I was glad though, because it was a novelty to see the officers and their wives and sweethearts all booted and spurred and a trifle muddy after a two-hour ride on Sunday morning. The best thing about the breakfast was an enormous strawberry shortcake (3-19-23).

All the while, Carter is busy with training flights. He writes about an eventful one to Mary Mann, rather than his parents:

> [Y]esterday one of my spark plugs blew out with a pop and [I] landed in a wheat field for repairs. I was flying to Smithville and I reckoned that I must be near Seguin, about 30 miles N.E. of San Antonio, on my course to Smithville. There was a house nearby, but it was deserted and a small Mexican boy and an old woman walked away from my questions as though I were an object of dread. Then I came on a Mexican plowing. He said "No speakee Ingles'." "No hablo mucho espanol,"

said I, and he grinned . . . Well, he understood "Monkey-wrench," and I screwed in my plug, tightened others, which a forgetful mechanic had left loose, cranked my own ship, and took off, with just 25 minutes delay (4-7-23).

2nd Lt. Landon Carter Catlett, Army Air Service, San Antonio, Texas, 1922.

By late April, Catharine has further difficulty:

> Catharine is just [up and] around after a severe case of measles and I am hobbling on a crutch with a sprained ankle. Fortunately my injury didn't occur until she began to get up some. She still lies down till dinner, but she takes a ride out in the afternoon . . .
>
> Hooray! In one more month we'll own our whole car. Then we'll begin saving for what Catharine calls "the picnic" in September . . .
>
> [Another wife] is in the same fix as Catharine but a month behind her. They . . . [have been] a great comfort to each other (5-3-23).

Finally, by mid-May Catharine is coming along well on a schedule of daily rest periods prescribed by the doctor:

> She complains that three hours of lying down in the day time leaves her no time for writing or anything else, and indeed it does not. I think she has better coloring now than she had before she was married and she is just as pretty and happy and full of fun as she can be (5-13-23).

In July, they are dealing with the prodigious heat of a Texas summer:

> The heat here has been more intense than ever—that is, there has been no breeze, so we keep the electric fan blowing on us most of the time . . .
>
> As usual lately, Catharine ate as much dinner as I did and seemed to enjoy it very much. Grapes, figs, Bartlett pears, and magnificent Elberta peaches are now on the market and she continually nibbles fruit between meals. I enjoy things too. I eat large pieces of watermelon now and again. We take Saturday and Sunday dinners in town this month. Only one more summer month to go! We'll be glad when *it* is over and we can get squared away for the pleasanter part of the year. Maybe by next summer we shall be in some other part of the world (7-29-23).

The next communication is a Western Union Telegram:

> San Antonio Tex Sept 2 1923
>
> L C Catlett, Gloucester Va
>
> Little Catharine arrived eleven Sunday night weighs seven pounds six ounces both doing well and all three glad it is over crying has not begun to influence our lives yet big Catharine was still talking when I left she is very proud of herself as am I
>
> Carter

Letters follow giving many details of daily life with their newborn, juxtaposing "dropping live bombs . . . and helping Catharine":

> All goes well with your eldest grandchild. She is now imbibing nourishment close to my elbow, lying on our porch couch, which is an army cot with a West Point blanket on it . . . [The baby's] bowels have done their fair share to day. When they get a little slow, she kicks and smacks boots and blankets all over the place. But she drinks a little warm water and soon follows an explosion, after which come clean clothes and sleep. That was yesterday. Today she has cried only at bathing time, when she almost stands up and jumps out of the tub. She likes it when turned on her stomach and scrubbed on the back however. It makes her purr like a kitten.
>
> I have been dropping live bombs during the week and helping Catharine in between. She rests plenty and awakens every morning fresh and full of pleasure at her "snookums'" antics, so I think she is doing finely. She certainly looks well. We have been driving slowly for short distances once or twice and been to the hospital on a weekly visit and to town to buy her a basket . . . [W]e are enjoying life here with our little scrap of humanity (9-23-23).

A week later Carter's letter home ranges from plans for their daughter's baptism, and their first socializing since her birth, to the success of their bedbug extermination efforts:

> Friday night we put Cathie to bed and went to a dance at Brooks. Mamie [our household helper] sat up with the water bottle

> ready, but after one change of raiment she never gave a grunt till we got home three hours later . . . We slept till 9 Saturday, except for feeding at 6 A.M., and neither Catharine showed any ill effects. Yesterday afternoon we [made calls] . . . and Catharine behaved very well lying in her basket in the back of the car. I changed one very soiled diaper while the other people were not looking and some warm water put her to sleep. Again we got back in three hours to feed her, which demonstrates how wonderful the age we live in is. We never drive anywhere save on smooth pavements and the whirring of the motor seems to put all babies to sleep quicker than anything . . .
>
> Apropos of nothing, Mamie tells us with pride that we are the one people on the row with no bedbugs . . . Surely we are reaping the fruits of our Herculean labors. The only ones we have seen were three in one day on or from a borrowed article, which was absentmindedly borrowed (by Catharine) and quickly returned with thanks. This climate is exceedingly favorable to insect life, but of course anybody can get rid of bugs who tries hard enough...Ours were all on the filthy old government cots and beds. By the way, everybody but us uses 2 single issued beds. We bought our own [double bed] and mean to carry it with us to the grave . . .
>
> Catharine says tell you that Catsy grins at me every day now. My face seems to inspire her with amusement. She is not prone to smile at her mother's, who goes to great lengths to induce her to. Such is the perversity of human nature, from the cradle to the grave(10-1-23).

Several weeks later in a letter to Mary Mann, Carter's remarks about the baby are not quite so rosy, and indicate some reservations about the joys of babyhood:

> Little Catharine is improving gradually from the disease of babyhood. In a year or two she'll look like something. Being a baby is about the rottenest job I know of, though being one in Texas isn't as bad as farther north. She lies outdoors in the sun all day long and it is fine for her. (Of course her face is

shaded.) We have her in a basket like little Moses, and it fits on the floor of the car (10-20-23).

Later, Carter reports that "little Catharine squalled all through the baptismal ceremony, but Mrs. Lee got her quiet just before the minister took her" (10-30-23). He and Catharine produce a version of the present-day mobile by tying "a piece of ribbon where . . . [the baby] can see it and she talks to it and grins when the air stirs it" (10-30-23).

In mid-November, some of the realities of the Air Service begin to intrude. Catharine writes in distress about the accidents that occurred in the recent "Air Carnival":

Kelly Field
Nov. 19th [1923]

Dear Mother Catlett—

. . . Carter hasn't been able to get in his weekly letters on account of being one of the committee to see to the restaurants, which was carried out at the Air Carnival yesterday. What a dreadful day it was! It was cold & rainy all day, but 4,000 people were out, so they tried to proceed with the program—two ships crashed and burned—the first one in the morning—the man was thrown clear, & scarcely hurt at all. The last accident, two ships collided when trying to gas in mid-air. One man did wonderful piloting and got clear. The other ship crashed—the two men in it were saved from the fire—but one was so badly injured, that he died several hours later. It was for the benefit of the Army Relief Work. They talk of having it over again but I truly hope they won't. Carter wasn't flying, I am glad to say . . .

It was so nice to get your long letter yesterday, in fact we always look forward to getting them, you are always so cheerful & encouraging.

We are well, & happy, & send lots of love to you & Father Catlett.

Devotedly—
Catharine

The family picture sent by Catharine and Carter to their Gloucester families, Christmas, 1923.

Soon after Thanksgiving, Carter is anticipating their eagerly desired home leave and reports with pride on their Thanksgiving dinner party:

> It rained four days out of seven last week and Catharine and I have done little but plan and talk about going home after we finish here. It is tantalizing not to know whether it will be Langley [Virginia] or the Philippines or any intermediate distance from home . . . We hope we shall hear something by Christmas though . . . We are afraid to put off asking leave until going to a new station, because it might be hard to get off after being assigned permanent duties. The Air Service is very short of officers, more so than any other branch . . .
>
> We had [Thanksgiving] dinner at night . . . We had turkey and oysters and trimmings. Our turkey was 13 ½ lbs minus the feathers and cost $4.00, which was cheap. It was a delicious young gobbler, ordered weeks ahead. We had the party, 3 meals and 3 soups from it, although Mamie ate a great quantity. Catharine cooked everything deliciously. Of course the oysters were not what we were used to, but probably the other people didn't know anything better. We all enjoyed the evening thoroughly, both boys and girls being congenial . . .
>
> The infant now weighs 12 lbs and Catharine is sitting up telling her how all her grandparents are going to love her and sending kisses to them. I am being told how sweet, innocent, etc., she is, so that it is very hard to write.
>
> I'm glad you are getting the furniture and boarders if you are also getting a cook, but I hate to think of your attempting six boarders without one (12-2-23).

So ends 1923, as Catharine and Carter prepare for their second Christmas apart from their Gloucester families, but this year they will celebrate with "little Catharine."

PART III

Home Leave and Hawaii
1924

Shortly before New Year's Day, Carter begins a series of cross-country training flights, the most ambitious of which is a flight to St. Louis with stops at five airfields along the way. Again, he writes his sisters, rather than his parents, about the experience:

> I flew to St. Louis taking turns with another pilot and during his shift we lost our landing gear . . . .The trouble was we flew till dark caught us and didn't have a candle to land by, so we ran into the dirt, fortunately a soft hay field. We both learned some sense. I fly with nobody after sundown hereafter (1-12-24).

Unable to fly their plane back to Kelly Field, Carter and fellow pilot have to wait in Missouri until January 3 for orders to return home.

From the beginning of the year, Carter, and particularly Catharine, are caught up in anticipating and planning for the long and eagerly awaited home leave. By now Carter knows his next assignment is Luke Field, Territory of Hawaii, so arrangements—complex and detailed—for the Texas-Virginia-Hawaii trip are a big undertaking. Catharine and baby are to precede Carter to Gloucester by a month in order to have ample time for extended visits with both the Catlett and Mott families. Their fervent anticipation is evident in many exchanges with Carter's parents. When there is some confusion about the date of their visit, Carter writes urgently, brushing aside worries about the possible whooping cough exposure awaiting baby Catharine in Gloucester:

> We never for a moment considered postponing the trip home. You "must don't know how bad we're home-struck" . . . Catharine will be with you for supper Saturday night. Kiss her roundly for me. I shall be missing her by then.

> I have plenty to do, getting our goods and chattels shipped to Frisco and attending to my supplies and flying on the side . . .
>
> [Fanny] . . . wrote in haste to enquire whether the whooping cough changed . . . [our] plans. Seeing that we have three cases of measles in this set of quarters and all the children around have been exposed to mumps, I think it more dangerous to stay than go. Whooping cough is also prevalent in town. Whenever . . . [the baby] is not in this house, she's in the open air, so I don't think she has been exposed to anything. She seems to grow more vigorous daily and is so fat she is a sight (3-23-24).

Before she leaves for Gloucester in late March, Catharine helps Carter with advance preparations for the overseas move, as he will be alone for a month in San Antonio before starting his two month leave covering most of May and June. Catharine writes her mother-in-law about the sewing she wishes to complete before the trip and her ingenious solution to the problem of diapers and train travel:

> We are both busy every minute of the day now. I am trying to get a lot of sewing finished up—have finished five pairs of rompers for baby, & have two more on the way & two dresses for my-self most done.
>
> Last night Carter helped me & we tore 180 diapers out of old sheets. Now I have to have them sterilized & baby will be well supplied for our entire trip, & I can destroy them, & not carry a lot of soiled diapers along, for washing them on a train is almost impossible. We got the sheets from the salvage.
>
> I want to spend the Saturday night of our arrival with you, so as you can get a peep at the baby (3-3-24).

By mid-March specifics of the Gloucester arrival are re-shuffled and Carter is at pains to have no hurt feelings result:

> Since Mr. Mott has the Ford truck and the whole family plan to come on Saturday night to meet the Catharines, we think the bus better bring the two C's to your house for supper and after supper Mr. Mott take them on to Toddsbury. That

> will save unpacking the "kiddy-koop" twice and the bottles and other things. When we planned to stay at your house overnight, we didn't know Mr. Mott would have the truck. I know you will understand that the change is to make the trip as easy as possible on the baby, as all our plans are. She can sleep in a clothes basket in the back of the truck going to Toddsbury and not awaken till morning (3-12-24).

Meanwhile, Carter is challenged at work by being appointed supply officer. The experience leads him to some observations about work in general:

> It is not my experience that most people love their work. Only one man in a hundred would still do the work he does if the pecuniary reward were not dependent upon the labor performed. I should still fly, but I should not handle supplies (3-3-24).

May and most of June are spent with the two Gloucester families, until the little family departs for Hawaii late June. A postcard from Carter to Fanny along the way notes the trials of train travel with an active ten month old: "[Baby Catharine] is busy crawling and walking around the . . . [compartment] now. She is entirely unawed by her surroundings and is a huge nuisance, but a cute one" (6-25-24).

They arrive in Honolulu in mid-July, and move into a house on Kuhio Ave. where they have enjoyable neighbors, a sweet and helpful Japanese maid and only a three-block walk to Waikiki Beach. They must immediately purchase household furnishings, but they are also intrigued with their new environment and want to introduce distant family to the very different climate:

> After a few months, when we get our house furnished . . . [we hope] to take some pictures around our little home. They will be all the more striking if they reach you in mid-winter, as we are assured that there is very little difference in seasons here. They have more rain in the winter. The showers now they call liquid sunshine. It sprinkles rather hard out of an almost

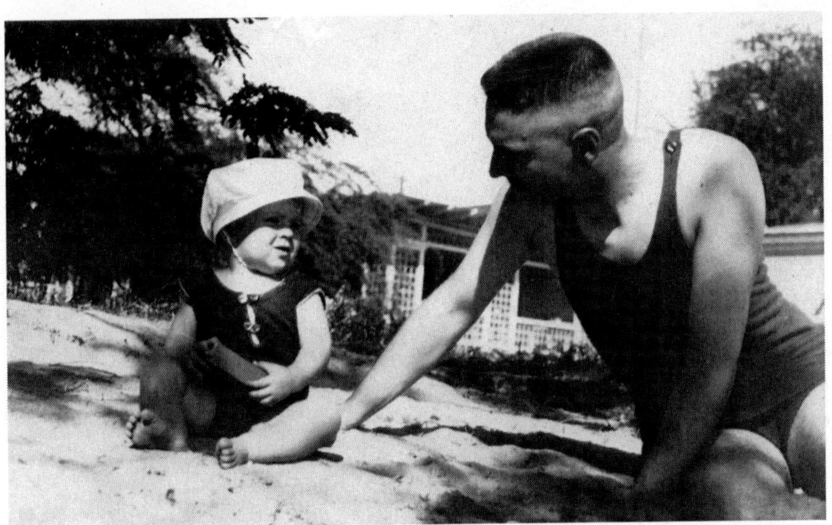

Carter and little Catharine, Waikiki Beach, 1924.

> clear sky with a bright sun and we have the most amazing rainbows every day, for it is always showering somewhere in the islands. It is warm rain and hardly wets you at all. It never lasts long either (7-25-24).

In early August—to their pleasure and relief—the Catlett car arrives on the transport:

> Our car came in good condition, so we are again counted among the rich who ride in chaises. We won't have to leave for church until a quarter to eleven and we shall not have to ride on the [trolley] cars here, which have wooden seats and make one's teeth chatter. They are all "summer cars", as they call them in Richmond . . .
>
> We had the most beautiful drive this afternoon that I ever imagined. We climbed a 2000-ft. mountain and saw the whole island around us, fringed by the purple ocean. Up near the top, we saw a cornfield and at the bottom rice paddies and cane fields (8-10-24)!

Catharine is enthusiastic about the scenery as well as glimpses of foreign cultures. In a letter to "Mother Catlett" she writes:

> The more we see of it here, the more beautiful it grows. I have never seen such a contrast of scenery—you never tire of it. There is so much that is interesting—the shops are full of all kinds of Chinese & Japanese Curios, linen, brass, & works of art. How I wish you could fly over & visit us, to enjoy it all with us (8-22-24).

Carter moves from the scenic beauty of Hawaii to its strategic importance for the United States:

> This afternoon we took the most wonderful mountain drive in the island, up Tantalus . . . The changes in scenery pass description.
>
> Almost up at the summit there are homes and summer camping places. I shouldn't care for it. My foot might slip. But it makes a wonderful drive, all the more because it is such a short distance from the heart of the city. Looking down on any other city you see squares of houses and streets, but the view of Honolulu is mainly of trees and flowers, with here and there a roof or street showing through. Its 80,000 people are mostly small potatoes and the Caucasian stores are few in number, but the glory of the city is its foliage and flora. I believe it is America's prettiest spot (this island), not the grandest or most beautiful, but from my point of view it is composed of oil tanks. The sole purpose of 30,000 soldiers being stationed here is to protect the navy's fuel supply. Of course that is only half of it. We must keep another nation from locating a fuel supply here, for this place is the key to the Pacific. It is about as close to the Panama Canal as New York or Frisco and it is the only harbour for 2000 miles in any direction (9-28-24).

Swimming becomes a daily delight for the whole family. Carter is impressed by the feats of the surf boarders, and means "[s]omeday . . . to get a surf board and learn to ride it." He describes Waikiki swimming to the Virginia family:

> The water is always cooler than I expected, cool enough to be bracing, but yet not chilling. You can swim for half a mile without getting over your head and yet a few feet from the

> shore it is deep enough to strike out. I thought when I saw the waves that we should be submerged with every crest, but one bobs over them without any effort and I can float on my back with my head pointed to the breakers and not ship a drop of salt water. It is surely wonderful swimming and the water is much more buoyant than our river water, because of the greater salt content. Little Catharine loves to be held where the waves will lap over her feet and up to her knees. She begins to kick her feet when she sees the wave coming and she dabbles them until it recedes (7-25-24).

By the fall he is writing with pride about little Catharine and the ocean:

> You just ought to see her now. She runs right out into the largest ocean in the world and lets the waves knock her down. Then she gets up just chuckling and runs out again (10-13-24).

Life in Honolulu is enjoyable in many ways, particularly the customs of welcome and departure, which Carter describes:

> You should see a transport leaving or arriving, with a host of brown boys diving and swimming around it, one or two bands playing on the dock, and hundreds of people with leis (wreathes) of flowers to put around the necks of friends arriving or departing. Some departing have more leis than neck. It really is unique. Incidentally everyone coming off the vessel has to step with both feet on a sterilized mat, to prevent importation of the "hoof and mouth" disease from California. That tickles Catharine's funny spot (8-10-24).

Friends and acquaintances from Carter's West Point and Kelly Field years arrive and depart on these transports conveying the picture of a long-distance community in which people weave in and out of each others' lives. Carter's old roommate, John Pitzer, is there when they arrive, and since he is on the army football team, supplies them with tickets for the Armistice Day game. "Pitzer took supper with us Sunday night. He is as amusing as ever" (11-11-24).

Throughout this busy time of settling-in, exploring new surroundings, attending to duty calls and welcoming new arrivals, Carter is working at Luke Field, not always flying as much as he would like:

> Time is hanging heavy on my hands to-day, as I have no flying scheduled and we are not allowed to take a ship up except when we have some definite mission to perform . . . I am always busy in the crowded waking hours that I spend at home, so I shall take to writing out here [at Luke Field] . . .
>
> Until to-day I have had daily flights and have gotten eight hours in the air, which is pretty good, considering all the other things I have had to do and the fact that I have been here only about half the month. Half of our ships are now under repair, so I hope we have prospects of doing more flying next month (7-25-24).

A month later, Carter writes his mother about a change in his duties:

> You must know that your son is [now] an adjutant, which means that he handles the office details for his commanding officer. Fortunately the commanding officer is a good fellow and the office a small one, because the details of office work are new to me and I have to stop and think a long time to decide where to send the letters and what to say in them. In my spare time I inspect the barracks for bedbugs and we find plenty. The surgeon came in and gave me some new points on finding them this morning. It made me feel pretty cheap and I found that we had a lot still to do. This climate suits . . . [bedbugs] and it is hard to clean every individual up when some of them have no great desire to clean up.
>
> Such are some of the harrowing details of my occupation . . . I find the life very stimulating and healthful and my chief complaint is that airplanes are rather scarce. Apart from that and the fact that living is rather expensive, especially at the start, the place is a paradise (8-21-24).

The following week Carter gives some details about flying in Hawaii:

> Last Monday I had my first inter-island trip and landed at Lanai and Molokai. They are mountainous islands devoted to cattle and sheep raising and Molokai contains the famous leper colony. We flew low over it but did not land. When the steamer stops at Molokai, passengers land by a small boat. It is called "The Lonely Isle." We saw beautiful green slopes and lofty mountains on Maui, next of the chain, called "The Garden Isle." They raise corn (and make whiskey) there. Our whole trip was a little over three hours of flying. While at Molokai we cleaned some brush off the field and chopped a 4 ft circle 50 feet in diameter to be covered with lime at some future date. I look forward with pleasure to the time when every village with any pretensions to progress will have a marked landing field. Then cross country flying will be 300% pleasanter than motoring. For enjoyment of scenery and appreciation of the beauties of nature, there is no comparison between the two . . . This morning I flew around in a formation of three ships. We lingered along the way and took 1 ½ hours (8-31-24).

By the end of September, he is engaged in maneuvers, which he describes in detail, reporting that they provided outstanding and very "worth-while flying training":

> This past week we have had a mimic war and I had to spend three nights away from home. My sole part in the maneuvers was a night bombing mission Wednesday night. It was the most worth-while flying training I ever had, beside being thoroughly enjoyable and slightly exciting. We flew across the island singly Wednesday afternoon, four bombers each with a crew of four, pilot, observer, mechanic, and radio operator. At Kahuku Point, the big wireless station of the Radio Corporation of America, we landed beside the mighty towers and went swimming in the surf. The sand there is made of bits of white shell, polished smooth like tiny Easter eggs. The waves will throw you thirty feet up on the beach if you swim in with them. We went in our birthday suits and had no cots or pup tents. I merely rolled in a blanket under a wing and slept soundly from eight till one. Promptly at two the first ship

> started, roaring down the beam of a big searchlight brought over on a truck for the purpose. He circled to the right. I followed and circled to the left. Our leader then took off and pressing a button light[ed] a wing tip flare, which made him resemble a sky rocket. We closed in V-formation behind him. The fourth ship was held in reserve. We flew over the island for two hours and a quarter and the artillery tried to find us with their searchlights. Only one of us was caught by them in all that time. The beam crossed me twice but they moved it so fast they didn't see me. Even if they saw us, their guns couldn't hit us. We are moving too fast and we can change direction so quickly.
>
> We ran into some nasty rain, but though lost for a few minutes, two of us joined again and the third man completed the mission separately. We had red, green, and white lights like a ship so the danger of collision was negligible after we got out of the storm. In the storm I never turned, but just plowed straight through. All the storms over here are local in nature.
>
> It was my first night formation and I found it quite easy. We landed on Luke Field by searchlight and I never landed better. The other two pilots were veteran night fliers and I was proud to be allowed to make the third.
>
> We had four parachute flares apiece in case of emergency. They light the whole country up for about fifteen minutes. Besides we had four wing tip flares, that are sufficient to land by, after the parachute flares have enabled you to pick a place (9-28-24).

Carter makes light of an accident that occurs right after the successful maneuvers:

> Just after the war closed on Friday, we had a regular comedy show on the field and I just happened to have a grandstand seat. A single seater lost a wheel in the air, so had to land in the water. He landed about 20 yards from a pier and I happened to hear of it in time to see him come down. He turned over of course and then the weight of the nose stuck the tail into the

> air. The pilot slid out and swam ashore, leaving his parachute floating on the water. It was highly entertaining; of course it cost the government money, but no lives. I don't know whether the parachute was ruined or not, but I should not like to use it (9-28-24).

But there are major deterrents to the smooth operation of the air field and the orderly pursuit of their work. He reports in late October that "Flying is at a standstill—whole field is almost out of gasoline. It is a ridiculous state of affairs" (10-27-24). Another development, however, is much to his liking:

> I am to take charge of high school and grammar school courses in the post school [for enlisted men], which starts Monday and runs six months. We have 24 pupils, all volunteers, in three general classes. I shall teach some and have four enlisted men, from whom to pick as assistants. The school runs every afternoon from 1 to 4. We have three classes a day. I may decide to change it to four. We have classes four times a week and the men study at night. This work, with my regular duties, will keep me pretty busy . . . I believe when I get the school going and get used to Capt. Griffin, so I know what he wants without asking him, I shall have the pleasantest combination of duties I could wish for. It is all work that amounts to something and affects the welfare and contentment of a good many men. I surely shall be glad when we can do some flying however. Not to fly takes the ginger out of work (10-19-24).

Just before taking over the post school, there is an abrupt interruption of the pleasant life the family is enjoying in Honolulu. Carter receives orders to leave the city and move to Luke Field, which is situated on Ford island in Pearl Harbor. He writes his mother the pros and cons of the new location:

> . . . Week before last we were paying off our calls and thinking about nothing in particular, when, bingo! The Post Adjutant asked me if I could move on the post October 1st. We begged to be excused and he let us off this time, but told us

to be prepared to move December 1, wherefore address your letters, hereafter to Luke Field and tell others the same, "Luke Field, T[erritory of] H[awaii]."

Luke Field on Ford Island, Pearl Harbor.

In some ways the move will be a help. We hope we can save money by it and I shall have the extra 2 ½ hours at home that I now spend commuting. And I can take the noon meal at home too. On the other hand, we give up the gas stove for coal and wood, we miss our daily trip to the beach, and we greatly fear that our little maid will not go so far with us. If she does not, leaving the post will be a problem. Marketing facilities out there are not the best and it may be that the

> added cost of living and of servants wages will balance the $30 difference in rent and fuel costs. We don't expect it to eat up the whole amount, though keeping up with the club and social obligations will cost a lot. The whole truth of the matter is that we would stay here if we could, but as we can't, we are reconciled. We are glad to get five months on the mainland before going on the island. The whole island is occupied by the army and naval air stations. It is about a mile long and half as broad. It is just 15 min. run by boat to the coal dock, where the officers have their garages, but waiting for the boat schedule makes getting to town an undertaking for a family with a small child (9-28-24).

It is mid-October before Carter can take Catharine for a daylight visit to their new quarters at Luke Field:

> It is a nice new house (two years old) and has a screened porch, dining room, 2 bedrooms, bath and servant's bedroom and bath. There are plenty of closets, a back porch, and a shower bath. The stove burns coal and wood, which is rather hot in this climate, especially as the wind always blows from the back of the house. Still all the houses on the post share that same objection (10-19-24).

To her mother-in-law, Catharine writes with regret about friends they are leaving behind, and makes disapproving observations of some guests' behavior at social gatherings.

> To-night we go over to Capt. Tenneys for dinner. They have certainly been nice to us & I hate to lose their friendship when we move on the Post . . . [In regard to] your speaking of having a drunk man—this place is the wettest I have ever seen—all the parties are overflowing with liquor, & many drunk men & women, in fact very few can enjoy them-selves with-out plenty to drink. We find very few who enjoy an evening as we do (10-14-24).

Catharine has further words to say about army life and they are dutifully sent on by Carter to his parents, though not fully shared by him:

> Catharine says I write home a false idea of army life, that I make everything appear pure and noble, when lots of the people we are thrown with are not the kind we would like to bring home. It is all too true. We certainly have our share of worthless specimens, yet I have sufficient love for my profession to believe that it develops some fine traits of character in almost every one who follows it. If I did not, I should be sad indeed at the example set by many officers of high rank whom we have seen or heard of (letter fragment, mid-November, 1924).

Carter and Catharine continue to speak of the higher cost of everything in Hawaii, but manage to live within their income, and Catharine writes of her plan to save regularly. She also gives a glimpse of her days, as well as her interest in preparing good food for her husband and child, and her enjoyment of the natural beauty of Hawaii:

> This is one of the weeks that Carter has to be out an hour earlier to drill, so we rose at 5:30 this A.M. It was just getting light, and the heavens were a lovely soft pink, green & blue, as a back ground for the Palms . . . I gave him breakfast of a papaya with a cut-up orange, salmon croquettes & toast—& fixed his lunch—Then I put little *C*'s cereal in the double boiler, & took a nap until nearly seven—when I fed *C*—Hariko came, & we started the mornings duties. The gas stove we have here is excellent—I can get breakfast in a few minutes on it—When we get on the Post we have coal stoves, in which we burn Chinese coal, & they say it is very dirty, & hard to get any heat from so I am enjoying this one to the fullest . . .
>
> Little *C* is still on powdered milk—all advice says not to give her cow's milk over here—the dairys are very dirty & unsanitary—so we buy six huge cans of DryCo every six weeks for $12.50. She is a picture of health, so it must agree with her. She has coddled eggs & baked potatoes now, and just loves them. My, how I wish she could have some of your nice eggs. Chickens & eggs here are *very very* poor—in fact some doctors say not to give a child Island eggs, but cold

> storage ones from California so in some ways the tropics are not an ideal place for the very young. I try to be as careful as possible, so trust none of us will get intestinal troubles. Every now & then a big *scare* will come up about it, but I don't think there is much danger (10-14-24).

Carter honors Catharine for her attentiveness:

> I want to pay a tribute to Catharine now while I think of it. She is the only wife I know of that gets up at six and eats a hot breakfast with her husband at half past. The other men get their own or go without. And I don't think she looks mistreated because the scales gave her 145 lbs—she says they are wrong, but she is getting to be quite a lapful (letter fragment, Fall, 1924).

There is news from both Gloucester families, and many letters from Hawaii are shared between them. At Toddsbury, they are overflowing with people—"some dozen boarders in the house at once " (7-25-24), while, in his family, Carter is "glad for [M]other to get some rest [from boarders], even if she was not taking in any money" (10-19-24). He is pleased with the good news about Mary getting a scholarship at Wellesley and Fanny passing her entrance exams:

> One of my first thoughts this Sunday morning was of Mary and Fanny. They will be leaving for Wellesley about the time this letter is received and I am sure they are about to experience one of the pleasantest years of their lives. It is a wonderful privilege for two sisters to attend such a fine school together. I surely wish we could visit them there. Maybe we can all motor up to Fanny's graduation. We shall anticipate it anyway. We are setting our hearts upon being back at Langley Field by then (8-31-24).

But he anticipates a lonely Christmas for his parents, since there is not enough money for the two girls to return home for the holidays (9-21-24).

Both Carter and Catharine always want news of their home community, and Catharine reports excitedly about seeing some

Gloucester people:

> This isn't so terribly far from home after all. This soon we have seen Gloucester people. Catharine Graham Lewis, & husband & Mrs. Graham passed through here on their way to the Phillipine Island[s]. While on the dock I kept looking at Mrs. Graham's back, & couldn't get over how much she looked like the Dimmock twins, & when she turned around, I couldn't believe my eyes! We had a nice chat with them, but didn't see more of them as they were sailing that night (8-22-24).

Little Catharine's development is tracked closely. When they arrive in Hawaii she is already walking, and developing right on schedule. They are challenged and delighted, but are also grateful for the baby-tending and household help given by their loving Japanese maid, Hariko:

> Little Catharine has been fretting to get up, so I have given her some of your letters to play with. She seems interested and rubs her fingers over the marks. She is even now scraping a pencil (unsharpened) over them. Her third tooth appeared yesterday. She is practically normal, but has a little less appetite than usual. I think we shall have a run of teeth now. She can slide off the bed feet foremost without hurting herself, so she isn't such a care...She will pick up a shoe tree, stocking or piece of clothing and carry it around the house for an hour. Consequently when I go to dress, I may find my socks in different rooms (8-10-24).

Her mother elaborates:

> Little *C* . . . keeps my house turned upside-down—as fast as I straighten the rugs, she comes along & rolls them all up, pulls the kitchen pans off the shelves, tears up all paper she gets her hands on, pulls the chairs all around the room, & thinks herself so smart! I just hate to think that all our home people are missing her, at this precious age . . . Hariko is such a help, & does the work so well. Little *C* loves her, & she is very good to little *C*. Every now and then she will get a fit of

chasing Hariko around to catch her bare feet & sandals, & it is a funny sight . . .

Baby *C* sends a real hug—she knows how now (8-22-24)!

Carter reports on the baby's first birthday and her capers:

Little Catharine is one year old today. She enjoyed the picnic and the other little girl thoroughly. She is not always such a squirmer as of yore. She has pensive moments when she will sit looking off into space and singing to herself and she will neither answer nor pay the slightest attention to words or shaking—decidedly like her grandmother, when her mind is engaged . . .

We have bought *C.* a little baby carriage and she loves it. Yesterday I called her to go riding in the car and held the front door open. Shoot me if she didn't toddle to the go-cart and push it to the door. I had to pull her away from it. She rolls it back and forth across the room and climbs in and out by the hour. She has six teeth now (9-2-24).

Hariko and little Catharine, Honolulu, 1924.

She stands on her head and looks through her legs at people and she just talks a blue streak without saying a word . . . She goes to the door and catches hold of the knob, hoping to be let out of doors. If you say "No!" she just collapses and cries like her heart . . . [is] broken (10-13-24).

Little Catharine gets more amusing every day, but her stubbornness is terrific. She gets angry and barks at her mother whenever she is crossed in any of her schemes. She is a regular touch-me-not when she is interested in something.

> Usually though she is very sweet and happy. She hasn't seen a bottle for two days and takes her milk only on condition that she may play in it with a spoon while fed from another. A ride in the car or a visit to the zoo is her greatest delight. She likes to occupy one side of the front seat alone. Her head is covered with brown ringlets now and she is quite pretty when her eyes sparkle and her six teeth show. Of course she is as brown as a berry (10-19-24).
>
> Little Catharine is as solid as a maul . . . She tries to dance now when we clap for her. And she comes up and holds my wrist to her ear to hear the watch tick. She surely is the best baby I ever saw, but she requires tactful handling, for she has a strong will and is hard to swerve from something she aspires to do.
>
> Hariko loves her. When she comes back from a half holiday, her first word is "Where baby?" and she trots through the house for a glimpse of her. Her affection is returned though little *C.* still prefers men to women and will leave anybody for me. She is truly the joy of our life, always radiantly happy, smiling through her tears after each little disappointment (letter fragment, Fall, 1924).
>
> Catharine just talks a blue streak now, but never an intelligible word except "Daddy," which she calls out the first thing in the morning and "Mum-mum-mum," which she groans when she is hungry, catching her mother by the skirt and impeding the preparations . . . [She] is crawling over me, playing with the stamps and ink bottle (11-11-24).

In moments of self-reflection, Carter speaks of the pleasure he takes in working on the Star, and his being oblivious to home furnishings and clothes, but not to Catharine's weight gain:

> I made some adjustments on the Star Sunday that I never knew how to make before. I am gradually learning so that my car costs me almost nothing except for gasoline and oil. About a year from now it will need a general overhaul and I expect to do a good deal of the work myself, working with a good mechanic. I was certainly born at the right time in the world's history, because I had much rather care for a motor

> than a horse. On the post, I shall [have] 2 ½ more hours a day to do my own work and help Catharine. She will need it because Hariko is not going with us (11-11-24).
>
> Our near neighbors have a $750 Chinese rug. I have walked on it many times and never noticed what it looks like! I never notice clothes. I do notice however that Catharine senior is splitting out of most of hers. She has gained 15 lbs since you saw her (11-11-24).

The final communication of the year is made by postcard to his father December 8:

> Don't know why I have failed to mention your letters. They have arrived regularly and are much enjoyed. Every day is moving day now. To night will be our last night in town. I am expecting a truck this morning, so stayed home from work. For the last week have been working hard to get quarters painted inside. Got the floors varnished and kitchen and bathroom painted white.

The next day, December 9th, the family makes its fourth move in little more than two years. Little Catharine loses beloved Hariko and Catharine faces a coal-fired kitchen stove, but Carter looks forward to having more time at home.

PART IV

A New Phase of Flying *1925*

The young family enjoys the stability that 1925 brings them—no more moves, enough flying hours to satisfy Carter, joy in their little daughter, and continuing pleasure in the beauty of Hawaii. There is also more than enough social activity. Yet the yearning for their next home-leave in a little over two years is always present, and reports of accidents with "the ships"—including two fatal ones—sound occasional somber notes in their letters home. But Carter sums up their general satisfaction when writing his mother in June with his exclamation, "How fast the happy days go by for those upon whose youth Dame Fortune smiles (6-16-25)!"

Reports on "little Catharine" are in almost every letter:

> Peggy Post [daughter of a neighboring pilot] and Catharine have become very much attached to each other. Peggy often runs away from home and turns up in our back yard where she is greeted with the utmost enthusiasm. Catharine tries to say "Peggy." Her best speech so far is "All gone" when her saucer is empty. She looks through the Geographic and mimics all the animals. She is always just as busy as can be, while Peggy will sit still and chuckle at her activities. Peggy's great stunt is to toddle over and sit in somebody's lap—she sits there too. Catharine sits down for the purpose of squirming and jumping up and down. Naturally Peggy, with her sedentary habits, weighs much more than Catharine (3-15-25).

> Catharine is a real little Tom boy. You should see her shin herself up on the ironing board, & in & out of the coal bin. She is such a busy little body & always wants to do what ever she sees me doing—from making the bed, sweeping & moping up the floor. She has a very nice habit of putting things back where she got them from. If I scold her for taking something

> she will run straight & put it back, & then come to be kissed. She thinks kissing will make anything well. Often she will run in from the back yard—dirty as a little pig & hold up a filthy little foot or finger to be kissed. Maybe she will have to run all over the house to find me—but as soon as it gets a kiss she forgets all about it, & runs out to play again (Letter from Catharine 3-28-25).
>
> Little Catharine had only ten teeth upon last examination. She squeezes one through every now and then. She calls "Peggy" by name constantly. They are very fond of each other, but Catharine will smack Peggy once in a while and Peggy will not retaliate, but lifts up her voice to the sky. Still if Catharine is carried off in disgrace, she bewails the separation (3-30-25).

On Mother's Day, Carter writes a particularly full report:

> When I hear of how Miss Lila and all the grandparents dote on news of her, I am stricken in conscience that I have sent some letters off without mentioning her. Life is not always a bed of roses for her. Noises of passing wagons disturb her naps and the teeth problem is still not settled permanently. Often she won't eat enough at meal time and later frets for "cay'cay" or "c'acker." But on the whole she is a very happy, healthy youngster, understands perfectly, obeys intermittently, and tries to talk incessantly. With Peggy she is always thoroughly happy. She tickles Peggy's knees and plays peek-a-boo when they take an auto ride together. Peggy sits still or watches the people in the car. Catharine takes in the car, the ships in the sea, and the ships in the air, and comments and points at them all. Every night she trots out and kisses us good night before going to bed. I don't try to sneak away when I leave the house. I kiss my hand to her and say "bye-bye" and she runs to the window and climbs into the rocker to wave and kiss her hand as long as she can see me. Her face is always serious then but she never cries unless she is cut up over something else.
>
> [The other day] [s]he was helping me make ice cream and every minute or two she'd sit down in the slush. I'd tell her

> to get up and she'd obey and in another minute sit down in the same place. You should see her putting ice and salt in the vacuum freezer for me. The first time "we" made cream she ate enough salt to cause a little upset of the stomach. This time she was more prudent (5-10-25).
>
> She is still a pest about books and magazines. She doesn't intentionally tear them. She just wears them all out. She loves to write on the margins with a pencil . . . Today she poured a glass of water in her mother's hand bag (6-4-25).
>
> The principal change the year has brought forth is little Catharine. Her teeth, her prattle, her little good-night kisses, and her eternal vigilance are more and more a delight. Catharine hates to think of her growing older before you see her, but I think the older she grows the more attractive she will be. A frank, whole-hearted, energetic child is never gawky or awkward, especially if taught to obey and to regard its parents with affection rather than fear. And Catharine surely holds her parents above everybody . . . If she thinks she is helping, carrying in wood or putting salt in the ice cream freezer, she just chuckles in glee (6-16-25).
>
> I raised my voice and said "No!" this morning. She sat down and burst into tears. I must try never to raise my voice in speaking to her. When we have a visitor with a loud voice, her eyes nearly pop out. Her mother is always quiet with her.
>
> Each day finds her more at home in the water. She rides on my back while I swim and she paddles too, but won't kick her feet yet. She complains when we let her head go under, but isn't frightened. She was much amused at seeing Catharine put her face under water and coming up beside us. It just struck her funny spot and she chuckled for several minutes. She attracts a lot of attention. Yesterday she took one hand off my neck to wave to an old fat gentleman and nearly lost her balance (letter fragment, 1925).

In April, Carter reconnects with his old love—baseball—by becoming coach for his squadron's team:

> My team played three baseball games last week and all our opponents were foemen worthy of our steel. We won one game and lost two, 3-1 and 11-10. Both were exciting and with fair umpiring we should have won the 3-1 game. The umpire was either very partial or very stupid. My team has certainly made rapid strides. At times they do so well that I get impatient when they have their bad days, as inexperienced teams are prone to do. I enjoy the work. I never played ball games as often before and never had my own team to manage, with uniforms, substitutes, and all trimmings (4-5-25).

Having lost Hariko's help, Catharine alternates between no help and having periodic assistance from a "striker" (enlisted man) who washes the dishes and cleans the house. They finally settle on a "part Hawaiian girl" who is "slow as death" in her work but wonderfully kind and playful with the little one. Catharine writes her mother-in-law:

> . . . [S]he and Catharine get on beautifully—for she spends most of her time playing with *C*, & I do the greatest part of the work . . . Yet it is a help to have her take C jr. out in the afternoon, so as I can get some sewing done. When I tell you I have made five dresses—you will know I haven't wasted any minutes . . . I made two voiles—a linen, a striped dimity & a broadcloth . . . which comes in very pretty stripes (4-5-25).

Carter asks rhetorically, or perhaps in answer to a query from home, "You wonder what we are doing with our money? We are saving to pay our insurance premium and take two weeks at the volcano in September" (5-27-25). This follows an accounting of his everyday uniform, which is inexpensive, beginning with khaki trousers which cost only $1.50 a pair. Because Catharine makes almost all her own clothes as well as the baby's, Carter figures "the electric [sewing] machine is rapidly paying for itself" (5-27-25).

Comments from home about strawberries being in season bring a reply about the special fruits of Hawaii:

> I too had some excellent strawberries this week, fresh from the garden and only 30 cents a quart, because there was no

> middleman between producers and consumer. And I brought home from Kauai an eight pound pineapple, which cost me nothing. Its rich green and gold adorns the tray the Fred Joneses gave us for a wedding present and ever and anon I walk over and sniff it. Each time it smells a little riper and better. Sunday we went calling and were presented with two "alligator pears," grown in a back yard in the city. They are tasteless, oily-fleshed things with a big stone in the middle, but cut in half and filled with french dressing they are a delicious salad, with soft rich meat right down to the thin purple skin (6-4-25).

Letters continue to express the ever-present longing to see family—to be home again in Gloucester, or at least nearby:

> A year ago today we were on the ocean. Two years from to day, we hope to be on leave in Gloucester, possibly with station at Langley Field. At any rate, the odds are in favor of a place farther east than Texas or Hawaii, and when we get settled the next time, we hope that it will be for four years and near home (7-6-25).

There are thoughts about the daffodil season:

> This letter will reach you at Eastertide, probably just as you are returning thanks for a completed jonquil harvest. I hope you hit Palm Sunday and Easter week this year . . . I trust you strike the best of everything and make one thousand dollars (3-30-25).

Carter details his insurance arrangements after explaining a recent notice about a bonus, which he anticipates will support little Catharine in her final year at college, though he errs on her graduation date:

> The document you enclosed was my Federal bonus. It is an endowment policy for $954 payable Jan. 1 1925. That will give little C. her final year in college—maybe more if she works her way. It is payable sooner in case of my death. I am now insured for $16,065, $4,000 with [F]ather as beneficiary and the rest payable to Catharine Sr., which is the best provision for accident that I have heard of on the part of any army man.

> Many do not carry the full $10,000 government insurance (3-30-25).

From time to time, letters home include reports on accidents involving Luke Field flyers:

> We lost a Martin in the harbor the other night all because a gasoline control lever became disconnected and the throttle closed. Fortunately nobody got scratched, though it was a black night and the ship was less than 200 feet high when the motor suddenly slowed down. The pilot did not have time to switch on his landing lights before the plane dived into the water. We went out in boats and got them. The plane was salvaged by the navy. We could use a few of those parts, but salt water ruined the motors of course. It was very encouraging that nobody was hurt in the most unfavorable combination of circumstances imaginable. Craig, the pilot, behaved with great coolness (4-20-25).

Not all accidents end that happily, as indicated in Carter's comments about the death of a good friend:

> [S]o I went alone Tuesday to the funeral of my friend and fellow-teacher, Sgt. Grosvenor, killed in an airplane accident last Friday. He was the best friend I ever lost that way. I can't get used to it, yet life goes on as if nothing has happened. Everybody tries to help the widow as much as possible and they appoint someone else to take up his duties. She has government insurance, bonus, and a home in Idaho, and her children are 12 and 8, so she will not be poverty stricken. The government gives six months pay and I think $35 a month compensation (as long as she remains unmarried). She is also able to teach school, I believe (2-23-25).

A month later, there is another fatal accident, and as she had on the occasion of pilot deaths at Kelly Field, Catharine expresses her distress to her parents-in-law:

> We are in the midst of a real storm to-night. It has been raining in torrents off & on all day—besides a terrific wind. And to add to it all one of the bachelors was killed in the storm this

> afternoon. We haven't heard the particulars, but suppose it is the usual case of no one ever knowing just what happened. Anyhow it is very heart-breaking. Carter was up early this morning, & said he never flew in such a wind—so he did not stay up for the usual time. Well, I did not mean to start with such news—but after an accident it takes some time to get it off my mind (3-28-25).

In May, Carter experiences mechanical difficulty on an attempted trip to another island:

> Our trip to Kauai is postponed until next Monday. My ship had to turn back last time because it threw out oil, due to a cork lodged in an oil pipe. It was not serious and the trouble was easily discovered (5-27-25).

Forced water landings are frequent enough to bring about a change in the flight uniform:

> We are now allowed to wear straight trousers for flying, so I never expect to buy any more boots or leggings. "Slacks" are much easier to kick off in the water, and the water is often the best place to land around here. It ruins the ship but it doesn't bruise the crew. We've had several men who lost a wheel in the air and landed in the water close to the dock, rather than try the flying field (5-27-25).

Again, uncertainties about the reliability of their ships dictate extra precaution when an expanse of water is to be crossed:

> I'm just back from Kauai, "the Garden Isle." That means I have landed on all the principal islands of the group . . . Only since the maneuvers have land planes been permitted to fly the 70-mile channel. We now are required to have a navy boat mid-way. It is a great comfort to see it. Eight pilots have now made the trip in bombers, all from our squadron, of course. Two-motored ships are best for over-the-water flying, because with one motor dead one loses altitude very slowly. The single motored ships (DH) hope to get permission to go next week (6-4-25).

Carter tries to keep his father informed about his work, especially when they are on maneuvers. He also speaks of his eagerness to accrue more flying hours:

> Friday night from 7 to 8 I flew a bomber for the anti-aircraft searchlights to practice on me. The flight surgeon accompanied me. It was his first night flight. I could not help but feel complimented in his electing to ride with me. I still have fewer hours in the air than most of those around me, but I am flying as much as any in the Martin bomber squadron and try to improve myself as much as possible. We had a pleasant little trip, with little sprinkles of rain, enough to make rainbow rings around the searchlight shadows of the plane on the cloud bank above us. It was all very pretty, with a half-moon winking through the scudding clouds. We landed without mishap a little after eight. It was a pretty cold ride (4-5-25).

> Yes, I flew a bomber all through [the maneuvers], #55. I take my regular time with all the boys and try to see that none of the squadron officers get more time in the air than I. If I am a little childish in my eagerness not to be outdone, I may be pardoned, because most of them have several years' start on me. Half of them have passed 1000 hours of flying and I have only 635. I am increasing it at the rate of 20 hours per month, which is a good steady climb. There are a dozen of us and only two that I rate as more daring and competent than I. And there are only two that I consider less competent than I. The rest of us are just steady, average pilots, not round-the-world trail blazers perhaps, but willing to do anything we are ordered to do and a little more if the chance offers (6-4-25).

Personal transportation requests from army officers—and demands to tow targets for anti-aircraft practice—are irritating to the bomber pilots and sometimes interfere with their training. Carter hopes that in due time the Air Service will be separated from the army:

> I flew to Molokai Sat. afternoon to bring back an artillery colonel and three dead deer and a dog. We are very much opposed to being used for such purposes because they

> interfere with our bombing training. We hope in a few years to gain our independence from the army. Right now they are trying to make us sacrifice a lot of our training just to pull targets for the anti-aircraft to shoot at and miss. It is a waste of time and money and no training to anybody, because towing a target in a straight line, over a known course, at known speed and altitude, is so different from actual warfare that it has no military value whatever. Even so, they never hit one over here, though they have broken the 2000 ft cable twice somewhere along its length. And you fly three or four hours on a black night just to have about a dozen shots fired at your sleeve target. They haven't done any actual firing since last spring, so I haven't towed a target yet, but I've flown night and day for them to aim at me. At night they really have great difficulty finding you with the searchlight and they have more trouble finding two planes than one, because the sounds conflict and make the location more difficult. I shudder to think what would happen to them if a big formation of bombers came over (6-16-25).

In a birthday letter to his father, Carter reflects on the lengthening human life span and envisions future beneficial developments in aviation:

> I have lately remembered that I have let your 68th birthday pass with no word of congratulation. Here it is. I heartily wish you many happy returns. May you live to be a great grandfather. The way human life is being lengthened by preventive medicine makes me believe that in a few more years centenarians will be common. They claim to have lengthened the average age attained by fifteen years in the last generation. Cutting down infant mortality, malaria, t.b., yellow fever, typhoid, small-pox, tetanus, diabetes, and diptheria have all played a big part. Surgery, of course has made wonderful progress too. Little Catharine has four living (grand) parents and three of them have had serious surgical operations . . . It is a wonderful age. The time will come when airplanes, containing operating rooms will fly to their country patients (4-20-25).

By April, Carter is unusually busy with a new assignment. As a result of the sudden illness of the engineer in charge of bomber maintenance, he is removed from his work as adjutant and placed in the engineer's position. This requires rapid learning on his part as well as respect for and trust in the enlisted personnel:

> I am assistant engineer officer and my chief is in the hospital indefinitely so I am in charge of the 50 men who work to keep the bombers in flying trim. This is the most interesting and responsible job I have had yet. Time alone will tell whether I can manage it. I haven't the technical knowledge. If I succeed it will be because my men are loyal and conscientious. They are a fine lot and their morale is high. I've known them nearly a year now and I'm attached to them (5-10-25).

Several weeks later, the engineer is able to return to his position, and Carter can "breathe better and worry less" (5-27-25). He stays on as assistant engineer.

Carter reports that he has "landed on Molokai, Lanai, Maui, and Hawaii at least twice each." Other than possible landings on two small islands, Nuhau, population 150, and Kahoolawe, which has "3 living souls, not counting the goats," he feels he has "no more worlds to conquer" (5-27-25).

Within a month, assignments are again shifted. Carter is philosophical about it, but feels a sharp loss at leaving his bomber-squadron mechanics. He also decides to request transfer to the pursuit squadron, wanting to broaden his skill and gain more flying hours, no longer being satisfied with the five hours a week in the bomber squadron:

> A year ago we were in San Francisco preparing to sail. I have had a great many and varied, valuable experiences during the past year and am now making a fresh start. I have been put in charge of Transportation, including the garage and the boat house. Thank goodness I didn't get the stables . . . Of course, I hated to leave the hangar and the ships and the men I have become attached to. For the first day I felt like

> the bottom had dropped out of everything, but I believe I can get interested in my job. I am asking to be transferred to a pursuit squadron, so as to get more flying. I have had enough experience in the bombers to feel master of the ship and I haven't had any single-seater flying for a long time. I have been to all the islands, so there is nothing new to be gained with the bombers and a great deal with the pursuit. They are getting in some overhauled ships from the states that will improve matters a lot (6-29-25).

Taking stock of what is ahead for them, Carter anticipates the family's activities in the coming months, and the next year:

> This is the month we pay our insurance and I am thankful to say that we have amassed the necessary hundred dollars in advance. The next thing is our trip to [the island of] Hawaii in September and then will come Christmas. There is always something ahead and usually it has been something pleasant. [Little] Catharine is becoming less of a problem to travel with and I think we shall really enjoy our trip to the Volcano. I'm sure she will. Capt. Fields is going with us and he and I will do some hunting. We shall take my car and drive over the whole island, for I do not expect to get back to the Big Island again during our tour. When we get back our tour will be almost half over (6-29-25).

Two days after the Fourth of July, Carter writes his father about his new work in the pursuit squadron, and his delight in his new squadron leader. He reports a very enjoyable July 4th picnic:

> I think I wrote to you last week about getting appointed Transportation Officer and transferring from the 23rd Bomb. to the 19th Pursuit Squadron. My new squadron commander, Lieut. Chenault, is a very remarkable man, a fine leader, and has a remarkable wife. They have six sons and a daughter living and have lost one child. All the others are remarkably athletic and the mother looks very robust, not a bit aged or careworn . . . They live at Pearl City and he rows across the harbor to work, about half a mile. He is one of the best pilots in the army and

one of the most athletic, sport-loving, outdoor men in the world . . . They are Louisiana people and he is a Creole. For the first time I am in a squadron, whose best pilot is its commander, a leader after the manner of the knights of old.

I have embarked on an entirely different phase of flying, the tiny, fast single-seater, and I can hardly claim to be comfortable as yet in my cramped quarters. It will take me several months to attain average proficiency as a pursuit pilot and I scarcely contemplate remaining in pursuit for more than one year. I am anxious to master every branch of the flying game and we are unusually fortunate here in being able to get all kinds of flying experience without changing our geographical location . . . I think that pursuit is the more difficult to master and bombing the more interesting to follow. The third branch, observation, is rather dull for the pilot. If I ever have an arm or leg shot off, I can be an observer. I got training in that at Kelly Field . . .

Catharine is busy preparing for the trip ordering many garments for self and off-spring from Montgomery Ward. She is also making a good many.

We have had two good rains in two days, very unusual and acceptable at this season of the year. Dust is very bad on the flying field. The propellers blow the soil away from grass roots and the sun browns them. We are on the lee shore. The windward side and the central mountains are much better watered . . .

[Little Catharine] runs around singing words she knows over and over like this "Ball—Daddy—Ball—Mudder—Ball—Peggy—night-night—Peggy—"cow-cow" (Japanese for eating, food, etc.). She constantly tries new combinations. Her best sentence so far is "Mudder, Peggy gone." This upon investigation, proved true.

We went for a wonderful picnic on the 4th. Unfortunately, I wasted two hours of the beautiful day sleeping after lunch, but I needed it. Catharine read and Advena and little C played in the sand and had a great time. A big wave came in and threw sand all over them, but the baby didn't seem to mind. She did a piece of shivering in the breeze, till we rolled her in a blanket. She is not a bit the worse for it . . . Our first view of her the following morning was when she was discovered trying to draw on her bathing suit over her clothes! So we took her down to the meager shore here and let her play. She lay on her stomach in the water.

Little Catharine and Peggy, 1925.

On July 17, the following is recorded by the Operations Officer in Carter's Pilot's Book:

Pilot killed.

Type of plane: MB-3A

Type of engine: Wright H-3

Type of work done: elementary pursuit training (crashed)

I certify that 661 hrs. 46 min. is Pilots Total Time as shown by the records of this office.

Signed. _________Slackburn
1st Lieut., A.S.
Operations Officer
Rated as a superior pilot.

I certify that the flying time of 8 hours 34 minutes for the month of July, 1925 is correct according to the records of this office. Total flying time to date 661 hours 46 minutes.

Albert L. Hegenberger
Group Operations Officer
5th Composite Group
Luke Field, Hawaii

To Mrs. Catharine M. Catlett:

I am expressing the universal opinion of the pilots of Luke Field when I say that we deeply grieve the loss of one who we considered a most enthusiastic, indefatigable, able and skillful officer. We are all the better for having known him. Please accept our heartfelt sympathies.

Albert T. Hegenberger

My dear, dear, precious Father,

What has happened?

How can it be that you didn't come home from the Field that Friday in July?

Silence. Only silence—and it does no good to beat against the fast-closed door. No matter how the heart aches, or how it breaks, there is only silence.

I go over and over that day, and those that followed. You kiss me good-bye, and I'm sure Mother, too, and I climb into the rocker by the window and wave and kiss my hand to you as long as I can see you. You and Mother—full of plans for your September vacation and the months and years beyond—delighting in your daughter and always anticipating, " . . . always something ahead and usually it has been something pleasant . . . " You, ever reaching for more worlds to conquer, eager to master every skill the Army Air Service has to offer, but—you assure family—always serious and careful in your flying, always doing good "headwork."

What happens in that plane Friday, July 17? Do you crash to earth and sea because of your inexperience in the "tiny, fast single-seater" pursuit plane in which you "can hardly claim to be comfortable as yet?" Or is it because of failure in the ship itself—one of those "overhauled ships from the states"—possibly not as reliable as it should be? Your letters speak of mechanical problems in flight that have nothing to do with the skill of the pilot—levers don't move as they should, wheels fall off, oil spews.

Just three and a half months earlier, Mother wrote about a pilot's fatal crash and commented, with all too much prescience, "We haven't heard the particulars, but suppose it is the usual case of no one ever knowing just what happened." Today, 80 years later, that would not be the case. Today the art and science of determining the cause of a fatal crash would give us an answer.

For the moment, these rational questions occupy my mind and protect me from the wrenching grief that shook me a half hour ago as I again read your obituary. I'm grateful to Grandmother Mott for placing it in her scrapbook, since that issue of the Gloucester Gazette *no longer exists.*

So many grieving people are present to me as I pore over this account. There are Mother and me arriving on "the funeral train at Lee Hall" and being met by "a military escort from [nearby] Langley Field." And there are Daddy Catlett and Granny, he bent with sorrow, she—small and erect—trying to be a strength to him, all the while bearing the almost unspeakable loss of you, her companion spirit. Your young sisters are there, in bewildered grief, as well as a number of Mother's family.

The afternoon of the next day, your funeral service is held at Ware Church, where you and Mother were married not quite three years earlier. The church overflows with grieving relatives and friends. As the newspaper says, "The sudden death of Lieut. Catlett is a great shock and sorrow to this community, where he was born and raised, and was known, greatly respected and admired by practically every resident." So afraid is Mother of another accident—another fatality—that she refuses to have Langley Field send formation-flying planes in a salute to you at the end of the funeral service.

Two years ago I was consumed by grief when I finished transcribing your letters. Now I can speak of your death to others without tears, and with a new confidence: "Yes, my father died, but I've heard his words, seen his heart, and known his presence."

But I may never be able to read this newspaper account—or show it to someone else—without tears. Despite coming through to the other side of that earlier terrible searing, your loss continues to sweep over me. The pain does not burn as it did earlier; it's simply there.

I know you would want me to progress beyond this point. Maybe some day I will succeed. But not yet.

LIEUT. CATLETT IS BURIED AT WARE

Body of Young Aviator Laid at Rest Tuesday.

1925

GREAT CROWD ATTENDS THE FUNERAL

The body of Lieut. Landon Carter Catlett, Jr., son of Mr. and Mrs. L. C. Catlett of Gloucester, who was killed in the crash of an airplane of which he was pilot, in Hawaii on July 17th, arrived in Gloucester Monday, accompanied by Mrs. L. C. Catlett, Jr., and their baby daughter. Lieut. Robinson, who was detailed to escort the body and widow home from Hawaii, and a military escort from Langley Field, which met the funeral train at Lee Hall, came with the casket.

Tuesday afternoon at 2:30 o'clock funeral services were held at Ware Episcopal Church, and all that was mortal of the gallant young officer was laid to rest in the churchyard, a gathering which was much too large to find seats in the spacious old colonial church having come to pay the last tribute of respect.

The funeral services were conducted by Rev. Douglas W. Neff, rector, and Rev. William B. Lee, rector emeritus, of Ware Parish, the last named of whom had also baptized the young man in infancy and been his rector at his confirmation at the same church. The flag-draped casket was borne by a detail from Langley Field, six commissioned officers, six non-commissioned officers and a firing squad having been sent by Major Westover, commandant of Langley Field, who was a comrade of Lieut. Carter at Kelly Field in Texas and was prevented from personal attendance at the funeral by an engagement which could not be broken.

The choir sang "The Aviator's Hymn," which was written by Mrs. Sally Nelson Robins, a cousin of Lieut. Catlett's, and a favorite hymn of the deceased, "The Son of God Goes Forth to War." Mr. Stewart, a veteran of of the World War, sang a solo, "Alleluia."

Following the beautiful and impressive burial service at the grave, a touching incident occurred when Lieut. Robinson handed the young widow her husband's cap and sword. There followed the salute of guns fired by the squad from Langley Field, the sounding of the requim by the bugler and the tender lowering of the body to its last resting place by men in uniform. Garlands of flowers about the grave were mute tokens of the love of the young officer's many friends.

Among those from out of the county attending the funeral were Dr. J. W. C. Jones and wife, Mrs. Marius Jones, Mrs. Ernest Rogers, Mr. and Mrs. Kemper Kellogg, of Newport News; Miss Sally Catlett, of Baltimore; Dr. and Mrs. Wm. McIlwain, of Petersburg; Mrs. Thos. Gordon, Mr. C. E. Picot and Miss Charlotte Picot, of Richmond; Miss Mary E. Nelson, Miss S. B. Nelson, Miss Byrd Nelson, Mrs. R. H. Nelson, Mr. Heber Nelson, Mr. Powell Catlett and Mr. George Nelson, of Henrico County; Mr. and Mrs. J. W. C. Catlett, of Stafford; Mr. and Mrs. Charles Catlett, of Hague; Mr. Robinson Nelson, of Orange; Mrs. Tilford, Miss Portia Baldwin, of Berryville, Va.; Miss Nora Moore, of Washington, Mr. Phillip Nelson, of Halltown, Va.; and Mr. Wm. Hutchinson, of New York.

Mr. Hutchinson was a comrade and devoted friend of Lieut. Catlett's in the World War service, they having received their commissions together in October, 1918.

Thought to be from the *Gloucester Gazette* August, 1925.

At least I'm facing the heartbreak full-square. And in these days, months and years of immersion in your written words, I've taken into myself your voice and your love, as I hope you have mine.

Your devoted daughter,

Catharine Carter

* * *

Dear Daddy,

There's more to tell you. I'm not so tranquil as the foregoing suggests, for now the terrible reality is penetrating the peace to which I thought I was coming. The reality is that I am at the end of your letters. There are no more discoveries to be made. There will be no new evidences of your love.

I rail against this ending, and don't want to make my peace with it. I don't want to give up the adventure of getting to know you and the comfort your letters often bring me. I struggle to accept the fact that your life has ended, as well as the present stage of our journey together, and to absorb the horror of your death in the ugly twisted mess of that pursuit plane. My mind arcs from the hideous circumstances of your death to the ugliness at the core of our Southern heritage. Clear as day, something comes to me: in life's fearful mix of love and cruelty, I can't have the joy without the ugliness and the heartbreak. They can't be separated; I must own them both.

It is in loving you, my father, that I reach a new understanding. I must cease disowning the horror in our Southern heritage. It, too, is a part of my life.

I know this new-found gut certainty—that life must be accepted in its wholeness—will free me up. In my adult years, I've strained against my inheritance of a culture permeated with the slave-owner mindset which pronounced black people inferior. We crippled them and we crippled ourselves. We stunted an untold number of lives. We built elaborate interior fences and didn't climb over them, or even try to. I came to hate this, to know that it was a terrible transgression. I wanted nothing to do with it. I wanted to divorce myself from it, to deny I was connected with it in any way.

And then I came to know you and love you with all my heart, and inexorably this love led me to your death. I'll never relinquish my love for you, so there is no way I can cease living with your death. The brutal brokenness of your ending abides along with the certainty of your love.

Alienation from my southern heritage—the monkey that's been clinging to my back most of my life—has come in the form of an inner voice of shame. It reminds me of the apartheid world in which I grew up, and starts a downward cycle that leaves me feeling an exile from the place and people who nurtured me.

Now I won't struggle. I accept my complicity with the evil, along with what is precious in my inheritance. I accept my humanness—and my part in the oppression of others. I will no longer struggle for a state of innocence and goodness—for the clean hands and heart I once sought to claim—because I'm a trespasser, too. Where formerly I wanted to establish before the world that I was different, that I didn't have anything to do with those aspects of my culture, I know now that the love and cruelty come bound together. I can't celebrate the love without owning the cruelty too. This acceptance is my doorway to freedom—hating the evil as much and more clearly than ever, but entering into the brutality and suffering of it with the rest of human-kind, rather than setting myself apart as pure and uncontaminated.

That frees me to affirm the rich and good parts of my heritage. To my amazement, no less than W. E. B. DuBois writes of them. Recently, when I revisited his book, The Souls of Black Folk, *with Eugene Genovese in* The Southern Tradition *as my guide, I was astonished to read these words:*

> *She [Atlanta] forgot the old ideal of the Southern gentleman,—that new world heir of the grace and courtliness of patrician,*

> *knight and noble; forgot his honor with his foibles, his kindliness with his carelessness, and stooped to apples of gold,—to men busier and sharper, thriftier and more unscrupulous . . .*
>
> *Atlanta must not lead the South to dream of material prosperity as the touchstone of success; already the fatal might of this idea is beginning to spread; it is replacing the finer type of Southerner with vulgar money-getters; it is burying the sweeter beauties of Southern life beneath pretence and ostentation.*

It is those "sweeter beauties of Southern life" that hold my heart: kith and kin in abundance; life and living rather than acquisition; love of the land and people—flowers and trees, talk and visits—in which the storyteller was especially valued; good food, mostly home-grown or from the surrounding waters, and good and gracious manners, the kind of manners, Daddy, for which you receive praise.

I even hear your words, my father, in those of DuBois. In your last letter, you hearken back to the world of your old favorite, The Idylls of the King, *a world that yet has a hold on you: "For the first time I am in a squadron, whose best pilot is its commander, a leader after the manner of the knights of old." However, you are richer and more complex in your approach to life—you practice the manners of the "patrician, knight, and noble," but prefer friendship with persons of character, whatever their origin and station in life.*

And there's another way you have changed my world. You and your acknowledgement of your "bright dreams" leads me to a self-respect that is new to me. You don't apologize for your dreams; rather, I think you treasure them, and hope they will lead to something "big" someday. I've never thought of myself as a dreamer, but as a rather hopeless idealist whom others could easily dismiss. Your respect for yourself helps me shed my self-denigration. Life has offered me special opportunities to take part in something big, like participating in the civil rights movement, and ending the practice of tying elders to their chairs and beds, and refusing to let social class and racial boundaries keep me from enjoying friendships wherever I find them.

Journeying with you has put me in a new place with new self-respect.

It's clear to me now that I've been looking for a life that doesn't exist in this world—looking for the good without the bad—whether it be my own, or my forbears'. But now, Daddy, you, and my journey with you, have schooled my heart. I revel in the joy of knowing you and being your daughter, even though I know that an ugly death in a flimsy, twisted airplane wrenches you out of my life, and breaks my heart. The shining happiness of this time with you insists that beauty and surpassing joy are always there too.

Thanks for bringing me to this peace.

With love,

Catharine Carter

"TOO DEEP FOR THE WORDS TO COME"

The day after the crash, Catharine writes Carter's mother:

> I am trying to be brave for I know he wants us to be—& Catharine & I will be with you just as soon as possible. A heartful of love to each.

And to her own mother she sends this note:

> Mother—it is hard to take it all in, but I am trying to hold up—and will get there as soon as possible & try to be a helping hand to his family.
>
> Everyone is very kind, & someone will come on with me—You will get a cable as to when I leave before this reaches you—and you can tell his Mother and Father & help them all you can.
>
> I tried to write a line to Mother Catlett, but it is all too deep for the words to come. Tell her I am thinking of them & will be so happy to get to them and all of you.
>
> Catharine

On the same day, Mrs. Post, the mother of Peggy, little Catharine's adored playmate, writes Carter's mother, despite the fact her letter will hardly reach Gloucester before Catharine arrives. She tells of the support and help being extended Catharine:

> I want you to know that everything is being done to help Catherine. She is remarkably brave and sensible and is anxious to be with you. She will leave here about Wednesday, July 22 and will reach Gloucester about twelve days later—but a message en route will tell you definitely. An officer from the Field will accompany her all the way—so she will be well taken care of (7-18-25).

The first written words of sympathy to reach Catharine are from John Pitzer, the rough-hewn West Point roommate whose honesty Carter valued. Pitzer writes from Military Camp on the island of Hawaii:

> July 18, 1925
>
> Dear Katherine:
>
> I hardly know what to say. My sergeant-major asked me this morning if I had heard of the Luke Field aviator being killed. I told him no and asked him who was it. He said Lt. Catlett. Well I just about fell out of my chair—you are his wife and are naturally sad. For the wild individual I have always been sorrow has nearly been unknown to me but honest I'm broken hearted. All the drunken bums still flying and old Carter dead.
>
> I say without qualification he was the "whitest and cleanest" man I ever knew. They don't come any better. Wish I could be over there to do something for you. Chaplain E. L. Branham is radioing you now. Express my sorrow to his mother too.
>
> With greatest sorrow,
> John Pitzer

Catharine disposes of most household furnishings, bringing only a few items with her beyond clothing and her wedding china and silver. On the day before her departure, a funeral service is held in Honolulu. It is described in detail by the Chaplain in a letter to

Catharine, apparently as requested by her because, in her state of shock, she might not remember it accurately:

Military Camp
Island of Hawaii
July 22, 1925

Mrs. L. C. Catlett
Gloucester, Va

Dear Catherine:-

The following is an accurate account of the funeral . . .

The funeral of 2nd Lt Landon C. Catlett Jr, 19th Pursuit Squadron, who was killed in an airplane accident near Fort Kamehameha, Hawaii, July 17th 1925, was held at the Army Service Club, Honolulu, Hawaii, at 2:30 PM, Tuesday July 21, 1925 under the direction of Chaplain Edw. L. Branham, assisted by Bishop John D. LaMother of the Episcopal Church.

Capt. Karl H. Gorman, 23d Squadron had charge of the military part of the funeral. A full platoon of the 19th Squadron, commanded by 1st Lt. Chas. M. Cummings acted as escort and the following officers of Luke Field were pall-bearers,—

Capt B. J. Peters
Capt Alfred Fields
Lt. C. L. Chennault
Lt. Leo F. Post
Lt. A. G. Hamilton
Lt. E. C. Langmead.

The entire personnel of the 19th Squadron and the 23rd Squadron were in attendance.

Placed upon the casket were the American Flag, the Saber, and the Cap of Lt. Catlett. There was also one beautiful wreath of white lilies on the casket while many lavish floral offerings were strewn about on the floor.

Following the service at the Service Club a procession was formed as follows,—The Band; The Escort; The Chaplain; The Caisson, Casket and Pall Bearers; the family; and Lt. Catlett's comrades. All marched slowly to Fort Armstrong where, with heads bowed and all soldiers at Parade Rest, the final tributes of respect were paid. The Chaplain spoke feelingly of the integrity and sterling manhood of Lt Catlett. Prayer was offered, the firing squad fired 3 volleys; The Bugler blew "taps" and the Chaplain pronounced the benediction.

During the march the Band played two solemn and impressive funeral dirges.

Side arms and the Service Uniform were worn by all officers and enlisted men. Officers also wore the badge of mourning on the left arm and on the saber.

When the entire service was completed the casket was lowered in the box and given in charge of the funeral director to prepare for shipment.

[Edw. L. Branham
Chaplain Luke Field, T.H.]

The next day—only five days after Carter's death—Catharine sets sail for San Francisco with her 22 ½ month-old daughter, and her husband's body in its casket, accompanied by Lt. Robinson, the officer from Luke Field assigned to give help and support throughout the almost two-week trip to Virginia by boat and train.

* * *

Meanwhile, during the days immediately after the crash, Carter's family in Gloucester suffers greatly, first with uncertainty, because they receive no official confirmation of his death for some time, and then with their inability to communicate with Catharine.

It is Carter's Aunt Mary, of The Cedars family, who happens to be visiting his parents, who first brings the awful news. She learns it from neighbors, the Rev. and Mrs. Lee, who show her the report of the crash in their newspaper. She writes Catharine the next day:

> The news of our dear one's going from us reached us yesterday [July 18] and we tried not to believe the worst. But several notices were received in yesterday's paper and I came over from Leeland to try to break the news to the dear father and mother. They were *brave* . . .
>
> We have heard nothing *officially* but trust that you are kept by . . . [God's] grace and that the friends will do everything for your comfort. We are so anxious to hear from you . . . My heart is too full for utterance (7-19-25).

Carter's parents write too, even though they know their words will not reach Catharine until she arrives home. In their desperate need and crushing sorrow, first his father and then his mother, pour out their hearts to her:

> July 19, 1925.
>
> My dear Catharine,
>
> We are thinking of you & the dear grand daughter all the time. We are crushed but we have much to be thankful for. We loved our boy so truly & we were so proud of him. I know you are glad you lavished your love upon him & I know you will cherish his memory as we will. There is no unpleasant thing in his life to remember. He was to me the most splendid man I knew.
>
> God comfort and keep you & the dear child. I am so glad you have her to love & cherish.
>
> We cannot yet realize that we shall never see our boy again.
>
> Everyone is so kind. Your father came up yesterday. A great many people have come to offer sympathy . . .

We slept pretty well & we are doing as Carter would have us do, that is we are going on with our same simple life. Oh Catharine, my daughter, I do wish I could write you something to comfort you. For his sake and little C's sake, be brave . . .

At first we hoped that some mistake had been made, but we cannot see how any mistake could be made. The papers have all the names & places right . . . Oh, I did not want to outlive any child of mine.

Kiss my little grand daughter for me & know always that our hearts are with you in love & sympathy.

Most affectionately
Father Catlett.

Carter's mother, in almost overwhelming distress, writes the next day, not always coherently:

My darling child,

We are bruised and strained beyond measure, & think all the time of *you* on the distant shore with our darling pressed to your heart. Only our saviour can comfort & I know the sympathizing friends, you have made, will do all they can for you.

My first thought when it dawned upon me that Carter was no more, in this world, was if God has taken him he was too good for earth, & he took him from trouble to come.

God help you, my child, & speed the day, that you, get back to our hearts. I have just heard of a poor woman, with three children, & another on the way, being *left*, by her husband. It must be our duty, to help them till we go to him.

God bless you,
Mother

She writes again the same day:

My only hope for you in this extreme hour is a loving heavenly Father, & youth & friends, & ever before you, what might be. I never thought I could stand his flying away, & be left on the field. I have always said if my son must fly I do not want him any nearer to Va. Now that you are called upon to meet the end alone I would that we were together . . .

I would give any amount of money, that I would have, to have one line cabled from you this hour, that is the craving of my heart to know you can speak to me & are not crashing into a suffering heap too . . .

All I can think of is *something* from you, & we are anxiously waiting for some word *directly,* from you . . . (7-20-25).

A week after Carter's death, direct word is finally received from Hawaii:

My darling child—

At last we have heard, that you are on the mighty deep, with our precious baby, & the earthly remains of him, so dear, to our bereaved hearts! Even that, is a comfort, & ever & anon has come to me the thought, "Be still. Know that I am God" . . .

I have not been able to write much to you, & when I did I said I couldn't feel, that what we were writing could ever reach you. The only definite news of you . . . is your mother's letter from Nora, which though brief, about covers the necessary ground. What we longed to hear, was that you could *stand,* & not be completely & absolutely crushed to earth. And she says you telegraphed for the necessary permissions & would leave. That is the most we could hope for and feel that if you find it necessary, you will telegraph from San Francisco, for your father, or Ellen, to come to meet you, (at your expense) knowing that the money is about the only thing that holds them back. We have considered your forlorn and heartbreaking situation from every point, & there was absolutely nothing we could see to do to reach your side a moment sooner than our government would arrange. If your father crossed the continent on the faster express & had a private yacht to board for Honolulu, he might miss you on the way, & you might leave before he got to the point you had left. A government like ours will do what is possible though forced to be deliberate & it is a comfort to feel that you will be given strength for the most trying hours of your life, and what you have done to comfort others will be done for you. God bless & keep you . . .

Your Mother Catlett

More than two weeks after the crash, Carter's father receives a letter from the Chief of Air Service:

WAR DEPARTMENT
Office of the Chief of Air Service
Washington

July 31, 1925.

My dear Mr. Catlett,-

I was very greatly grieved when the news came that your son, Lieut. Catlett, was killed in Hawaii on the 17th of July. These sad accidents which happen in the Air Service from time to time distress me and I know, of course, that they bring to the loved ones of those who thus gave their lives the keenest of sorrow.

I do want you and your family to know how deeply I sympathize with you in your loss and that I speak not for myself alone but for all of the Air Service and particularly for the officers who were associated with your son.

Just as soon as I have any further details concerning this most unfortunate accident, I shall send them to you. My office has been notified that your son's wife is coming back with his remains and I have already telegraphed to my representative at San Francisco to see that she is met and assisted in every way in connection with the landing and the continuance of her sad journey across the continent. If there is anything else

> which I can do or which any of my officers can do, please believe that we stand ready to be of aid.
>
> Again with my sympathy to you and yours, I am
>
> Very sincerely,
> Mason M. Patrick,
> Major General, A.S.
> Chief of Air Service.

By the time Carter's parents receive General Patrick's letter, the long days of awaiting Catharine's arrival are almost over. On August 3, they meet her train at Lee Hall, the station closest to Gloucester and a second funeral service is held the next day at Ware Church.

Letters of sympathy come to Catharine and to Carter's parents in a steady stream as friends read the account of Carter's death in the *New York Times* and other papers. One of Carter's early flying instructors writes from Connecticut, his Fort Sam Houston chaplain from Texas, an Air Service cousin from Ohio, and other friends from across the country.

The day after the crash, Carlisle Penfield, upon seeing the notice in the *Times,* writes that "Landon C. Catlett Jr. came to me as my first student, and our brief moments together in the air are still happy memories. He never knew the satisfaction his work gave me and how proud I was the day he soloed."

Chaplain Westcott of Fort Sam Houston expresses a mixture of sorrow and indignation at losing "so splendid a man." His indignation is perhaps generated by what many considered inadequate congressional appropriations for the Air Service:

> Our grief at Carter's going on cannot be expressed in words. And to try to write a word of comfort to you seems mockery. He was so splendid a man that his departure calls from me one more protest against the international selfishness that compels our nation to develop an army in the spirit of preparedness [paper torn] so to endanger some choice young men. Many

> could be spared better than Carter can be. I may seem rebellious but we admired him and you immeasurably . . .

A distant relative, Augustine Warner Robins, Commanding Officer of Fairfield Air Intermediate Depot in Ohio, sends a portion of a letter received from an officer at Luke Field, which purports to give first-hand information about Carter's crash:

> Lieut. Catlett had very recently, in fact since July 1, transferred from a heavy bombardment (23rd) to a pursuit squadron (19th)—he was an excellent bomber and D.C. pilot and bade well to become a first rate pursuit pilot flying an M.B. but was lacking in experience required for this type of flying. He was out this morning with another officer in another M.B. practicing cross over turns and for some reason or other, went into a spin at about 1200 feet—unable to pull out and crashed into the water. The location as given in the paper ["the reef about 100 yards off shore at Fort Kamehameha"] is substantially correct. Certainly is too bad for we all thought a lot of Lieut. Catlett (Peters 7-18-25).

Catharine hears from many people who became her and Carter's friends in their Air Service years. The shock of Carter's death is palpable, as well as the ensuing deep sorrow over the loss of "our beloved and gallant aviator," as an acquaintance writes Catharine from Missouri:

> I have just seen in *The New York Times* the crushing news of Lt. Catlett's fatal accident . . .
>
> Knowing you and Lt. Catlett was one of the delights of our stay in Honolulu—and the memory of that last Sunday when we were your guests in that drive up Tantalus—and our adieu to you at the end of the car line—will remain with us for all time . . .
>
> You have given up a beloved and loving husband; little Catherine has lost a father of whom she will retain but a proud memory; his parents mourn a son of whom they must have been very proud—and his friends—a worth while companion

> but our country has lost a bulwark that was holding back the wave of lawlessness sweeping over her. His going has left us all bereft—wife, child, parents—friends and fellow citizens . . . (7-20-25).

From Mrs. Wolcott, a friend with ties in Gloucester whom Carter and Catharine saw in their Texas days, comes another distressed letter:

> The terribly sad news has just come to us. Oh Catharine how my heart aches for you; and have you anyone there to help and comfort you? . . . I felt like rushing to you when we got the word. Even now I have a faint hope, because Emily, who sent me the clipping from the paper, says that no direct word has come from you. I have always felt that you and Carter were belonging to me in some way and I cannot bear to sit here and do nothing for you. Pray and pray dear child and just talk your heart out to God and help will come to you; there isn't any other way. Underneath are the Everlasting Arms, don't forget that honey—dear love to you and Mr Wolcott sends all the love & sympathy in the world. We shall be thinking of you every day and praying for you.

After Carter's funeral, Catharine hears from Mrs. Lockwood who had befriended the young couple in Texas:

> You know our warm affection for Carter and how both Joe and I feel about him. We *honored* him and were proud to be counted among his friends. He held a place all his own in our estimation and affection. I am so thankful you have the little Catharine. She promised to grow very like her Father (8-8-25).

In a letter to Catharine, Billy McIlwain writes of Carter's approach to life, saying he "love[d] life to the full, unselfishly, intensely, joyously, soberly," and telling Catharine she was his "deepest treasure" (7-20-25).

Friends struggle with a sense of incomprehensible loss. One Gloucester friend traveling in Europe writes:

> I don't know whether you will want this letter or not. I had not heard until Ellen's letter reached us in Naples three weeks ago of your Carter's death. My dear, I feel helpless: to tell you that I feel for you with my whole heart is nothing . . . [Y]our Carter with his life before him; it seems incredible...I can't tell it to you well, but I feel sure that God did not mean to take your happiness from you . . .
>
> Ellen says you bear your sorrow like a queen (Tucker Bryan, 12-26-25).

Then, in January, a full six months after Carter's death, a letter arrives from the mother of Earl Gruver, Carter's West Point roommate:

> January 9, 1926
>
> Dear Folks—
>
> It is in great sorrow I send you this note for some information. Earl learned at Army Headquarters that your son had been killed in an accident over Hawaii some time in September he has never heard from anyone that gave us facts.
>
> I think we loved Carter next to our own son and thought he was the most wonderful boy we ever met. You know he visited us three times in our home.
>
> I was with him a number of times at Camp Dix and West Point.
>
> Earl was his room mate all the time he spent at West Point. He simply is stunned and I could not get him to write. I was sorry I never had the pleasure to meet you all, but we know what a lovely family you must be by your son.
>
> He wrote Earl he knew he was in dangerous work but if anything ever happened his life had been so full of good things he was ready to go . . .
>
> Kindly give us information and remember we will always be a friend for the family of one we loved dearly.
>
> Mrs. W. S. Gruver.

Following the Catlett family reply, Mrs. Gruver writes a second time, conveying the impression that Earl was in shock after the news of Carter's death reached him:

> I will never be able to thank you enough for the information you gave us in regard to Carters death. I think next to my own family I have grieved over his death more than I could for any of Earl's boy friends and he has a great many friends . . . I sent your letter to Earl and he sent it back he intends keeping it in his Army book the book is just full of Carter's photos and quotations. We have his West Point photo and will always cherish it. Truly I must say we never met a young man to be his equal my own son included. I have lots of respect for Earls hard work and he has been a good son to us but he was never given the brains Carter had . . .
>
> [Earl] . . . said when he first heard the news for about 1 ½ hours he was dazed and he wrote me nearly a week later he said, he still hardly could realize what he was doing. At Christmas he simply would have nothing to say and said he could not write you (1-26-26).

* * *

Catharine and daughter stay at Toddsbury with her family until late September when they move to Newington to live with Carter's parents for the winter, a plan Catharine has made with the hope that the presence of the little one will be a solace to the grandparents. She writes her mother-in-law:

[Toddsbury
September 8, 1925]

Dearest Mother Catlett,

Nothing has touched me, or meant quite so much, as your sweet note, which I got in the mail as we came home yesterday. No one knows the aches & loneliness that sweep over me—but "tomorrow is another day!" I do not want to renew my youth. I only want courage and strength enough to face the future, & give little Catharine the life her Father would want her to have—& to be of some use to others myself.

I am proud to have been Carter's wife—I have so many wonderful things to remember about him, & our life together. I only wish I could feel that I had meant half to him what he has meant & will continue to mean to me. I feel closer & closer to him each day, even though he is not with me in person & I feel sure he is going to help us from where he is.

I am going to be very happy with you & Father Catlett this winter—& I do want to be of all help I can—for if I keep busy—my mind does not have time to think too hard. And I do want you to help me with Catharine—to give her the splendid foundation in life which you gave Carter.

A heartful of love,

Catharine

Dear Daddy,

I desperately need to talk to you. I have come upon some words in the condolence letter from Earl Gruver's mother that take me to a place I do not want to be—a place of separation from you. Here are the words:

> *[Carter] wrote Earl he knew he was in dangerous work but if anything ever happened his life had been so full of good things he was ready to go.*

Ready to go?

At age 25 or 26 you were ready to go? With a wife and daughter, you were ready to go? I know Mother accepted your plans to enter aviation, but what about me? I'm disregarded, left to fend for myself, because my father is "ready to go." I suppose I was one of those "good things" that filled your life.

Your words take me back to that dreadful poem you quoted to your parents in Fall, 1917:

> *But youth's fair form, though fallen, is ever fair,*
> *And beautiful in death the boy appears,*
> *The hero boy, that dies in blooming years:*
> *In man's regret he lives, and woman's tears,*
> *More sacred than in life, and lovelier far,*
> *For having perished in the front of war.*

So there it is from the outset: the romantic glory of sacrificing all—including life—for one's country, coupled with your decision to join the Air Service.

Well, you achieved it, didn't you—I mean, you achieved that ultimate sacrifice. When I think back over things you have said, considered your deep commitment to honor and country, your absorption in Arthurian romance, your dismissal of men who fail to give their all to their chosen profession, your love affair with "glorious adventure," your stubborn determination to be an aviator, and your message to your father inviting him and anyone else to "say whatever you feel on the subject [of my becoming an aviator] without fear of intruding" because "I shall make . . . [my decision] regardless of what anyone else may say to me"—when I think of all these things, why am I thrown by your words quoted by Mrs. Gruver?

Because I wanted you—I want *you to be my father—and not this adventurer rushing toward an engagement with death.*

I know that my feeling is partly shaped by this time in our country's history. I see young men and women ordered into a war in Iraq, a war that I can in no way support. I see lives of both Americans and Iraqis wasted. These young people are not "More sacred than in life and lovelier far, For having perished in the front of war." The sentiment revolts me.

But my understanding of the pull "glorious adventure" has on you continues to grow. As I've written you earlier, it has been a help to hear similar words from astronauts, the flight pioneers of our age, as you were in yours. I think your pioneering was more dangerous than theirs; certainly on a daily basis it was.

What comes relentlessly between us is your feeling that your life "had been so full of good things" that "if anything ever happened" you were "ready to go."

It's as though you are pushing forward to keep your appointment with death. Your very decision to request a transfer to the pursuit squadron reinforces that feeling. You are a highly skilled bomber pilot, but that is not enough. And you've seen all the Islands, so there is little left to explore by air—so you must seek new challenges.

I understand fully now that flying is what makes you feel really alive—it is the "ginger" of life. It presents the physical and mental challenges you crave. So why does this "ready to go" statement take me to a place of raw pain? Why is the hurt so great?

Because it feels as though you are willing to discard me. You must know there is in me still that very little girl whose Daddy disappeared. That little girl could hardly talk, much less weep and mourn. And now her long-untended wound is laid bare.

Who can tend it?

* * *

Sometimes when the day has been a hard one, I sense your presence in the moments before I fall asleep. I am embraced, comforted and consoled. It's as though I'm sitting in your lap, leaning against your strong body, being reassured by your love. It's not big, eighty-two-year- old me, but a little girl snuggling against her father, knowing love and protection. Is it body memory?

I know exactly when you were first present to me in this way. Six years ago we were in St. Louis at a meeting of nursing home advocates, and the day had been full of stress and strain as we struggled to become a cohesive group. I was exhausted and tearful, but as I lay in bed, ever so gradually a warmth and peace embraced me, and I felt cared for as a small one wants to be—protected, comforted by a loving parent. I knew the source was you. I cannot bid you come, but you are often present to me at day's end, especially when the going has been rough.

* * *

Now this is new: I'm not in bed at the end of a long hard day, but working in my study in broad daylight, and the same sense of your closeness embraces me. The thought comes that death was not your choice, that you did not want to leave Mother and me, but death was a risk you willingly faced in the line of duty, and I know how deeply you honored duty. My heart knows these things.

I know too that I mustn't blow up your remark out of context—in fact, I have no idea what the context was, or when you wrote it. It might have been a note to Earl when you were working in a summer camp just before your wedding. It may have been written long before I appeared on the scene.

So I move forward, slowly and deliberately, with love and care for the little girl who suffered loss, and had no means of understanding it. I'm tending her with your love.

Now, my father, shall we continue our journey?

Always in love,

Catharine Carter

8

THE DEMISE OF LETTER-WRITING

Wendy Lustbader

Handwritten letters are becoming a thing of the past. Everyone still delights in the discovery of a letter in the mailbox amidst the bills and advertisements, but dwindling numbers of us remain who actually write letters. We oddballs like to scribble our thoughts on paper, address the envelope, and put on a stamp. We find satisfaction in the thump of the mailbox, the start of a journey that will culminate in a loved one's pleasure.

While in her early 70's, Carter Catlett Williams found a treasure trove of letters written by the father she lost when she was not quite two years old. The letters were in a box in her attic, having dwelled there and in other attics for decades. She ended up spending several years reading, transcribing, and responding to these letters. During this undertaking, she entered into a living relationship with her father. How can words inscribed on yellowing paper have this kind of power? It turned out that Carter's father had left enough of himself behind in these letters that she could truly know him.

Another friend recently read through the World War II letters her father had sent daily to her mother, getting a feel for the sensitive and passionate side of the restrained man who had raised her and later slipped into Alzheimer's disease. I am afraid that such life-changing reclamations will never happen again in human history, once all letter-writing has ceased. We have e-mail now, but the two forms of mail have little in common. Sadly, the myth that e-mail can take the place of the old kind of mail tends to weaken whatever inclinations toward letter-writing still exist.

It is true that e-mail from cherished friends can be printed out and given the heft of paper. I have done this. I then place each e-mail in a file folder labeled with the friend's name. But I prefer my shabby boxes filled with thirty years' worth of letters from these same friends. When I open one of the boxes, I am greeted by envelopes of different colors and shapes, stamps of all varieties, and postmarks from places near and far. I see my name written in familiar handwriting, addressed to apartments and houses of my past, and I am transported back to earlier eras of my life. When I open a file folder of accumulated e-mail, I remain unmoved as I flip through pages of bloodless, typed uniformity.

Handwriting ties us to our beloved like nothing else. Somehow it calls forth the person more than a photograph or even a video clip. I get tearful when I glimpse the envelope containing the birthday card my Aunt Judy sent me a few days before she died last August. I have plenty of photos of her, but seeing my name in her handwriting is what evokes the sweetness of grief. Perhaps it is the evidence of having been addressed by her, the personal salutation—"Dear Wendy." Not too long ago, she held a pen in her hand and wrote my name.

E-mailers almost never bother to fashion a greeting beyond "Hi," and many do not put in a closing at all. "Dear, dear Mother" is how Carter's father addressed his mother while away at boarding school for the first time at age sixteen. Often, he closed his letters home, "With a heart full of love." Now e-mailers tend to come to an abrupt halt with their last sentence, as though signing off with a name attached to a sentiment is just too *retro.* For me, ending with "Love, Wendy" is an occasion for tenderness when communicating with a friend, even in an e-mail's rush to convey a message and be done with it.

E-mail is about hurry and transience. *It's so much easier.* I can dash off a few thoughts to a friend and send it instantaneously. This kind of writing is actually much closer to speaking than the old kind of letter-writing. It is spontaneous utterance, as opposed to sitting with pen in hand and pondering how to convey what is in one's heart. Carter's father wrote ornate sentences, full of finely observed details about people and places, ailments, longings and worries. One has the sense he is being with his parents as he writes to them, and thus it feels, a century later, that one is spending time with him while reading what he has written in so intimate a manner.

Place matters in a letter, while it is literally immaterial in an e-mail. A letter takes place within the life being lived. The letter-writer needs to remark how the light is beaming in through the window and lighting up the page, or how delightfully the smell of baking scones is suffusing the air around the kitchen table. This feeling of being together through words in a certain time and place is the grounding of a letter. The reader becomes situated along with the writer, easing into the mood as much as the context where the letter is being written. *I'm sitting in a café downtown, with a double espresso and your latest letter in front of me.* Such locating passages are almost never included in an e-mail, even if a laptop were to sit on the same café table. The sensory dimension of life comes with the letter-writer's willingness to sit with what is there and spend time.

Letters are rooted in time, the way life is. It takes time to sit down, pick up pen and paper, and compose one's thoughts. More time accrues in preparing the envelope and getting the thing over to a mailbox. Days elapse as the missive travels, and then it lingers for a bit longer until the recipient gets home. Finally, the letter is torn open. The person must slow the forward rush of life in order to read what someone else has taken the time to inscribe. Then writing back takes more time. Often, I will carry a letter around in my purse for weeks, until I have an interlude and setting suitable for responding. Re-reading the letter, I like to glance back and forth between different sections to be sure I have taken in the details where the pain resides. All of this is part of encompassing the gift that a friend has finally unburdened herself.

The blurted voice rarely muses or ventures the way the written voice does, tending more toward instrumental than exploratory purposes. When I receive a paper letter, I like to spread out the pages and take in the whole—as can the writer. When I compose or read a long e-mail, I find the screen cuts off the flow and causes me to get lost when I have to scroll through digressions. There is usually more depth and cohesion with writing on paper, arising chiefly from the freedom to wander away from the original point and yet be able to find the way back.

Writing by hand on paper is how I find out what I am thinking. The first several drafts of this essay were written by hand. "I need to feel the words run through my fingers," admitted a fellow writer I once knew. Typing is so disembodied and impersonal that we may fail to invest sufficiently in our sentences. Quick electronic deletions cause us to lose words or phrases that should have been kept. When I write on paper, I frequently return to crossed-out sections in another frame of mind and find a phrase or two that well deserve rescue. Sometimes these almost-discarded thoughts spur the best sentences of all.

Carter's father wrote home from army flight school in July of 1918: "A bold innocent face, a controlled tongue and watchful waiting keeps me out of trouble in the army." He had missed roll call that morning when he had gone off without permission to the YMCA library. These words capture a young man's dance with military culture, all in a single sentence. Throughout his letters, there is this same careful and expressive use of words. I only wish we had the abundant love letters he must have written to Carter's mother, which surely would have been masterpieces of the form. Carter does not know when her mother threw these into the fireplace.

Are there any lovers anywhere who still wait for the mail? The waiting was part of it—watching for the letter-carrier down the block or listening for the creak of the mail box lid. Between letters, there was time to yearn and doubt. E-mail or text messages blurt their declarations, making the slow dignity of the letter laughable. Time for pondering and questioning, days on end for discerning exactly what one feels, belong to the days when people labored over letters. Whole courtships were carried on by letter. I have the fourteen-page tome Edna Whitman received in 1904 from Victor Chittick declaring his love for her and his wish to spend the rest of his life with her. It was found in her nursing home night table after she died at the age of 101. She had outlived their marriage of seven decades by twelve years, but this letter accompanied her to the end.

A generation is coming of age now in which it would be difficult to find even one sixteen year old boy away from home who writes letters to his parents, much less one who would conclude, "With a heart full of love." My granddaughter, Sophie, who is just learning how to write, may never know how it feels to see a friend's handwriting on an envelope that she pulls from her mailbox. Handwritten letters speaking the language of the soul will be the rarest of treasures, but those that are saved may speak again when a desk is cleaned months later, or when a daughter seeks to know her father seventy years hence.

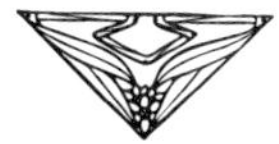

Endnotes

Chapter One: Prologue, and a Message to My Father

Page 6, para. 1. At the National Citizens Coalition for Nursing Home Reform in Washington, DC, Elma Holder, Barbara Frank and Sarah Greene Burger were immediately receptive to the information about restraint-free care which I brought back from Gothenburg. Largely because of their referrals, opportunities developed for me to speak around the country.

Doris Schwartz, Professor Emeritus of Nursing, Cornell University Medical College, referred me to Neville Strumpf, PhD and Lois Evans, DNSc, of the University of Pennsylvania School of Nursing faculty. Neville and Lois introduced me to their and others' research on the effects of restraint use on patients and nurses, and were generous in their sharing of developments in the fledgling movement to rid nursing homes of physical restraints.

Page 8, para. 1. Subsequently my cousin, Letitia Montague Grant, found 100 more letters from my father to his sisters stashed in an old trunk. Excerpts from these letters have now been included in the text.

Chapter Two: Carter, the Schoolboy and Letters from Home

Page 9, para. 1. The Episcopal High School (EHS) was founded in 1839, and, since it was the first high school in the state, was often referred to simply as The High School. It was adjacent to the Virginia Theological Seminary where High School boys attended church services. The Seminary was also a source for speakers for EHS, both from the faculty and visiting lecturers, which exposed the boys to wide-ranging opinions.

Page 19, para. 1. Both Harris and Page published many books in the late 19th and early 20th centuries. Of those written by Joel Chandler Harris, the following were particularly popular: *Uncle Remus: His Songs and His Sayings,* first published in 1880 (New York: D. Appleton and Company, 1930); *Nights with Uncle Remus: Myths and Legends of the Old Plantation* (New York: Houghton Mifflin, Singing Tree Press, 1883) and *New Stories of the Old Plantation* (New York: McClure, Phillips, 1905).

Popular titles by Thomas Nelson Page included *In Ole Virginia* (New York: Scribner's Sons, 1896), *The Old South, Essays Social and Political* (New York: Scribner's Sons, 1892), and *Red Rock, A Chronicle of Reconstruction* (New York: Scribner, 1906). The *Encyclopedia of Southern Culture* states that Page "created of the antebellum South a mythical would be land of noble gentlemen and ladies, of contented slaves, a society ordered by the laws of chivalry." (Anne E. Rowe in *Encyclopedia of Southern Culture,* edited by C. R. Wilson and W. Ferris. Chapel Hill: University of North Carolina Press, 1989, 891.)

In the Catlett family the following essay by my great uncle, Maryus Jones, probably composed in the early 1900s, is an example of the wide-spread romanticizing of antebellum days. The "servants" he speaks of were slaves:

Gloucester in Other Days

To write of the life in Gloucester in those halcyon days of yore fills me, thrills me with fantastic visions of a past that can never come again to her sons and daughters.

Many of the homes were handsome, yea luxurious, all were snug and comfortable. The inmates contented with breathing an atmosphere of refinement and culture. In many instances families retained the same home for several generations. The same servants in attendance from the cradle to the grave. Every thing went on smoothly and noiselessly with such accomplished cooks, house-maids, seamstresses and dining-room servants, who always knew their places, yet were true friends of the family in the "Great House". The landlord, almost without exception, was a professional man who employed an overseer, whose business it was to receive orders and to have them enforced on the plantation. Should he prove unkind, he was promptly dismissed.

Think of the lord of the manor mounting his thoroughbred steed at any hour it suited him during the day and riding, leisurely, over his broad acres to view the growing crops.

The young people of to-day can scarcely realize such conditions ever existed.

Much entertaining was done in most stately and elegant manner. Gloucester was always far-famed for good living, the lands yielding an abundance of fruits and vegetables and the waters, in turn, an abundance of the "nonpareil" bivalves [oysters] as well as other kinds of sea-food.

When large parties were given, the whole lower floor was thrown open to the guests and the magnificent supper was spread in a room upstairs. Old ham, round of beef, saddle of mutton, oysters, all sorts of cakes and jellies, every thing prepared in the wonderful kitchen of the plantation. Then champagne flowed freely and all were as merry as a marriage-bell.

The ladies bedecked in gorgeous silks and velvets and the gentlemen, in swallow-tail coats, at one time adorned with brass buttons, made a dazzling spectacle.

The fiddlers never seemed to grow weary and the dancers flew on through the entire night and were sorry when morning came. Then, perhaps, a drive of many miles, which seemed just a matter-of-course. But often many guests remained for breakfast with the untiring host and hostess. My mother told me she had breakfasted as many as forty people after a party. Such a thing would be impossible

> in these strenuous days but there is no occasion for repining or living in the past. "Let us, then, be up and doing" and put our shoulders to the wheel and help move the world toward Peace-everlasting Peace—with no booming of cannon or rattling of musketry again so long as Time shall last . . .

A story from the other half of the Gloucester population contrasts the viewpoints of black and white people in this society, and exposes a deep fault line that whites did not perceive. In 1916, Rosewell, a grand house on the York River where legend has it that Thomas Jefferson wrote an early draft of the Declaration of Independence, caught fire. A frantic young woman called to an elderly black man working in the Rosewell fields, as he had most of his life, "Don't you see the house is burning—come help!" His reply: "Let it burn."

Page 20, para. 1. Landon Carter Catlett Dies Suddenly, The *Gloucester Gazette*, March 16, 1933

Page 22, para. 3. Here, and in other instances, Carter's mother holds up Revolutionary and Civil War leaders as exemplars of behavior.

Page 27, para. 1. Page 29, para. 3. Scott's Emulsion was a preparation of cod liver oil highly regarded by Carter's mother. She wrote Carter that Mark Twain said "he lived on it till he was a big boy so I thought it must have agreed with brain work," and she repeatedly urged Carter to take it regularly (LNC 3-3-15). Liquid creosote, an expectorant derived from wood-tar, was prescribed in small amounts to relieve the congestion of chronic bronchitis. (Hobart Amory Hare, M.D., *A Text-Book of Practical Therapeutics*. Philadelphia: Lea & Febiger, 1909, 225-226.)

Information on potash is less clear. One 19th century text warns that "Great caution is necessary in tasting and handling it, as it rapidly destroys organic tissues." My father speaks of taking it in tablet form, but what good it was thought to do remains a mystery. (*The Pharmacopoeia of the United States of America,*

Seventh Decennial Revision, 1890. Philadelphia: J. B. Lippincott Company, 1893, 311.)

Page 28, para. 1. Alfred Lord Tennyson, "Lady Clara Vere de Vere" in *The Home Book of Verse*, Burton Egbert Stevens, comp. Ninth Edition. (New York: Holt, Rinehart and Winston, 1952, 835-837).

Page 31, para. 2. When the memorial to Carter was being written by his friend William Morton for an Academy publication, his father wrote twice detailing Carter's ancestry:

> Landon Carter Catlett, Jr., the oldest child & only son of Landon Carter Catlett & Letitia Nelson was born at the home of his parents, Newington, in Gloucester Co. Feb. 11, 1898. His paternal grandfather was John Walker Carter Catlett a direct descendant of Robert (called King) Carter and Betty Landon his wife. His paternal grandmother was Fanny King Burwell daughter of Col. Armistead Burwell who served in the War of 1812. His maternal grandfather was Reginald Heber Nelson a direct descendant of William Nelson of Yorktown, known as President Nelson. His maternal grandmother was Sally Berkeley Nelson a direct descendant of Thos. Nelson of Yorktown a signer of the Declaration of Independence, governor of Va. & Major General in the revolutionary army (LCC, Sr. 4-1-30).

Lt. Morton managed a condensation:

> [Carter] . . . sprang from a long line of distinguished ancestors who played a prominent part in the making of his state and nation. *Sixty-First Annual Report of the Association of Graduates of the United States Military Academy*, (West Point, N. Y., June 11, 1930).

Page 32, para. 5. Langston Hughes catches the essence of the minstrel show:

Minstrel Man

Because my mouth
is wide with laughter
and my throat
is deep with song,
you do not think
I suffer after
I have held my pain
so long?

Because my mouth
Is wide with laughter,
you do not hear
my inner cry?
Because my feet
are gay with dancing,
you do not know
I die?

Langston Hughes, "Minstrel Man," *The Collected Poems of Langston Hughes,* Arnold Rampersad (ed.), 1995 (New York: Vintage Books), 61.

Page 33, para. 2. The quotation is from a review by Christopher Lehman-Haupt of the novel *Jacob's Ladder,* by Donald McCaig: "A Sweet World and the Horror That Kept It Going," the *New York Times,* August 6, 1998.

Chapter Three: University and War

Page 44, para. 2. Closing lines of "Martial Elegy" by the seventh-century B.C.E. Greek poet, Tyrtaeus, translated by Thomas Campbell, in *Greek Poets in English Verse.* William Hyde Appleton, ed. (Cambridge: Riverside Press, 1893).

Page 48, para. 3. See Thomas Calhoun Walker, *The Honey-Pod Tree, The Life Story of Thomas Calhoun Walker* (New York: The John Day Company, 1958).

Chapter Four: Aviation

Page 57, para. 1. The Curtiss plane JN4-D, nicknamed "Jenny," and the somewhat faster JN4-H, both manufactured in Hammondsport, New York, were the training planes for World War I pilots. In *Jenny, The Airplane That Taught America to Fly,* David Weitzman describes the construction of the JN4-D:

> Each [Jenny] was made of carefully chosen sticks of spruce, ash, birch, and pine dried in kilns. These woods are so strong that frame members like the longerons (the long horizontal sticks) only needed to be 1 ½ inches by 1 ¼ inches thick. The frame was fitted and fastened together by hand, glued, and then varnished like a fine cabinet. Wire cables, stretched diagonally in all directions and tightened with turnbuckles, tied the longerons and struts (vertical sticks) together into a rigid box that could resist the jolts, stresses and vibrations of flight.
>
> The Jenny had quite a wingspan. The upper wing was over forty-four feet long, and the lower almost thirty-four feet from tip to tip. The long heavy pieces, called spars, tied together all the compression ribs that gave the wing its shape—curved on top, flat on the bottom. The ribs were sawn out of plywood and holes were cut to reduce weight. Each wing panel could easily be lifted and moved around by two people. . . .
>
> The wonder of these airplanes was that huge, strong structures were made up of small sticks. The wings and fuselage were covered with cotton, or sometimes, linen. Narrow lengths of fabric were machine sewn together into pieces big enough to cover a wing panel. After the fabric had been stretched smooth and tight over the wing and stitched together by hand, the whole wing was sprayed with water. As the cloth dried it shrank, and became taut, drum taut. Finally the wing was brushed with five or six coats of dope, which made it waterproof and airtight (and smelled terrible) . . .

> [To meet the war demand] Mr. Curtiss . . . began turning out Jennys by the hundreds, and then thousands.

David Weitzman, *Jenny, The Airplane That Taught America to Fly.* (Brookfield, CT: Roaring Brook Press, 2002) [unpaginated].

Chapter Five: The West Point Years

Page 91, para. 1. Stephen Ambrose, in his history of West Point, explains that before the Civil War, plebes upon admission went directly into summer camp. After the war, a new practice was instituted:

> [T]hey first spent a three-week period segregated in the barracks, with a few upper classmen there to teach them saluting, marching and other basic elements of military life. This undertaking was soon marked more by an introduction to hazing than to the profession of arms and became known as "Beast Barracks." Stephen E. Ambrose, *Duty, Honor, Country, A History of West Point. (*Baltimore: The Johns Hopkins Press, 1966) p. 225).

Under the guise of teaching plebes "unquestioning and instant obedience" (225), degrading practices developed that the administration was unable to curtail, despite strong measures. A Superintendent of the Academy, Hugh L. Scott, said in a 1910 Senate hearing "I believe if a cadet is made to do menial service, if he is browbeaten and humiliated, it is injurious to his character. It is just the same with cadets as with anybody else" (227).

Ambrose, after describing various physical hazing acts, such as being forced to drink Tabasco sauce, "permitting hot grease to be dropped on the feet . . . being pulled from bed without warning . . . and sitting at meals with the feet raised to the bottom of the table" (226), adds the following:

> For the plebe, perhaps the worst feature of his life was not the physical hazing but the isolation. At no time was he allowed to feel a real part of the Corps, a procedure that

> did make becoming a Third Classman and being accepted into the community more appealing but still meant that the plebe's first year was a difficult and constant test . . . when the cadets "cut" a plebe, months would literally pass without anyone's speaking to him . . . [As his Fourth Class year drew to a close, one plebe observed that] the plebe and the cadet of the upper classes are separated by a gulf of infinite width (228).

Page 95, para. 1. A study of Col. Landon Carter, an 18th century Carter family luminary and great-great uncle of Carter, was recently published: Rhys Issac, *Landon Carter's Uneasy Kingdom: Revolution and Rebellion on a Virginia Plantation.* (New York: Oxford University Press, 2004). Robert "King" Carter, about whom much has been written, was Carter's great-great-great grandfather. For an article detailing his often brutal treatment of his slaves, see Lorena S. Walsh's "Slavery at Carter's Grove" in *Virginia Cavalcade,* Vol. 47 (3), 110-125. He is also remembered as the donor of Christ Church, Lancaster County, which is now preserved by a foundation. His imperious ways at Anglican church services—other members are said to have awaited his arrival before entering the church—contributed to his nickname "King."

Page 97, para. 3. The Air Force Academy was not established until 1955.

Page 99, para. 1. The Beast Barracks experience, lengthened to six weeks, is still in place at West Point. The significant change that occurred under Superintendent Douglas MacArthur in 1920 that caused Carter to say "[Beast barracks] has been abolished," was the removal of upper classmen from the scene. Instead, officers were now to train the plebes.

Page 104, para. 1. Ellen Newbold LaMotte, *The Backwash of War: The Human Wreckage of the Battlefield as Witnessed by an American Hospital Nurse* (New York: G. P. Putnam's Sons, 1916).

Page 105, para. 1. For an account of the civil rights movement in Chapel Hill, NC, see John Ehle, *The Free Men* (New York: Harper & Row, 1965).

Page 115, para. 1. West Point film archives are meager and include none from 1920.

Page 121, para. 3. See "The Freedom Fighter a Nation Nearly Forgot," *Adventist Review,* Online Edition.

Page 122, para. 4. "The Day Slavery Bowed to Conscience," *The Washington Post,* July 21, 1991, F1, F4.

Page 122, para. 3. "Cover [Picture]: *Henry Darnall III,* by Justus Engelhardt Kuhn, ca 1710. In a vivid depiction of the eighteenth-century relationship of slave and owner, the young slave carries a bird felled by his master's bow and wears a silver collar symbolic of his servitude. (Collection of the Maryland Historical Society)" *Virginia Cavalcade,* Vol. 47 (3).

Page 123, para. 1. Lorena Walsh, "Slavery at Carter's Grove in the Early Eighteenth Century," *Virginia Cavalcade,* Vol. 47 (3), 110-125.

Page 123, para. 2. Thomas Dixon, *The Clansman, An Historical Romance of the Ku Klux Klan.* Introduction by Thomas D. Clark (Lexington: University of Kentucky Press, 1990) and *The Leopard's Spots, A Romance of the White Man's Burden* (Ridgewood, NJ: Gregg Press, 1967).

For a critique of Dixon's books see "Controversial History: Thomas Dixon and the Klan Trilogy" at http://docsouth.unc.edu/highlights/dixon.html

Page 123, para. 3. Robert A. Gibson, *The Negro Holocaust: Lynching and Race Riots in the United States, 1880-1950* (Yale-New Haven Teachers' Institute, May, 2006)

Page 124, para. 1. Hunter Dickinson Farish, *Journal & Letters of Philip Vickers Fifthian, 1773-1774: A Plantation Tutor of the Old Dominion* (Williamsburg, Virginia: Colonial Williamsburg, Incorporated, 1943), 51.

Page 125, para. 1. Andrew Levy, "The Anti-Jefferson: Why Robert Carter III Freed His Slaves, (And Why We Couldn't Care Less)" *The American Scholar,* Vol. 70 (2), 15-35.

Page 25, para. 1, pp. 16 and 18 in the above article. Professor Levy has now published a biography of Robert Carter: *The First Emancipator, The Forgotten Story of Robert Carter III, the Founding Father Who Freed His Slaves* (New York: Random House, 2005).

Chapter Six: Family and Flying

Page 176, para. 1. Langley Field, an army airbase about 35 miles from Gloucester, had been commissioned in 1917.

Page 183, para. 1. These conditions may be manifestations of the meager support given the Air Service by Congress. Gen. Billy Mitchell, who had been Chief of Air Service in World War I, was certain air power was of utmost importance, and, in the years after the war, pressed for increased appropriations and a separate air service which would be coequal with the Army and the Navy. (Roger Burlingame, *General Billy Mitchell, Champion of Air Defense* (New York: McGraw-Hill Book Company, Inc., 1952), 113). But Mitchell was thwarted by the "old brass" who denied the relevance of this new kind of warfare. A commission appointed by the Secretary of War went to Europe and brought back findings completely corroborating Mitchell's words. But by the time the hearings on the commission's findings were completed in February, 1920, "It was too late. Already the Army had reduced its Air Service, the Navy had abolished its Air Division. Admiral Williams S. Benson was shouting "Aviation was just a lot of noise. [And] Pershing, returning from Europe amid accolades, had announced, to Mitchell's great disappointment, that he was opposed to a separate air force" (Burlingame, 114). Carter appears to have been very much on Mitchell's side (see his enthusiasm for an Air Academy, page 119), but does not mention him by name.

Page 198, para. 2. By the mid-1920s the raising of daffodils (jonquils) had become a means of supplementing many Gloucester family incomes. My grandfather, Landon Carter Catlett, Sr., described the preparation of the flowers for shipping by steamer to Baltimore:

The flowers were taken to the house in large baskets and tied with soft strings 25 to a bunch. Large water troughs were provided in which the flowers were set for two hours before being packed upright in large baskets holding 100 bunches. The baskets were covered with cheese cloth [and dispatched on the afternoon boat to Baltimore, arriving in time for next day's morning market.] (L. C. Catlett, Sr., *Somebody's Hometown Magazine,* Fanny B. Catlett, ed, (Wellesley, MA, 1926), 26.

Page 204, para. 2. In World War II, Gen. Claire Chenault was famous as the Commander of the Flying Tigers whose mission was to protect the Burma Road, the supply route to China.

Page 210, para. 6. My father was flying a Thomas Morse MB-3 pursuit plane at the time of his fatal crash. A piece of the engine remains from the crash, apparently given to my mother before we left Hawaii. She used it as the door-stop in her bedroom, and it was another of those givens in my life, so much a part of the daily scene I never thought anything about it. It never occurred to me to ask her who gave it to her and what that person said in presenting it.

Piston and broken valve from the wreckage of my father's plane.

Dr. Kevin Kochersberger, mechanical engineer and early-plane expert, has looked at the engine piece. He tells me it is a piston with a broken valve embedded in the top. It appears to him "that the valve broke, and power was lost."

My further thought is that the selection of this particular part of the engine is itself a mute message. My conjecture is that the mechanics who dismantled the engine chose the damaged piston to present to my mother because it tells the informed viewer what happened.

So far, I have been unable to discover any official report on the crash.

Page 211, para. 3. Along with my father's obituary, Grandmother Mott also clipped from the *Gloucester Gazette* this sonnet written by my father, date of composition unknown:

SEMPER PLUS ULTRA

(Always More Beyond)

Who thinks himself secure must fear a fall,
For thus decrees the Guide Book to the proud.
So say the annals of great nations all
And so our own experience shows. A crowd
Has borne us on triumphant shoulders! Sing
In praise of him to whom the world has bowed.
So gloats proud youth—his halls with plaudits ring,
Yet earth forgets him ere he fills his shroud.

O Youth! desir'st thou wealth or place or fame,
Then strive, and when men see thy victory near
And praise, then waver not in goal or aim,
Or rest, content with laurels gained. Nor cheer
Nor blame may halt thee. Scorn the Present's rage
And gain increasing laud from age to age.

Page 213, para. 4. W. E. Burghardt DuBois, *The Souls of Black Folk.* (Connecticut: Greenwich, Fawcett Publications, 1961), p. 67.

GENEALOGY

Catlett Family

Home: "Newington", at Gloucester Court House

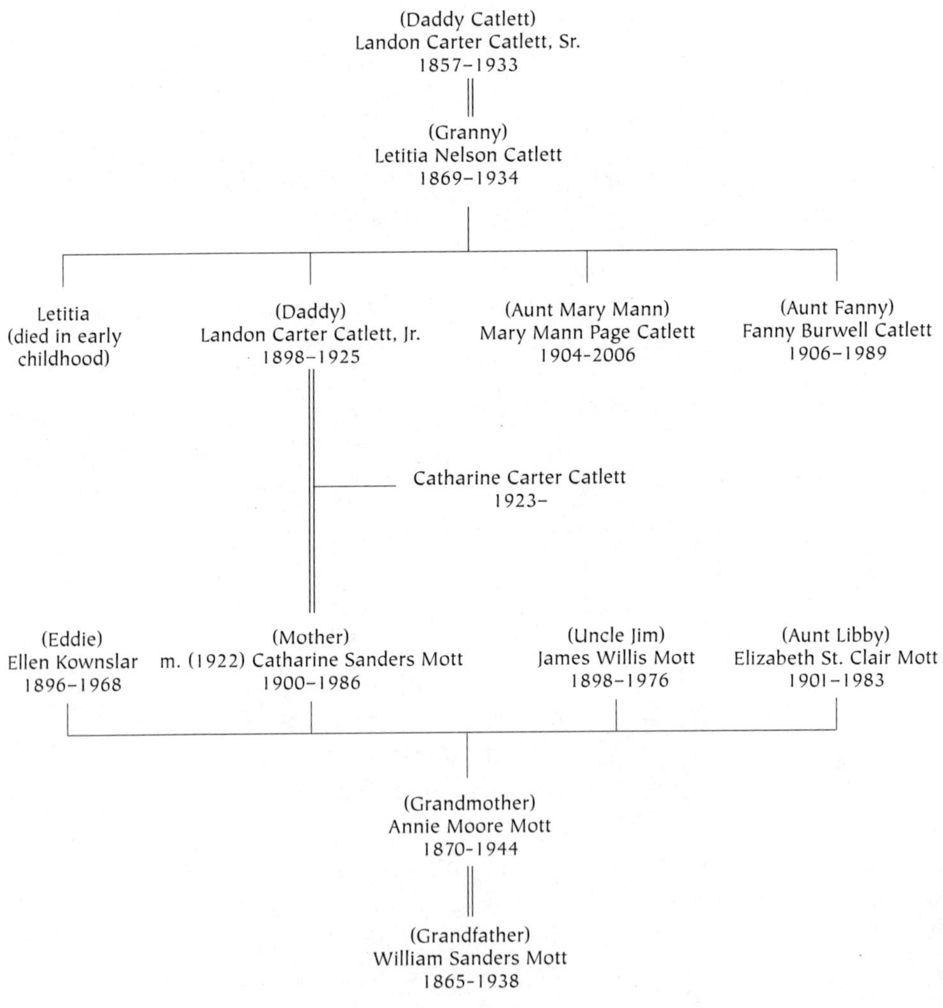

Mott Family

Home: "Toddsbury", on the North River